Palgrave Critical Studies in Human Rights and Criminology

There is growing interest in the connection between criminal justice concerns and human rights, including in topics from global migration and youth justice to mass imprisonment. This series combines the latest theory and research in criminology, criminal justice, and related fields with a critical perspective on the theory and practice of human rights. It explores in depth what human rights can bring to criminology and what criminology and related disciplines can bring to our understanding of the real-world practice of human rights. Books in the series link specific human rights instruments and institutions with core criminological settings such as policing, youth justice, prisons and courts to critically explore how they have influenced criminal justice policy, practice and theory. Alongside contributions that see human rights applied in these criminal justice contexts, the series welcomes contributions that critique human rights in the context of what justice is, and who defines it, and how this may matter to cutting-edge debates such as gender equality, Black Lives Matter, decolonising criminology and others. The intention is for these books to be accessible to a wide audience via e-books, short Palgrave Pivot books as well as full-length books. Authors from the Global South are particularly encouraged to submit proposals and translations of suitable works already published in languages other than English. The series invites both monographs and edited collections on well-defined groups of rights including youth rights, disability rights and Indigenous rights, as well as on topics that stretch the boundaries of the discipline such as border control, environmental regulation, global crime and international development, when viewed through a criminological lens.

Book proposals are invited to the Editor: Josephine.Taylor@palgrave.com. Palgrave Macmillan will work actively with authors to explore opportunities for open access funding.

Ursula Kilkelly · Louise Forde ·
Sharon Lambert · Katharina Swirak

Children in Conflict with the Law

Rights, Research and Progressive Youth Justice

palgrave
macmillan

Ursula Kilkelly
School of Law
University College Cork
Cork, Ireland

Louise Forde
Brunel Law School
Brunel University London
Uxbridge, UK

Sharon Lambert
School of Applied Psychology
University College Cork
Cork, Ireland

Katharina Swirak
Department of Sociology
and Criminology
University College Cork
Cork, Ireland

ISSN 2731-412X ISSN 2731-4138 (electronic)
Palgrave Critical Studies in Human Rights and Criminology
ISBN 978-3-031-36651-2 ISBN 978-3-031-36652-9 (eBook)
https://doi.org/10.1007/978-3-031-36652-9

This Palgrave Macmillan imprint is published by the registered company Springer Nature Switzerland AG
The registered company address is: Gewerbestrasse 11, 6330 Cham, Switzerland

Acknowledgements

This research has its origins in research funding awarded to the authors at University College Cork by the Irish Research Council COALESCE scheme. The original aim of the study, supported by the Irish Department of Children and Youth Affairs, was to enhance the understanding of pathways into and out of offending behaviour by young people, mapping the Irish experience against international children's rights standards and research evidence. The project involved a mixed methodology including consultation with young people and an analysis of the data drawn from Growing Up in Ireland—Ireland's national longitudinal study of children and young people, and it was undertaken with the helpful support of an international steering group, a youth advisory group and a research advisory group including colleagues from relevant government departments all of whom contributed to its outcomes and ensured its relevance to a policy audience.

We are extremely grateful to the Irish Research Council for its grant support, to our colleagues in the (now) Department of Children, Equality, Disability, Integration and Youth Research and Evaluation Unit—Dr Kasey Treadwell Shine and Grainne Collins who provided important guidance throughout. Our thanks also to the following who contributed to aspects of that study—specifically Dr Siobhan Buckley and Dr Emma Hurley and Deirdre Kelleher. We are particularly grateful to the young people who participated in the research both as advisors and as participants. They shed a light on the research issues that was both compelling and authentic.

Expanding, updating and reframing our analysis for this book was also a collaborative endeavour and it required the input and support of many colleagues at University College Cork and at Palgrave Macmillan. Thank you to Josie Taylor, senior commissioning editor at Palgrave, for her constant enthusiasm and interest, and to Ashwini Erlango for keeping us on track. At UCC, we are grateful for the collegial support and interest from the School of Law (Ursula), the School of Applied Psychology (Sharon) and the Department of Sociology and Criminology (Katharina), as well as Brunel University Law School where Louise is now based. Finally, we are extremely grateful for the expertise provided by Clara Paul, without whose research support we would have been lost.

This book highlights the range and complexity of issues that children face when they come into conflict with the law and the terrible consequences this can have on their life chances. Although, as academics, we come from different disciplinary backgrounds and perspectives, together we share a passion that we can and must do better to protect the rights of children in such circumstances. We believe that rights and research are key to advancing the progressive reform of youth justice internationally, and we hope that this book makes a valuable if modest contribution to the sharing of knowledge, to this end.

Contents

CHAPTER 1

Introduction

Abstract For decades—since the Geneva Declaration on the Rights of the Child in 1924—the international community has been developing and adopting standards for the treatment of children in conflict with the law and highlighting ways in which states should prioritise the welfare of these children. Since then, a large body of international standards to respect, protect and fulfil the rights of children in conflict with the law has been developed. Alongside this, there has been significant research—from psychology to law, education to sociology—about these children, their circumstances and their pathways in and out of the justice system. However, there has been little study of the overlap or interplay between these two bodies of knowledge—the international standards and the research. The purpose of this book is to address this gap and bring together the best research on children in conflict with the law, mapping it against the international children's rights standards.

Keywords International children's rights · Children in conflict with the law · Juvenile justice · Inter-disciplinarity

For decades, the international community has been developing and adopting standards relating to the treatment of children in conflict with

U. Kilkelly et al., *Children in Conflict with the Law*, Palgrave Critical Studies in Human Rights and Criminology, https://doi.org/10.1007/978-3-031-36652-9_1

the law. The earliest instrument—the Geneva Declaration on the Rights of the Child adopted by the League of Nations in 1924—implored states to 'reclaim' 'the delinquent child', and from then on, the focus has been on identifying ways in which states should prioritise the welfare of children in trouble with the law. The rights-basis for this approach emerged through the adoption of numerous recommendations and guidelines from bodies such as the United Nations and the Council of Europe and it was consolidated in 1989 when the United Nations adopted the Convention on the Rights of the Child (CRC). The CRC confirms that children in conflict with the law, like all children, are entitled to dignity and respect for their rights. This includes the right to development, to non-discrimination in the enjoyment of their rights, to have their best interests treated as a primary consideration in all actions concerning children and to have their views taken into account in all matters affecting them. The CRC also provides express protections for children in conflict with the law—identifying general principles that must guide state action to ensure children's rights are recognised throughout this process. These legally binding standards have been developed and clarified further by the Committee on the Rights of the Child, the body that monitors implementation of the CRC, and others including the Council of Europe.

The process of developing and adopting international standards is inherently political (Kilkelly, 2008; Liefaard, 2016). Taking place in consultative inter-governmental fora, it invariably involves academic and professional experts, non-governmental organisations and advocates, and political representatives and appointees working together to generate from knowledge and experience a statement that reflects the generally accepted consensus on the issues. Whether legally binding or not, the process has to strike a balance between what states—the parties to these instruments—will accept, in light of their legal, political, cultural and economic circumstances while on the other hand, ensuring the highest possible standards of protection for the rights of the child. While a high level of consensus has generally surrounded standard setting in children's rights (Hammarberg, 1990), this does not always extend to children in conflict with the law, where concern for the public interest, including the victims of crime, can pull against more progressive approaches, especially where children are involved in violent offending (Lynch et al., 2022). In truth, the diversity of approaches to youth justice around the world has meant that consensus has been difficult to achieve. Viewed against these considerations, however, the body of international children's rights standards relevant to children in conflict with the law is impressive—in its clarity, consistency and adherence to rights principles (Liefaard, 2020). Although not perfect—they have been criticised for lacking detail and coherence in places (Hespel et al., 2012) and for setting standards too low, such as with respect to the minimum age for criminal responsibility—as a body of law, the international children's rights standards nonetheless offer an effective 'north star' to states committed to a progressive approach to children in conflict with the law, and to campaigners advocating for such an approach (Kilkelly, 2008).

During the decades that children's rights standard setting has been taking place, significant advances have been made in research about children in conflict with the law—their circumstances and pathways in and out of the justice system. Small and large empirical studies have sought to document the lives of children who come into conflict with the law, seeking to understand the impact on the lives, and life chances of these young people, of the interventions and approaches, policies and programmes designed to respond to their behaviour. Across jurisdictions and academic disciplines—from psychology to law, education to sociology—an expansive and diverse body of scholarship now exists on children in conflict with the law. The frontiers of the field have continued to expand, with the introduction of the relatively new specialist field of youth studies and criminology and the inclusion of disciplines like neuroscience into the mix. Whether framed as child justice or youth crime, the broad subject is ripe for the benefits of inter-disciplinarity academic study, while both policy impact and practitioner engagement are common themes. A wide range of methodologies are now in use—using quantitative and qualitative methods, social-legal approaches and ethnographic studies for instance—and the increasing use of participative approaches, involving children directly in the research not just as subjects but as research participants, has begun to enable a more child-centred approach (Lundy & McEvoy, 2012). The growth in children's rights research, which seeks to evaluate the extent to which international children's rights standards are protected in state responses to children in conflict with the law, has also helped advance the agenda of children's rights implementation more broadly (Liefaard, 2020).

Despite the obvious common ground between the research on youth crime and justice and the development of international children's rights standards, there has been little study to date of the overlap or interplay between these two bodies of knowledge. There has been a similar dearth in rights-based studies that ensure children's views and experiences are taken into account. Although the process of developing instruments like the Beijing Rules (UN General Assembly, 1985), the European Guidelines on Child-friendly Justice (Committee of Ministers, 2010) and the Convention on the Rights of the Child, and collaborations like the UN Global Study on Children deprived of Liberty (Nowak, 2019) undoubtedly took account of the leading research in the area, no major study has yet examined the synergy between children's rights standards and the academic literature. Such a study is important for several reasons. First, international children's rights standards carry both legal and moral weight. Adopted almost universally, they are understood to represent the international consensus on the treatment of children in conflict with the law. This position is undoubtedly strengthened by research that documents the ways in which the rights-based approach is supported by scientific evidence. Second, and conversely, drawing a clear connection between internationally adopted children's rights standards and the research on child justice also serves to reinforce the relevance of the latter giving the research added significance in the policy sphere. Overall, advocacy to promote progressive approaches to children in conflict with the law is strengthened by aligning the best research with the most widely accepted international children's rights standards.

Admittedly, there are some challenges with this approach. The research on children in conflict with the law is voluminous, diverse and sometimes contradictory. It includes copious small-scale studies, extensive programme evaluations with little international comparability and compelling, but scientifically light, advocacy reports. For students and policymakers alike, the field can seem vast and impenetrable and of varying quality, factors that can make it difficult to decipher key lessons and messages. Nor are the international children's rights standards easy to navigate—adopted at different times, with varying formats and goals, they range from the high-level instruments like the Convention on the Rights of the Child to more specific guidelines that address particular aspects of the justice system. Nor are they free from inconsistencies or contradictions, and much remains to be worked out in their application and interpretation.

Taking account of these challenges, the purpose of this book is to bring together the best research on children in conflict with the law, mapping it against the international children's rights standards. Drawing on the most authoritative published works in the field, in the fields of law, psychology and the social sciences, the book aims to situate the contemporary research on children's pathways into and out of the justice system, in the context of the international children's rights standards. The book has the following structure. Chapter 2 introduces the international children's rights standards relevant to children and the justice system, setting out the benchmarks against which the research literature will be presented in the three chapters that follow. Like the children's rights standards, the research cannot always be neatly divided into distinct stages of the child's involvement with the justice system and some overlap or intersection—between prevention and diversion for instance—cannot be avoided. For the purposes of this book, however, the material is presented in three phases or stages—Prevention, Diversion and Justice, and Reintegration—with the view to promote a more systematic rights-based approach. Chapter 3 begins by identifying the research that makes the case for the protection of children's rights as a means of preventing them from coming into conflict with the law. Chapter 4 builds on this approach, considering the research that supports children's rights to diversion, as well as regard for the child's procedural rights where they come into contact with the justice system. Chapter 5 then considers the research in support of reintegration, a core child rights principle, helping to clarify the approaches most likely to support the child to move away from offending behaviour, and as a result, move towards more hopeful futures. Finally, Chapter 6 presents some conclusions, identifying the learning from the study at hand, including some gaps in the research and the children's rights standards, respectively. It concludes with a message for how research in this area might achieve a more robust, rights-based approach.

Finally, a brief note on terminology. In any interdisciplinary study, the diverse terms used to describe children, their behaviour and circumstances are a challenge as language continues to evolve along disciplinary and cultural norms. The scholarly literature is replete with references to 'youth', 'juveniles', 'young offenders', 'delinquency' and 'criminal behaviour' to describe the children impacted by this study. While it is understandable that every discipline will use the language most familiar with their field, in line with the rights-based approach, specifically General Comment No. 24 (Committee on the Rights of the Child, 2019, paras. 7–8), this book seeks where possible to avoid using terms that could judge or label, using the neutral term 'child' or 'young person' to refer to those under 18 years (Article 1 CRC), and 'children in conflict with the law' as those who come into contact with the justice system.

Bibliography

Committee of Ministers. (2010). *Guidelines of the Committee of Ministers of the Council of Europe on child-friendly justice.* Adopted by the Committee of Ministers of the Council of Europe on 17 November 2010 and explanatory memorandum.

Committee on the Rights of the Child. (2019). *General comment No. 24 (2019) on children's rights in the child justice system*, 19 September 2019, CRC/C/GC/24.

Hammarberg, T. (1990). The Convention on the Rights of the Child and how to make it work. *Human Rights Quarterly, 12*, 97–105.

Hespel, S., Put, J., & Rom, M. (2012). Navigating the maze. The interrelation of international legal norms, with illustrations from international juvenile justice standards. *Human Rights and International Legal Discourse, 6*, 329–365.

Kilkelly, U. (2008). Justice and children's rights: Measuring compliance with international standards. *Youth Justice, 8*(3), 187–192.

Liefaard, T. (2016). Child-friendly justice; protection and participation of children in the justice system. *Temple Law Review, 88*, 905–927.

Liefaard, T. (2020). Juvenile justice. In J. Todres & S. M. King (Eds.), *The Oxford handbook of children's rights law* (pp. 279–306). Oxford University Press.

Lundy, L., & McEvoy, L. (2012). Children's rights and research processes: Assisting children to (in)formed views. *Childhood, 19*(1), 129–144.

Lynch, N., van den Brink, Y., & Forde, L. (Eds.). (2022). *Responses to serious offending by children: Principles, practice and global perspectives*. Routledge.

Nowak, M. (2019). *Global study on children deprived of liberty*, A/74/136.

UN General Assembly. (1985). *United Nations standard minimum rules for the administration of juvenile justice ("The Beijing Rules")*, 29 November 1985, 40/33.

CHAPTER 2

Children in Conflict with the Law: The Rights-Based Framework

Abstract Throughout recent decades, a large body of children's rights standards has been developed, setting a clear benchmark for the protection of children's rights in the justice system. These instruments include the Convention on the Rights of the Child, the Beijing Rules, the Riyadh Guidelines, the Havana Rules and the European Guidelines on Child-friendly Justice. This chapter brings together these instruments to present a framework for the protection of the rights of children in conflict with the law. After setting out the general principles of children's rights, it outlines the children's rights principles and provisions that have specific relevance to children in conflict with the law and presents the elements of a rights-based framework for the treatment of children in such circumstances. Underlining the importance of a rights-based approach to the care and treatment of children in conflict with the law, this chapter proposes three themes or phases—Prevention, Diversion and Justice, and Reintegration—that will be used as an integrated rights- and evidence-based approach to the analysis and development of youth justice.

Keywords Children's rights · Children in conflict with the law · Youth justice

U. Kilkelly et al., *Children in Conflict with the Law*, Palgrave Critical Studies in Human Rights and Criminology, https://doi.org/10.1007/978-3-031-36652-9_2

Introduction

The adoption of the Convention on the Rights of the Child (the CRC) by the United Nations in 1989 marked a significant milestone in the development of children's rights standards by the international community. The CRC represents a comprehensive statement of the rights to which all children are entitled across all areas of their lives, and it contains precise protections that apply to children in conflict with the law. The significance of the CRC—the most widely ratified instrument in international law—lies in its comprehensive and legally binding nature. In terms of children and the justice system, the Convention contains a number of important provisions and, together with the General Comments of the Committee on the Rights of the Child (in particular, Committee on the Rights of the Child, 2007a, 2019), it sets important standards for states parties with respect to the duty to respect, protect and fulfil the rights of the child in this situation (Liefaard, 2020). Both before and since the adoption of the Convention, multiple other instruments have been adopted to recognise particular aspects of children's experience in the justice system. They include the 1985 Beijing Rules (UN General Assembly, 1985), the 1990 Riyadh Guidelines (UN General Assembly, 1990a) and Havana Rules (UN General Assembly, 1990b) and the 2010 European Guidelines on Child-friendly Justice (Committee of Ministers, 2010). Together, these and many other documents set down a clear benchmark for the protection of children's rights in the justice system (Kilkelly, 2008). Established through dialogue and standard setting, they represent the consensus of the international community with respect to the treatment of children in conflict with the law.

The aim of this chapter is to bring together the relevant international instruments in order to present a framework for the protection of children's rights with regard to children in conflict with the law. It begins by setting out the general principles of children's rights that emanate from these standards, before moving on to outline the principles and provisions that have specific relevance to children in conflict with the law. The chapter will then present the elements of a rights-based framework for the treatment of children who come into contact with the justice system. Framed in three phases—Prevention, Diversion and Justice, and Reintegration—the final section will provide the structure for the chapters that follow, which will present the research evidence under each phase in support of a rights- and evidence-based approach to youth justice.

The General Principles of Children's Rights

This first section sets out the general children's rights principles that apply to children in all circumstances, including those in conflict with the law. According to the Committee on the Rights of the Child (the Committee), the treaty body that monitors implementation of the Convention, there are four general principles in the CRC. They are: the right to development in Article 6, the right to enjoy CRC rights without discrimination in Article 2, the requirement that the child's best interests must be a primary consideration in all actions concerning the child in Article 3 and finally, in Article 12, the right of the child to have their views taken into account in all matters affecting the child in accordance with their age and maturity (Committee on the Rights of the Child, 2003a, para. 12). According to the Committee, states parties are required to apply these general principles systematically in the administration of child justice (Committee on the Rights of the Child, 2007a, para. 5).

Non-discrimination

With respect to the principle of non-discrimination, states must take measures to ensure that all children in conflict with the law are treated equally before the law, paying attention to de facto discrimination and other disparities which may impact on children depending on their ethnic background, gender, vulnerability or those who are being drawn deeper into the justice system (Committee on the Rights of the Child, 2007a, para. 6). As a result, the European Guidelines on Child-friendly Justice provide that states may need to grant 'special protection and assistance' to more marginalised children, 'such as migrant children, refugee and asylum-seeking children, unaccompanied children, children with disabilities, homeless and street children, Roma children, and children in residential institutions' (Committee of Ministers, 2010, para. II.D.1). The standards are relatively muted on the issue of disproportionate minority contact with the justice system, which is surprising given the fact that issues relating to race and ethnic background, and disproportionate contact of children from marginalised groups, dominate the youth justice landscape in many jurisdictions (Mallett, 2018). At the same time, the standards recognise that girls, who are in a minority in the justice system, can also have their needs overlooked, causing the Committee on the Rights of the Child to recommend that they are paid special attention (Committee on the Rights of the Child, 2019, para. 50). This is underlined in the Beijing Rules, which provide that girls in conflict with the law who are placed in an institution deserve 'special attention as to their personal needs and problems' and should receive fair treatment in relation to 'care, protection, assistance, treatment and training' (UN General Assembly, 1985, rule 26.4). More generally, the standards require that states should take measures to prevent children becoming victims of discrimination as a result of their contact with the justice system, and should enact legislation to prevent 'further stigmatization, victimization and criminalization' of children whose behaviour or circumstances may bring them into contact with the law (Committee on the Rights of the Child, 2007a, paras. 8–9; citing also UN General Assembly, 1990a, article 56). Such legislation should ensure that conduct that is not considered an offence or penalised if committed by an adult is not when committed by a child (UN General Assembly, 1990a, article 56; see also Committee of Ministers, 2010, commentary para. 47).

The Best Interests of the Child

Noting that Article 3 of the CRC encompasses a right, a procedural rule and a principle (Committee on the Rights of the Child, 2013, para. 6), the Committee has reflected on the special application of the child's best interests to children in conflict with the law. In particular, the Committee has highlighted that the child's best interests must be an essential component of any child justice policy, noting that, in this context, Article 3 requires that 'the traditional objectives of criminal justice, such as repression/retribution, must give way to rehabilitation and restorative justice objectives in dealing with child[ren]' (Committee on the Rights of the Child, 2007b, para. 10). Drawing on the Beijing Rules (UN General Assembly, 1985), the Committee considers one of the consequences of the best interests principle to be that the focus should remain on rehabilitation and reintegration for all children (Committee on the Rights of the Child, 2016, para. 88). Indeed, even where children have committed serious offences, the Committee emphasises that in decision-making, weight should be given both to the child's best interests and to the need to promote reintegration (Committee on the Rights of the Child, 2019, para. 76; see also Kilkelly & Liefaard, 2022). This is highlighted in the Beijing Rules, according to which children in conflict with the law should be provided with 'necessary assistance' at all stages of the proceedings to 'facilitate the rehabilitative process' (UN General Assembly, 1985, rule 24.1). This emphasises the importance of providing children with the necessary assistance to further their best interests throughout the rehabilitative process (UN General Assembly, 1985, rule 24.1 commentary). Moreover, the Havana Rules show a similar objective for children who are deprived of their liberty (UN General Assembly, 1990b, rule 12). Throughout a child's contact with the youth justice system, the child's best interests should be protected through the use of procedural safeguards and also taken into account in decision-making, particularly where a child is deprived of liberty. Proceedings should be conducive to the best interests of children in conflict with the law (UN General Assembly, 1985, rule 14.2). In addition, the Committee on the Rights of the Child has emphasised that adequate realisation of a child's rights under Article 3 requires states to adopt a rights-respecting approach to all of the rights protected within the Convention and to 'secure the holistic physical, psychological, moral and spiritual integrity of the child and promote his or her human dignity' (Committee on the Rights of the Child, 2013, section I.A.).

This approach reinforces the need to take a holistic approach to ensuring children's rights are respected and protected where children are in conflict with the law. The European Guidelines on Child-friendly Justice follow this by promoting the development of multidisciplinary methods to assess the best interests of the child (Committee of Ministers, 2010, explanatory memorandum para. 36). They state that, in assessing children's best interests, all their other rights should be respected at all times (Committee of Ministers, 2010, para. III.B.2.b). They add that authorities should adopt a comprehensive approach, taking into account all interests at stake, including the 'psychological and physical well-being and legal, social and economic interests of the child' (Committee of Ministers, 2010, para. III.B.2.c).

Finally, the importance of prevention and early intervention is also an aspect of protecting the child's best interests within the justice system insofar as these approaches ensure that children are kept out of formal contact with the law. Such measures should involve 'safeguarding the well-being, development, rights and interests of all young persons' (UN General Assembly, 1990a, article 5(d)). It is clear therefore that the best interests principle has application at all stages of decision-making in relation to children in conflict with the law, both through prevention and early intervention efforts, and throughout all decision-making made when children are in contact with the justice system. Moreover, having regard to the best interests of the child also underlines the importance of the child having access to universal services, including their fulfilment of CRC rights more generally.

The Right to Life, Survival and Development

The next general principle—the child's right to life, survival and development protected by Article 6 of the CRC—also has special resonance to the circumstances of children in conflict with the law. The Committee has noted that children's experience of coming into conflict with the law has very negative effects on their development, requiring, consequently, that policies in this area should support the child's development while minimising harmful impacts (Committee on the Rights of the Child, 2007a, para. 11). The Beijing Rules also underline that, in the administration of juvenile justice, states should endeavour to develop conditions that foster a process of personal development and education for the child (UN General Assembly, 1985, rule 1.2). Children's development should be considered in the elaboration of prevention policies and measures, as highlighted in the Riyadh Guidelines (UN General Assembly, 1990a, articles 5(a), 5(d), 10). In relation to responses to children in conflict with the law, the European Guidelines on Child-friendly Justice provide that measures and sanctions should bear in mind, among other things, the child's physical and mental well-being and development (para. IV.82). As the Committee notes, exposure to the criminal justice system has been demonstrated to cause harm to children, limiting their chances of becoming responsible adults, a principle that reinforces the importance of both diversion and early intervention. According to the Committee, children's differences from adults in terms of physical and psychological development form the basis for recognising their 'lesser culpability, and for a separate system with a differentiated, individualized approach' (Committee on the Rights of the Child, 2019, para. 2). This links also to the minimum age of criminal responsibility, considered further below.

The Right to Be Heard

The right of the child to have their views taken into account in matters that affect them under Article 12 of the CRC also applies to children in conflict with the law. As the Committee has noted, this right must be respected and fulfilled throughout every stage of the justice process, and in this regard, the principle clearly aligns with the due process guarantees set out in Article 40 (Committee on the Rights of the Child, 2007a, para. 12; 2019, para. 44). The possibility for children in conflict with the law to participate and express their views freely in justice proceedings was already enshrined in the Beijing Rules (UN General Assembly, rule 14.2). In line with recent developments, including in European human rights law, the child has a right to participate effectively in such proceedings, in order to benefit from what is now established as 'child-friendly justice' (Liefaard & Kilkelly, 2018). As the Committee explains,

> [d]evelopments in child-friendly justice provide an impetus towards child-friendly language at all stages, child-friendly layouts of interviewing spaces and courts, support by appropriate adults, removal of intimidating legal attire and adaptation of proceedings, including accommodation for children with disabilities. (Committee on the Rights of the Child, 2019, para. 46)

The European Guidelines on Child-friendly Justice further enshrine children's 'right to be informed about their rights, to be given appropriate ways to access justice, and to be consulted and heard in proceedings involving or affecting them'. This includes giving children's views due weight, bearing in mind their 'maturity and any communication difficulties' to make their participation in the legal process meaningful (Committee of Ministers, 2010, para. III.A.1). According to the Guidelines, children should be consulted on how they would like to be heard, and the means used should be adapted to the individual child and the circumstances of the case (Committee of Ministers, 2010, para. IV.44). Children should receive all necessary information to effectively exercise this right, including the fact that their views will not necessarily determine final decisions (Committee of Ministers, 2010, para. IV. 48). The Guidelines underline that the right to participate in the process is a right, not a duty (Committee of Ministers, 2010, para. IV. 47). Another aspect of this right is that decisions affecting children should be reasoned and explained to them in language they can understand (Committee of Ministers, 2010, para. IV. 49).

The principle of the child's participation in decision-making also has a wider significance in the context of child justice, given that children in conflict with the law are, as a group, often ignored and seldom heard. In this regard, the Committee has noted with approval that 'the voices of children involved in the juvenile justice system are increasingly becoming a powerful force for improvements and reform, and for the fulfilment of their rights' (Committee on the Rights of the Child 2007a, para. 12). Elsewhere, the Committee has articulated the importance of children's participation in research (Committee on the Rights of the Child, 2009), and it is also clear that research affecting children in conflict with the law must ensure their rights are respected and their views taken into account, in line with Article 12 (Lundy & McEvoy, 2012).

Children's Rights Applied to Children in Conflict with the Law

While specific rights in the Convention are directly applicable to children in conflict with the law and are discussed in the following section, it is important that the Convention's other substantive rights apply also to children in such circumstances. This is clear from the CRC's general principles, discussed in the previous section. Also relevant are a whole range of rights of wider significance to children in conflict with the law. Article 27, for instance, builds on Article 6 of the CRC in requiring states parties to assure to children a standard of living 'adequate for the child's physical, mental, spiritual, moral and social development'. This clearly resonates with children in conflict with the law whose development can be hindered by an absence of early childhood care and support, while their contact with the justice system can have a similarly negative impact on their lives. This is highlighted in the European Guidelines on Child-friendly Justice's definition of the concept of child-friendly justice as 'justice systems which guarantee the respect and the effective implementation of all children's rights at the highest attainable level [...]' (Committee of Ministers, 2010, para. II.c).

The Importance of Parents and Family Care

Parents play a very important role in the fulfilment of children's rights, and this is recognised in several ways in the CRC. First, the Convention's Preamble recognises that the child's 'full and harmonious development' depends on them growing up in a 'family environment, in an atmosphere of happiness, love and understanding'. This is no less important for children in conflict with the law; indeed, the lack of such care—both before and during their contact with the justice system—can accentuate the vulnerability of children in such circumstances. Article 5 builds on this principle, recognising the duty of the state to respect the 'responsibility, rights and duties of parents' to provide the child with 'appropriate direction and guidance' in the exercise of their rights (Kilkelly, 2020). This principle is especially important in the context of children in conflict with the law, not least given that, as Article 40(2) of the CRC illustrates, parents have a valuable role to play in supporting the child through the justice process (Committee on the Rights of the Child, 2019, paras. 47, 56).

This supportive role is also highlighted in other international standards applicable to children in conflict with the law. The Beijing Rules provide that parents (or guardians) should be notified of a child's apprehension (UN General Assembly, 1985, rule 10.1) and are entitled to participate in proceedings, unless contrary to the child's interests (UN General Assembly, 1985, 15.2). In particular, rule 18.2 points to the importance of the child's family, requiring that a child's separation from their parents be used only as a last resort (UN General Assembly, 1985, commentary rule 18.2). For children who are deprived of their liberty or are institutionalised, the international standards recognise the importance of guaranteeing access for children's parents (Committee of Ministers, 2010, para. IV.21.a; UN General Assembly, 1985, rule 26.5) and of communication between children and their families and friends (Committee of Ministers, 2010, para. IV.21.a; UN General Assembly, 1990b, rule 59). Similarly, the European Guidelines on Child-friendly Justice highlight parents' role in relation to access to information (Committee of Ministers, 2010, paras. II.E.3, II.E.5), children's apprehension and questioning by the police (Committee of Ministers, 2010, paras. IV.28–30) as well as a child's parent's presence in justice proceedings (Committee of Ministers, 2010, para. IV.58).

Further, Article 18(2) of the CRC requires states parties to provide 'appropriate assistance' to parents and those who care for children in the fulfilment of their parental responsibilities, requiring the development of 'institutions, facilities and services for the care of children'. The Committee on the Rights of the Child is keen to stress the importance of involving parents in measures and programmes designed to prevent children from coming into contact with the justice system, noting that the research supports both family- and community-based measures that provide important safeguards to children and families in such situations (Committee on the Rights of the Child, 2019, para. 9). The value of programmes that provide early, universal supports to children and families is particularly noted and programmes that are 'evidence-based' should be developed, according to the Committee, in order to reflect the 'multiple psychosocial causes' of children's behaviour, but also 'the protective factors that may strengthen resilience' (Committee on the Rights of the Child, 2019, para. 11). As an absolute priority, children should be supported in their families (Committee on the Rights of the Child, 2019, para. 11). Similarly, the Riyadh Guidelines consider that states should provide families with opportunities to learn about parental role and obligations regarding child development and childcare and take measures to promote family cohesion and discourage separation of children from their parents (UN General Assembly, 1990a, articles 16–17). They highlight the important role of the family and communities in preventive policies that facilitate the successful socialisation and integration of all children (UN General Assembly, 1990a, article 10, section IV.A, section IV.C).

Just as the CRC makes specific provision for children to be supported by their parents in the fulfilment of their rights, it also recognises the role of the state in the provision of appropriate alternative care for children deprived of a family environment. Article 20 of the Convention recognises the right of such children to 'special care and assistance', including foster care and adoption that takes account of the 'desirability of continuity in a child's upbringing' and their ethnic, religious, cultural and linguistic background. According to the Committee, children should be supported within their families and communities as 'an absolute priority' and where, as an exceptional measure, an out of home placement is required, family-based care should be preferred, with residential care only used where it is necessary to provide professional services (Committee on the Rights of the Child, 2019, para. 11). Such placements should, nonetheless, be used only as a measure of last resort and for the shortest appropriate period of time and, in line with Article 25, they should be subject to periodic review (Committee on the Rights of the Child, 2019, para. 11). The role of the state in the provision of appropriate alternative care is also recognised in the Riyadh Guidelines, which provide that alternative placements, including foster care and adoption, should be considered where the child does not have a 'stable and settled family environment', community efforts to assist the child's parents have failed and the child cannot be cared for by their extended family (UN General Assembly, 1990a, article 14).

Special Protection for the Rights of Children with Disabilities

Children with disabilities are also the subject of special rights protections under Article 23 of the CRC including the right to enjoy 'a full and decent life', in conditions that promote dignity and self-reliance and active participation in the community. Children with disabilities are entitled to special care that is appropriate to the child's needs under Article 23(2), with effective access under Article 23(3) to education, training, healthcare, preparation for employment and recreation that is conducive to the fulfilment of the child's development. Although no specific reference is made in the Convention to children with disabilities who are in conflict with the law, the Committee has made clear that the Convention's specific provisions—Articles 37 and 40—apply equally to such children who have additional vulnerabilities (Committee on the Rights of the Child, 2007b, para. 73). According to the Committee, specialised supports and services are required to ensure that children with disabilities benefit from an adapted justice process and diversion from both the judicial process and detention in order to ensure the rights of such children are protected (Committee on the Rights of the Child, 2007b, para. 74). This is reasserted in the European Guidelines on Child-friendly Justice, which provide that specific protection and assistance may need to be granted for more marginalised children, including children with disabilities (Committee of Ministers, 2010, para. III.B.2).

Prevention, Reintegration and the Right to Education

Although fundamental rights for every child, the rights to education and health have very particular significance for children in conflict with the law. Article 28 of the CRC makes provision for the child's right to education, including 'primary education' (Article 28(1)(a)), 'all forms of secondary education including general and vocational education, that is available and accessible to every child (Article 28(1)(b)) and 'higher education accessible to all on the basis of capacity by every appropriate means' (Article 28(1)(c)). While noting the relevance of the requirement that education must be 'available and accessible', of specific relevance to children in conflict with the law is the duty on states parties under Article

28(1)(e) to take measures to encourage regular school attendance and reduce drop-out rates. Also important in this context is the requirement under Article 28(2) to take all appropriate measures to ensure that school discipline is administered in a manner consistent with the child's human dignity and the Convention. Meanwhile, Article 29 requires that a child's education must be directed at the development of their 'personality, talents and mental and physical abilities to their fullest potential'. It must also develop respect for human rights, respect for the natural environment and the preparation of the child for responsible life in a free society. These are important general and indeed preventive measures with respect to children who come into conflict with the law according to the Committee (Committee on the Rights of the Child, 2019, para. 9). Linked with the role of parents, already outlined, the Committee has highlighted the importance under the CRC of ensuring parental partnerships with schools to ensure children who are at risk of no longer attending school or of not completing their education receive the necessary supports (Committee on the Rights of the Child, 2019, paras. 9–10).

The Riyadh Guidelines also consider education as one of the core measures that must be emphasised for the development of policies designed to facilitate the successful socialisation and integration of children (see UN General Assembly, 1990a, section IV.B). Similar to Article 29 of the CRC, it sets out the principles to which education systems should 'devote particular attention', such as teaching basic values and developing children's respect for human rights and fundamental freedoms (UN General Assembly, 1990a, article 21(a)). They also emphasise the role of parents in education, providing that educational systems should seek to work together with parents (UN General Assembly, 1990a, article 22). They address the need to promote children's attendance in school, by giving special assistance to children who struggle with attendance (UN General Assembly, 1990a, article 31). They also contain provisions aimed at children in vulnerable situations, considering that children who are at 'social risk' should receive particular care and attention from educational systems (UN General Assembly, 1990a, article 24), and that teachers and students should be especially sensitised to the 'problems, needs and perceptions' of young people from 'underprivileged, disadvantaged, ethnic or other minority and low-income groups' (UN General Assembly, 1990a, article 27). Linked to this, they provide that comprehensive policies for the prevention of 'alcohol, drug and other substance abuse' should be given special attention and students, teachers and other professionals should be provided with information on how to prevent and respond to these issues (UN General Assembly, 1990a, article 25). Similar focus is found in the European Rules for Juvenile Offenders Subject to Sanctions and Measures (Committee of Ministers, 2008); in providing for a set of basic principles, these Rules state unequivocally that any sanctions or measures imposed on children should be 'based on principles of social integration and education and the prevention of re-offending' (Committee of Ministers, 2008, I.A.2). The Rules recognise the rights of children in respect of their education should not be limited by the imposition of community sanctions (Committee of Ministers, 2008, II.C.28), and equal priority should be given to the provision of education where children are deprived of their liberty (Committee of Ministers, 2008, III.E10.77).

At the other end of the spectrum, the Committee has highlighted the importance of education for children deprived of liberty, identifying its integral connection with the child's right to be supported to reintegrate into their community following release. In particular, it has emphasised in this context that every child has the right to education suited to their needs and abilities and designed to prepare them for return to society (Committee on the Rights of the Child, 2019, para. 95). It similarly notes the importance that such children receive vocational training in occupations likely to prepare them for future employment (Committee on the Rights of the Child, 2019, para. 95). This is highlighted in the Havana Rules, which recall that '[e]very juvenile of compulsory school age has the right to education suited to his or her needs and abilities and designed to prepare him or her for return to society' (UN General Assembly, 1990b, rule 38) and the right to receive vocational training (UN General Assembly, 1990b, rule 42). The Rules also include specific provisions on how education and vocational training should be administered for children deprived of their liberty, such as access to an adequately stocked library (UN General Assembly, 1990b, rule 41), provision of education by qualified teachers and integrated in the national education system, or the right to special education (UN General Assembly, 1990b, rule 38). In addition, the Rules specify that diplomas or certificates awarded to children while in detention should not indicate that the child was in detention (UN General Assembly, 1990b, rule 40). The Beijing Rules also recall that children shall receive educational and vocational assistance while in custody (UN General Assembly, 1985, rule 13.5) and in institutions (UN General Assembly, 1985, rule 26.2). European Rules for Juveniles Subject to Sanctions and Measures emphasise that priority should be given to school and vocational training over work within the activities provided for in institutions where children are deprived of their liberty, recommending that young people should be facilitated to attend school and training activities in the community where possible (Committee of Ministers, 2008, III.E10.78). Planning, including educational planning, should be focused on enabling children to 'make the best use of their time and to develop skills and competences that enable them to reintegrate into society' (Committee of Ministers, 2008, III.E10.79.2). Finally, the European Guidelines on Child-friendly Justice also underscore the right of children deprived of their liberty to receive 'appropriate education, vocational guidance and training' (Committee of Ministers, 2010, para. IV.21.b), which should always be guaranteed for children in conflict with the law (Committee of Ministers, 2010, para. IV.82).

Health Rights and Children in Conflict with the Law

The right to health is, similarly, important both as a measure to prevent children coming into contact with the justice system and as a means to promote a child's reintegration into society following such contact (Committee on the Rights of the Child, 2019, para. 18). Contact with the justice system entails risks to children's right to health, and therefore, a focus on health is important as part of a broader strategy of prevention. Under Article 24(1) of the CRC, the child has the right to enjoy the 'highest attainable standard of health and to facilities for the treatment of illness and rehabilitation of health'. Full implementation of this right requires that states parties take measures to combat disease and malnutrition, develop preventive healthcare and promote health education to children and parents alike. In addition to recognising the important role played by preventive healthcare, the Committee has also highlighted the particular challenges to a child's health and development experienced during adolescence (Committee on the Rights of the Child, 2003b). In particular, it has noted that children at this stage of development can be exposed to particular risks of violence and exploitation as well as to threats to their well-being and moral and physical integrity that require investment in research to inform the adoption of effective policies and programmes (Committee on the Rights of the Child, 2003b, para. 8). The Committee has also drawn attention to the need to ensure that adolescents affected by poverty are not criminalised (Committee on the Rights of the Child, 2003b, para. 8); taking account of the increased vulnerability of children who are socially excluded requires that they receive the appropriate services and facilities to support healthy life choices (Committee on the Rights of the Child, 2003b, para. 30). Specific threats to children's health that can lead children into contact with the justice system—such as homelessness (Committee on the Rights of the Child, 2003b, para. 32)—require dedicated strategies and resources, while those who have experienced exploitation, including sexual abuse and trauma, require health and counselling rather than criminalisation (Committee on the Rights of the Child, 2003b, para. 33). The link between the right to health and preventing children coming into contact with the justice system is also highlighted in the Riyadh Guidelines. In fact, they provide that comprehensive prevention plans should involve health education agencies in preventive actions (UN General Assembly, 1990a, article 9(g)). States should also provide sufficient funds and other resources for the 'effective delivery of services, facilities and staff for adequate medical and mental health care, nutrition, housing and other relevant services, including drug and alcohol abuse prevention and treatment' (UN General Assembly, 1990a, article 45).

Health is also linked to the child's reintegration into their community following contact with the justice system, including the deprivation of liberty. In this context, the Committee has highlighted the need for courts to take account of the child's health needs as part of their reaction to their offending behaviour ensuring that their mental health needs, for instance, are weighed in the balance in such circumstances (Committee on the Rights of the Child, 2019, para. 85). The Committee has placed significant emphasis on the child's right to health and healthcare in the case of children who spend time in detention, drawing on the Havana Rules to accentuate the child's right to receive adequate healthcare in line with their assessed needs (Committee on the Rights of the Child, 2019, para. 108). The Havana Rules underline that details of known physical and mental problems, including drug and alcohol use, of children deprived of liberty should be recorded (UN General Assembly, 1990b, rule 21(e)). Detention should only take place under conditions that take full account of the child's particular needs, status and special requirements, including according to their mental and physical health (UN General Assembly, 1990b, rule 28). Facilities and services have to meet the requirements of health and human dignity (UN General Assembly, 1990b, rule 31), including in relation to clothing (rule 36) and food and water (rule 37). While in detention, children also have the right to receive adequate medical care 'both preventive and remedial' (UN General Assembly, 1990b, rule 49) in circumstances detailed in the Havana Rules (UN General Assembly, 1990b, section H).

Protection from Harm

More generally, the child's right to protection from harm—recognised in strong terms in Article 19 of the CRC—has very particular significance for children in conflict with the law, with respect to both understanding the vulnerability of children in such circumstances and recognising the harm that contact with the justice system can cause (Committee on the Rights of the Child, 2011, para. 3; UN General Assembly, 1985, commentary rule 1 and rule 10.3). This also explains the prohibition in Article 37 of the CRC of torture or other cruel, inhuman or degrading treatment or punishment, which reflects the particular vulnerability of children in the justice system where they are often denied protection from such harms (Committee on the Rights of the Child, 2011, para. 26). The Committee has repeatedly noted that violence 'occurs in all phases of the juvenile justice process' from first contact with the police to the deprivation of liberty (Committee on the Rights of the Child, 2019, para. 15; Nowak, 2019). As such, the Beijing Rules provide that contacts between law enforcement agencies and children in conflict with the law should be managed in a way to 'avoid' harm to the child (UN General Assembly, 1985, rule 10.3). Harm can also be incurred during judicial proceedings, for example, through the disclosure of harmful images or information to the child (see Committee of Ministers, 2010, para. IV.60). For children deprived of their liberty, the Havana Rules provide that recourse to instruments of restraint or to force for any purpose should be prohibited, except in limited circumstances laid down in the rules (UN General Assembly, 1990b, rule 63). If it is used, it should not cause 'humiliation or degradation' and should be used for the shortest possible period of time (UN General Assembly, 1990b, rule 64). Likewise, all disciplinary measures constituting cruel, inhuman or degrading treatment should be strictly prohibited, 'including corporal punishment, placement in a dark cell, closed or solitary confinement or any other punishment that may compromise the physical or mental health' of the child (UN General Assembly, 1990b, rule 67). The Havana Rules also try to protect children deprived of liberty from violence inflicted by staff by prohibiting them to carry and use weapons in facilities (UN General Assembly, 1990b, rule 65). The European Guidelines on Child-friendly Justice provide that children should be protected from harm, 'including intimidation, reprisals and secondary victimisation', in all judicial and non-judicial proceedings and other interventions (Committee of Ministers, 2010, para. IV.11). This understanding informs the priority given in the CRC to diverting children from the justice system altogether while it also informs the principle in Article 37(d) of the CRC that detention, where such harm can occur, is to be a measure of last resort used for the shortest appropriate period of time. As the Committee notes, this harm can be caused by peers, through the use of physical restraint, or abuse by adults in positions of authority (Committee on the Rights of the Child, 2019, para. 108).

The Committee's appreciation of the impact that violence has on children's development and their well-being also underpins the emphasis given to the wide range of measures necessary to ensure children are protected from all forms of violence (Committee on the Rights of the Child, 2011, para. 15). These are particularly acute with respect to the violence experienced by children in the justice system where the closed nature of the environment requires independent complaint and inspection mechanisms to be in place to provide adequate oversight and redress where required (Committee on the Rights of the Child, 2019, para. 95). Article 19(2) of the CRC requires the adoption of measures that prevent violence, while requiring states to take effective measures that enable the 'identification, reporting, referral, investigation, treatment and follow-up of instances of child maltreatment' (Committee on the Rights of the Child, 2011, paras. 49–58). To prevent the occurrence of harm, the European Guidelines on Child-friendly Justice recommend that professionals working with and for children should, where necessary, be subject to regular vetting (Committee of Ministers, 2010, para. VI.12). The Havana Rules provide that qualified inspectors should be empowered to conduct inspections of detention facilities (UN General Assembly, 1990b, rule 72). They also grant children deprived of their liberty the opportunity to make requests or complaints to the director of the detention facility, their representative, the central administration, the judicial authority or other proper authorities through approved channels (UN General Assembly, 1990b, rules 75–76). They encourage the establishment of an 'ombudsman' to receive and investigate such complaints (UN General Assembly, 1990b, rule 77). Also relevant here is Article 39 of the CRC, which requires states parties to take measures that ensure the right of the child who has suffered abuse or exploitation to access measures and supports aimed at their physical and psychological recovery and reintegration. According to the CRC, this recovery must take place in an environment that fosters the health, self-respect and dignity of the child.

The Rights of Children in Conflict with the Law

In addition to the general rights which apply to all children, Articles 37 and 40 of the CRC set out a number of specific principles relevant to children in conflict with the law and their contact with the justice system. Most importantly, Article 40(1) provides that states parties to the Convention recognise the right of every child:

> alleged or, accused of or recognised as having infringed the penal law to be treated in a manner consistent with the promotion of the child's sense of dignity and worth, which reinforces the child's respect for the human rights and fundamental freedoms of others and which takes into account the child's age and the desirability of promoting the child's reintegration and the child's assuming a constructive role in society.

There are a number of important principles to be found in this provision which inform the rights-based and child-centred approach to children in conflict with the law. First, it is clear from Article 40(1) that its protections apply to all children who have been accused, adjudicated or convicted of having infringed the law and nothing in the provision suggests any deviation from this general principle on the basis of the crime committed or its circumstances. In this regard, a child accused or convicted of a serious offence is entitled to enjoy the same rights protections as the child involved in low-level offending and states are not permitted to distinguish between children on these terms (Kilkelly & Liefaard, 2022; Lynch & Liefaard, 2020). Similarly, there is nothing here to support the approach of states parties that prefer to treat older children more punitively. At the same time, Article 40(1) recognises the principle that children in conflict with the law are entitled to age-appropriate treatment that reinforces the importance of a child-centred and individualised approach. The Havana Rules recall this in relation to children deprived of their liberty, stating that detention should only take place under conditions taking full account of the particular needs, status and special requirements according to, among other things, their age (UN General Assembly, 1990b, rule 28). Related to this is the principle that children must be treated in a manner that takes account of their age and that promotes their reintegration into society, enabling them to fulfil their potential. According to the Committee, the requirement of age-appropriate treatment applies through every stage of the justice process and can only be fulfilled where the professionals involved are knowledgeable about 'child development, the dynamic and continuing growth of children, what is appropriate to their well-being, and the pervasive forms of violence against children' (Committee on the Rights of the Child, 2019, para. 15). The requirement of age-appropriate treatment is also underlined in the European Guidelines on Child-friendly Justice, as child-friendly justice is justice that is 'accessible, age appropriate, [...] adapted to and focused on the needs and rights of the child [...]' (Committee of Ministers, 2010, para. II.c). A final general principle under Article 40(1) is that children in conflict with the law must receive care and education that is consistent both with their rights and with the development of respect for the rights of others. This is an important acknowledgement that a rights-respecting approach to children in conflict with the law must also involve children learning to respect the rights of others, in line with Article 29 of the CRC and the broader principles of the UN Charter (Committee on the Rights of the Child, 2019, para. 15). Although not mentioned expressly in the Convention, this also reflects the value of a restorative approach where children are supported to take responsibility for the harm they may have caused others (Committee on the Rights of the Child, 2019, paras. 1 and 8).

Youth Justice Processes and Children's Rights

Building on the general principle in Article 40(1) above, Article 40(2) of the CRC sets out a list of important procedural safeguards that apply to all children in contact with the youth justice system. It sets out children's right to be presumed innocent until proven guilty, and it has been emphasised that suspicious behaviour should not lead to an assumption of guilt without proof of the child's involvement beyond a reasonable doubt, as 'lack of understanding of the process, immaturity, fear or other reasons' may lead the child to engage in behaviour which may be perceived as suspicious by adults (Committee on the Rights of the Child, 2019, para. 43). The Committee on the Rights of the Child has emphasised that the list of specific requirements in Article 40(2) represent minimum requirements, and that states 'can and should try to establish and observe higher standards' (Committee on the Rights of the Child, 2019, para. 38). Indeed, when read together with the requirements for effective participation, as required under Article 12 of the CRC, discussed above, it is clear that the Article 40(2) requirements are indeed a floor rather than a ceiling.

In order to respect the right of the child to participate effectively (Article 40(2)(iv)), adjustments to the proceedings are required to create an 'atmosphere of understanding', including adjustments to language, 'child-friendly layouts' of courts and interviewing spaces, removal of intimidating attire, and making sure that support from both appropriate adults and all practitioners involved in the proceedings is available to the child (Committee on the Rights of the Child, 2019, para. 46). In ensuring that prompt and direct information is given to the child about any charges, the Committee has emphasised that while assistance to support the child's understanding from a parent or guardian is important, the duty ultimately lies with the authorities to make sure a child is supported to understand any information given (Committee on the Rights of the Child, 2019, para. 48). While the CRC itself refers to 'legal or other appropriate assistance' throughout the course of the proceedings, the Committee on the Rights of the Child has expressed concern that children would be afforded less protection than adults. In this regard, it has reiterated the importance of free and effective legal representation for the child from the outset of the formal legal process. (Committee on the Rights of the Child, 2019, paras. 49–53). Practices and processes, it says, should safeguard children's rights 'from the moment of contact with the system', and it highlights that the need for 'continuous and systematic training of professionals' is particularly crucial, including training in relation to the special needs of marginalised children (Committee on the Rights of the Child, 2019, paras. 39 and 41). Article 40(2)(vii) of the CRC also guarantees children's right to privacy throughout the proceedings, which should be read in line with the goals of reintegration and age-appropriate treatment set out in Article 40(1). This guarantee of privacy should, according to the Committee, entail 'lifelong protection from publication' across all forms of media and social media, to ensure that the child is protected from potential harm and can access employment and educational opportunities so that their opportunities for reintegration are not impeded (Committee on the Rights of the Child, 2019, para. 70).

Specialisation and Community-Based Services

Other important principles include the requirement contained in Article 40(3) of the CRC for states to ensure that children in conflict with the law receive the care and support of specialised laws, procedures, authorities and institutions. According to the Committee, this includes the development of specialised divisions within the police, the courts and those providing legal representation (Committee on the Rights of the Child 2007a, para. 92), while it also supports specialised services and facilities such as probation, counselling, supervision and residential care (Committee on the Rights of the Child, 2007a, para. 94). Regarding the training of professionals, the Riyadh Guidelines provide that law enforcement and other relevant personnel should be familiar and use 'to the maximum extent possible' programmes and referral possibilities for diversion (UN General Assembly, 1990a, article 58). Individual and community-based services are also considered important (Committee on the Rights of the Child 2019, paras. 105–109). Specialisation is supported by the European Guidelines on Child-friendly Justice in relation to courts, procedures and institutions for children in conflict with the law, as far as possible (Committee of Ministers, 2010, para. IV.63), as well as specialised judges, lawyers and support and information services (Committee of Ministers, 2010, para. V.f and k). Moreover, the important role of the community in the prevention of children coming into contact with the justice system is highlighted in the Riyadh Guidelines (UN General Assembly, 1990a, section C). This is strongly linked to diversion which is examined in the next section.

Fulfilling Children's Rights Through Opportunities for Diversion

Article 40 of the CRC mandates the child's diversion from the justice system where 'appropriate and desirable' and as long as 'human rights and legal safeguards are fully respected'. According to the Committee, diversion should be the 'preferred manner of dealing with children in the majority of cases' given that it 'yields good results for children' and is cost effective and consistent with public safety (Committee on the Rights of the Child, 2019, para. 15). While the exact nature and form of diversion method are left to states parties, the Committee considers that opportunities for diversion should be available from 'as early as possible after contact with the system, and at various stages throughout the process'.

Diversion, the Committee says, should be 'an integral part of the child justice system' (Committee on the Rights of the Child, 2019, para. 16).

In the implementation of the principle of diversion—specifically in the avoidance of detention—Article 40(4) of the CRC requires that a variety of community-based measures must be put in place as alternatives to institutional care. In this regard, the CRC prescribes that measures such as 'care, guidance and supervision orders; counselling; probation; foster care; education and vocational training programmes' must be available in order to ensure that children are dealt with in a manner appropriate to their well-being and proportionate to both their circumstances and the offence. The strength of provision for diversion within the Convention makes it clear that this is a fundamental principle of a rights-based approach. This reference to the child's well-being reprises the importance of the child's best interests under Article 3 of the CRC in the specific context of child justice, while the requirement of proportionality—with regard to the child's circumstances and their offending behaviour—is an important reminder that this general principle of criminal justice also applies, with specific adaptations, to children (UN General Assembly, 1985, rule 5.1).

The use of diversion for children in the conflict with the law is also included in other international standards. For instance, the Beijing Rules state that considerations should be given, wherever appropriate, to dealing with children in conflict with the law through diversion (UN General Assembly, 1985, rule 11.1). They consider that 'diversion at the outset and without referral to alternative (social) services may be the optimal response', especially when the offence is non-serious and where the child's family, school or other informal social control institutions have reacted or are likely to react in an appropriate and constructive manner (UN General Assembly, 1985, commentary rule 11). To facilitate this, Rule 11.4 considers that efforts should be made to provide for community programmes, such as temporary supervision and guidance, restitution and compensation of victims. Rule 11.3 requires the consent of the child, or their parents or guardian to be given, and underlines that care is needed to minimise the potential for coercion or intimidation during the diversionary process (UN General Assembly, 1985, commentary rule 11). The European Guidelines on Child-friendly Justice also refer to diversion, providing that alternatives to judicial proceedings should be encouraged when they may best serve the child's best interests (Committee of Ministers, 2010, para. IV.24). They underline the importance of children being thoroughly informed and consulted on the use of diversion, including its possible consequences (Committee of Ministers, 2010, para. IV.25).

Age Limits and Children in Conflict with the Law

As part of the requirement to establish specialised laws and approaches for children in conflict with the law, Article 40(3) of the CRC requires states parties to establish a minimum age of criminal responsibility below which the child shall be presumed not to have the capacity to commit a criminal offence. Although an important measure designed to keep the child away from the justice system, the failure of the drafters to agree a minimum age has been the subject of criticism (McDiarmid, 2013). The Beijing Rules had previously indicated that the minimum age should not be fixed at too low an age level, bearing in mind the facts of emotional, mental and intellectual maturity (UN General Assembly, 1985, rule 4.1). Likewise, the European Guidelines on Child-friendly Justice state that this age should not be too low (Committee of Ministers, 2010, para. IV.23). In this respect, the Committee in its first General Comment recommended 12 years as the minimum age (Committee on the Rights of the Child, 2007a, para. 32), revising this upwards to a recommendation of 14 years in 2019 (Committee on the Rights of the Child, 2019, para. 22). One of the reasons for the revision was to take account of recent developments in neuroscience and child development research which emphasise that children's capacity for abstract reasoning is still developing in younger adolescents (Committee on the Rights of the Child, 2019, para. 22). It is an important reminder that rather than being set in stone, such standards are dynamic concepts that evolve in line with the advances of research and scientific evidence.

Article 1 of the CRC defines a child as every human being below the age of 18 years unless, under the law applicable to the child, majority is attained earlier. This obviously gives states parties discretion to limit the application of the CRC to children below the age of 18 years, an issue of particular importance to children in conflict with the law who may lose the protections of the CRC in states where such age limits apply. The Committee has sought to limit the impact of such measures by recommending, for instance, that states should ensure that the protections of the child justice system apply to all children above the minimum age of criminal responsibility up to 18 years (Committee on the Rights of the Child, 2019, para. 29), including applying to those who were below the age of 18 at the time of the commission of the offence but who turn 18 during the trial or sentencing process (Committee on the Rights of the Child, 2019, para. 31). The European Guidelines on Child-friendly Justice sought to remedy this risk, by defining a child as any person under the age of 18 years (Committee of Ministers, 2010, para. II.a), thus making its recommendations applicable to all children under 18. Likewise, the Havana Rules define a 'juvenile' as every person under 18 years old (UN General Assembly, 1990b, rule 11(a)), while the Beijing Rules define a 'juvenile' as a 'child or young person who, under the respective legal systems, may be dealt with for an offence in a manner which is different from an adult' (UN General Assembly, 1985, rule 2.2(a)). Reflecting this approach, the Committee commends states parties that allow the application of the child justice system to persons aged 18 and older, whether as a general rule or by way of exception, describing this approach as 'in keeping with the developmental and neuroscience evidence that shows that brain development continues into the early twenties' (Committee on the Rights of the Child, 2019, para. 32). Overall, the Committee recommends that the protection of the Convention extends to the maximum extent possible to children in conflict with the law, regardless of their age or the nature of the harms caused. This is considered in line with the rights-based and child-centred approach.

Implementation of Children's Rights in the Justice System

Article 4 of the CRC requires states parties to take 'all appropriate legislative, administrative, and other measures for the implementation of the rights' in the CRC and the Committee has set out its guidance in this area in its General Comment No. 5 (Committee on the Rights of the Child, 2003a). These measures have been found to have an 'incremental and transformative' effect on the legal implementation of the CRC at a national level (Kilkelly, 2019), and according to the Committee, they include both legal and non-legal measures designed to give the CRC the force of domestic law and to shift the treatment of children from passive recipients of charity to holders of rights with legal entitlements against the state (Committee on the Rights of the Child, 2003a, p. 3). The Committee recommends the incorporation of the CRC into domestic law, so that it can inform policymaking and be directly invoked before the courts (Committee on the Rights of the Child, 2003a, para. 20).

It emphasises that domestic law should reflect the CRC's general principles and considers it important that sectoral laws such as those on the justice system should reflect the principles and provisions of the Convention (Committee on the Rights of the Child, 2003a, para. 22). In this way, enshrining the CRC's provisions and principles in national law is considered key to its implementation.

In addition to the measures that support the CRC's standing in domestic law, the Committee recommends the adoption of non-legal measures to further implementation at national level. Its key advice for states parties is to ensure cross-sectoral co-ordination, as well as regular monitoring of implementation, with the involvement of national human rights institutions, non-governmental organisations (NGOs) and others (Committee on the Rights of the Child, 2003a, para. 27). In recognition of the important role of national policy, the Committee has strongly recommended the adoption of a unified, comprehensive national strategy or action plan, rooted in the CRC, highlighting that developing such a strategy must take account of the views of children including those heard less often (Committee on the Rights of the Child, 2003a, para. 30). The Committee also advocates a process of child impact assessment, to evaluate the impact of proposed policy and budget decision-making on children, and promotes self-monitoring and evaluation as a government obligation but one in which it is important for others—parliamentary committees, academic institutions, NGOs and independent human rights institutions—to also participate (Committee on the Rights of the Child, 2003a, paras. 45–47).

The child's right to information about their rights in Article 42 of the CRC draws a unique connection between children's awareness of their rights and their effective realisation, and by extension, the Committee has consistently recommended that the training and capacity building of those who work with and for children should be systematic and ongoing, emphasising the status of the child as a holder of rights and encouraging active respect of the child's rights (Committee on the Rights of the Child, 2003a, para. 53). This has been a particularly important recommendation in relation to children in conflict with the law, and the Committee has recommended repeatedly that there should be 'continuous and systematic training' of all professionals who work in the justice system—including police, judiciary, prosecutors and those working in residential and detention settings—regarding the vulnerability of children in conflict with the law, as well as children's rights and child development more broadly (Committee on the Rights of the Child, 2019, para. 49). As such, the Riyadh Guidelines provide that law enforcement and other relevant personnel should be trained to respond to the special needs of young people (UN General Assembly, 1990a, article 58) and that teachers should be trained to prevent and deal with children's problems with substance use (UN General Assembly, 1990a, article 25). According to the Havana Rules, staff of detention facilities should receive training to enable them to carry out their responsibilities effectively, 'in particular training in child psychology, child welfare and international standards and norms of human rights and the rights of the child, including the present Rules' (UN General Assembly, 1990b, rule 85). The training of professionals working with and for children is also considered as one of the general elements of child-friendly justice by the European Guidelines on Child-friendly Justice (Committee of Ministers, 2010, section IV.4). Staff who have direct contact with children should receive interdisciplinary training on the rights and needs of children of different age groups, on proceedings adapted to those needs and on ways to communicate with children of different ages and stages of development (Committee of Ministers, 2010, paras. IV.14–15).

The Rights-Based Framework

As this chapter demonstrates, the international children's rights standards recognise the importance of the rights-based approach to the care and treatment of children in conflict with the law. Although not perfect, considering these various instruments were developed by different international bodies at different times and with different emphases, they present a remarkably clear and coherent framework for the protection and promotion of children's rights in this area. The detail and comprehensive nature of the standards are considerable, although that can make it difficult to establish a single roadmap for reform for those seeking to advocate for or implement progressive, rights-based policies. To aid this process, the final section in this chapter sets out a framework according to which the standards are grouped into three themes or phases as part of a rights-based model for the treatment of children in conflict with the law:

these are Prevention, Diversion and Justice, and Reintegration, explained as follows:

- 'Prevention' includes the whole range of rights which, if protected, can serve to help children avoid coming into conflict with the law. In particular, securing the child's rights to education and health, to protection from harm and to strong family relationships all help to prevent children coming into contact with the justice system. These rights are not unique to children in these circumstances, but rather are fundamental rights to which all children are entitled, provided through the provision of universal services. Highlighting them here acknowledges that these rights are particularly important for children in especially vulnerable circumstances.
- 'Diversion and Justice' includes measures that prevent the harm that the justice system can cause—both the diversion of the child from the justice system and the protection of the child's legal rights while in that system. This category includes the right to early intervention and care, as well as a range of measures that seek to divert a child from more formal or deeper contact with the justice system. It also acknowledges that a child in contact with the justice system may struggle to have their due process rights protected 'due to vulnerabilities, reduced capacities and the complexity of the process'. Consequently, this phase also includes the requirement that the procedures and processes experienced by the child are child-friendly and age-appropriate, as well as being specific to the individual needs of the child. Child-friendly justice is vital to ensure the child is treated as a child throughout the process.
- 'Reintegration' includes the rights of the child associated with the child's return to their families and communities following contact with the justice system. Ranging from measures that highlight the importance of post-institutional care that helps a child avoid further contact with the justice system, to measures that reinforce those rights—to education and healthcare for instance—that serve to promote the child's reintegration into society supported to play a constructive role with positive life chances.

Underpinning all of these approaches is respect for the rights of the child, specifically, the general principles that require regard for the child's best interests in line with their age and development, their right to participate in decision-making and their equal entitlement to rights protections regardless of their backgrounds or circumstances. Together, these approaches reflect the rights-based approach to children in conflict with the law, articulating what this requires from states parties before, during and after a child's contact with the justice system.

Conclusion

In setting out the rights of the child in conflict with the law, this chapter reinforced that children's rights apply to all children, without exception or condition. It highlighted that universal rights—like education, healthcare, family support and the protection from harm—have particular resonance for children in conflict with the law, while international standards also recognise that such children enjoy additional rights, as a result of their vulnerable circumstances and reduced capacity. As a body of international standards, children's rights are diverse and wide ranging, drawn from different instruments and standard setting bodies over several decades. Despite this diversity, the standards nonetheless provide a strong overarching framework of protection for the rights of children in such circumstances. As the chapter established, these rights are important to help children avoid contact with the justice system, to protect them from the harm the system can cause and to promote their reintegration into society on release. To this end, the three themes identified—Prevention, Diversion and Justice, and Reintegration—will now be used in the chapters that follow in order to help structure the research literature that underpins these rights.

Bibliography

Committee of Ministers. (2008). *Recommendation CM/Rec(2008)11 of the Committee of Ministers to member states on the European Rules for juvenile offenders subject to sanctions or measures*. Adopted by the Committee of Ministers on 5 November 2008 at the 1040th meeting of the Ministers' Deputies.

Committee of Ministers. (2010). *Guidelines of the Committee of Ministers of the Council of Europe on child-friendly justice*. Adopted by the Committee of Ministers of the Council of Europe on 17 November 2010 and explanatory memorandum.

Committee on the Rights of the Child. (2003a). *General comment No. 5 (2003): General measures of implementation of the Convention on the Rights of the Child (arts. 4, 42 and 44, para. 6)*, 27 November 2003, CRC/GC/2003/5.
Committee on the Rights of the Child. (2003b). *General comment No. 4 (2003): Adolescent health and development in the context of the Convention on the Rights of the Child*, 1 July 2003, CRC/GC/2003/4.
Committee on the Rights of the Child. (2007a). *General comment No. 10 (2007): Children's rights in juvenile justice*, 25 April 2007, CRC/C/GC/10.
Committee on the Rights of the Child. (2007b). *General comment No. 9 (2006): The rights of children with disabilities*, 27 February 2007, CRC/C/GC/9.
Committee on the Rights of the Child. (2009). *General comment No. 12 (2009): The right of the child to be heard*, 20 July 2009, CRC/C/GC/12.
Committee on the Rights of the Child. (2011). *General comment No. 13 (2011): The right of the child to freedom from all forms of violence*, 18 April 2011, CRC/C/GC/13.
Committee on the Rights of the Child. (2013). *General comment No. 14 (2013) on the right of the child to have his or her best interests taken as a primary consideration (art. 3, para. 1)*, 29 May 2013, CRC/C/GC/14.
Committee on the Rights of the Child. (2016). *General comment No. 20 (2016) on the implementation of the rights of the child during adolescence*, 06 December 2016, CRC/C/GC/20.
Committee on the Rights of the Child. (2019). *General comment No. 24 (2019) on children's rights in the child justice system*, 19 September 2019, CRC/C/GC/24.
Kilkelly, U. (2008). Youth justice and children's rights: Measuring compliance with international standards. *Youth Justice, 8*(3), 187–192. https://doi.org/10.1177/1473225408096458
Kilkelly, U. (2019). The UN convention on the rights of the child: Incremental and transformative approaches to legal implementation. *The International Journal of Children's Rights, 23*(3), 323–337. https://doi.org/10.1080/13642987.2018.1558974
Kilkelly, U. (2020). "Evolving capacities" and "parental guidance" in the context of youth justice. *The International Journal of Children's Rights, 28*(3), 500–520. https://doi.org/10.1163/15718182-02803004
Kilkelly, U., & Liefaard, T. (2022). International children's rights principles and responses to serious offending by children. Recent developments, topical issues and global challenges. In N. Lynch, Y. van den Brink, & L. Forde (Eds.), *Responses to serious offending by children. Principles, practice and global perspectives*. Routledge.
Liefaard, T. (2020). Juvenile justice. In J. Todres & S.M. King (Eds.), *The Oxford handbook of children's rights law* (pp. 279–306). Oxford University Press.

Liefaard T., & Kilkelly U. (2018). Child-friendly justice: Past, present and future. In. B. Goldson (Ed.), *Juvenile justice in Europe. Past, present and future* (pp. 57–73). Routledge.

Lundy, L., & McEvoy, L. (2012). Children's rights and research processes: Assisting children to (in)formed views. *Childhood, 19*(1), 129–144. https://doi.org/10.1177/0907568211409078

Lynch, N., & Liefaard, T. (2020). What is left in the "too hard basket"? Developments and challenges for the rights of children in conflict with the law. *The International Journal of Children's Rights, 28*(1), 89–110. https://doi.org/10.1163/15718182-02801007

Mallett, C. (2018). Disproportionate minority contact in juvenile justice: Today's, and yesterdays, problems. *Criminal Justice Studies, 3*(3), 230–248,

McDiarmid, C. (2013). An age of complexity: Children and criminal responsibility in law. *Youth Justice, 13*(2), 145–160. https://doi.org/10.1177/1473225413492056

Nowak, M. (2019). *Global study on children deprived of liberty*, A/74/136.

UN General Assembly. (1985). *United Nations standard minimum rules for the administration of juvenile justice ("The Beijing Rules")*, 29 November 1985. 40/33.

UN General Assembly. (1990a). *United Nations guidelines for the prevention of juvenile delinquency (The Riyadh Guidelines)*, 14 December 1990, 45/112.

UN General Assembly. (1990b). *United Nations rules for the protection of juveniles deprived of their liberty (The Havana Rules)*, 14 December 1990, 45/113.

CHAPTER 3

Prevention

Abstract This chapter aims to explain the research underpinning the rights-based approach in the category of 'Prevention' rights as they relate to children in conflict with the law. The child has a right to enjoy universal protections of their fundamental rights, which are integral to child development and especially important in preventing children from coming into conflict with the law. This chapter explains the link between these rights and the research literature, demonstrating how a denial of these rights can play a role in bringing children into contact with the justice system and conversely the fulfilment of these rights can work to prevent children having such contact. As such, it considers the relationship between child development and offending behaviour, marginalisation of specific groups of children, particularly children from ethnic and minority backgrounds and those with care experience, as well as the question of the voice of young people. It explores the research on the child's substantive rights—health, education, play and protection from harm—and their relevance to preventing the child from coming into conflict with the law. It concludes with some observations about the lessons to be from this study.

Keywords Prevention · Family care · Non-discrimination · Children's rights · Children in conflict with the law · Child development

U. Kilkelly et al., *Children in Conflict with the Law*, Palgrave Critical Studies in Human Rights and Criminology, https://doi.org/10.1007/978-3-031-36652-9_3

Introduction

Chapter 2 set out the international children's rights standards that are relevant to children in conflict with the law noting the importance of both general and specific rights to children in such circumstances. The chapter introduced the category of 'Prevention' rights, including the rights to health, education, family support and right to protection from harm, as integral to preventing the child from coming into contact with the law. It is the aim of this chapter to explore the international research that underpins the rights-based approach in this area.

As explained in Chapter 2, the child has a right to enjoy universal protections of their fundamental rights, and as this chapter shows, these rights are both integral to child development and especially important in preventing children from coming into conflict with the law. The aim of this chapter, therefore, is to explain the link between these rights and the research literature, demonstrating how a denial of these rights can play a role in bringing children into contact with the justice system and conversely, how the fulfilment of these rights can work to prevent children having such contact. In this regard, the first section considers some of the major themes in the literature that speak to children's rights in this area: first, the relationship between child development and offending behaviour; second, the issue of disproportionate minority contact; and third, the question of marginalisation and the voice of young people. The second main section of the chapter details the research on the child's substantive rights—health, education, living standards, family, protection from harm and play—and their relevance to preventing the child from coming into conflict with the law. The chapter concludes with some observations about the lessons to be learned from the analysis.

Child Development and Offending Behaviour

As the international standards indicate, there is a strong relationship between protecting the child's best interests, advancing the child's right to development and preventing children from coming into conflict with the law. As is well understood, involvement in offending represents a threat to a child's development and best interests, meaning that preventing a child from coming into conflict with the law will, conversely, serve to advance the child's rights and life chances. Specific developmental factors can also play a role in young people's involvement in offending behaviour. Research highlights that while adolescence is generally a time of high-sensation seeking and under-developed self-regulation, individual factors such as variations in levels of impulsivity and low self-control are important developmental features that are linked to involvement in offending behaviour (McAra & McVie, 2010; Salmi & Kivivuori, 2006; Smith & McVie, 2003). The resulting preference in the international standards, therefore, is for an approach where—all children—are treated as children with equal protection of all their rights. These themes are now explored in more detail.

Understanding Child Development and Behaviour

The age-crime curve posits that offending behaviour peaks during the teenage years, after which a young person tends to grow out of offending (Farrington, 1986; Loeber et al., 2012). While there are copious studies that seek to explain why this is the case—examining individual, peer, family and community factors—a significant body of research now makes clear that the relationship between brain development and behaviour during adolescence is very important (Steinberg, 2017; Steinberg et al., 2018). Neuroscience has established that the prefrontal cortex—the area of the brain associated with emotional regulation, executive functioning and decision-making—does not fully mature until early adulthood, with several periods of sensitive development from birth until maturation (Kolk & Rakic, 2022). Research indicates that sensation-seeking tendencies increase among adolescents after puberty and remain high into the early 20s, after which they begin to decline (Steinberg et al., 2018), with brain development across adolescence a potential reason. Other studies highlight a significant increase in risky or rebellious behaviour as a normative part of development between adolescence and mid-twenties (Blankenstein et al., 2020). This combination of high-sensation seeking and undeveloped impulse self-regulation can contribute to adolescents engaging in risky, including offending behaviour (Steinberg, 2017; Steinberg et al., 2018). This pattern—demonstrating a heightened propensity towards risk taking during adolescence—has been found to be similar across jurisdictions (Cohen, 2016; Duell et al., 2018; Hill et al., 2018; Icenogle et al., 2019; Steinberg et al., 2018).

Another key component of youth offending is the role of the endocrine system. In this regard, individual differences in factors such as testosterone (Cooke et al., 2020), cortisol reactivity (Figueiredo et al., 2020) and dehydroepiandrosterone (Taylor-Cavelier et al., 2021) have all been associated with several types of risky and/or offending behaviour within differing developmental contexts, demonstrating the complexity of the issues here. Moreover, studies have found some links between certain types of neuropsychological and behavioural risks and later involvement in offending, with research establishing a link between disruptive behaviour difficulties and involvement in offending behaviour (Lay et al., 2005). However, other studies have highlighted that having behavioural problems during childhood was not significantly associated with continuous reoffending, whereas factors such as early alcohol use, early behavioural problems and family arrest were significant in increasing the likelihood of recidivism among a cohort of sentenced adolescents in the US (Ozkan, 2016). While research evidence such as this indicates that developmental factors such as neuropsychological risks and behavioural difficulties are linked to later offending, the picture is complex.

As this indicates, taken together, a large body of knowledge helps to clarify the relationship between a child's development and associated behavioural tendencies including offending behaviour. In certain jurisdictions, this research has begun to shape how the courts view the culpability of young people, leading to the development of tailored approaches to sentencing among other approaches (Schmidt & Skelton, 2022; Scott, 2013). More generally, however, the research is a reminder of both the particular vulnerability of adolescence as recognised by the children's rights standards (Committee on the Rights of the Child, 2016) and the importance of maximising the protections of children's rights during that period. In this regard, while the CRC applies to everyone below the age of 18 years under Article 1, the Committee has additionally commended those states parties whose youth justice rules and regulations apply to persons aged 18 and, in some instances, up to 21, whether as a general rule or by way of exception (Committee on the Rights of the Child, 2019, para. 42).

Child Development and Offending Trajectories

Research demonstrates that the amount or intensity of risk-taking behaviour is informed by the context of youth, with factors such as peers, health, parenting, self-esteem and socio-cultural context all playing a role in the trajectory of the behaviour (Leather, 2009). While there is strong consensus about the link between child development and offending behaviour, different trajectories are evident depending on whether the problematic behaviour began in early childhood (when it is typically associated with childhood adversity) or adolescence, where it is more commonly viewed as a matter of 'temporary maladjustment', involving mental health or substance use for instance (Moffitt, 1993). In this latter respect, the role of coping skills, especially with regard to external stressors including criminal behaviour, is important, if little studied (Aebi et al., 2014).

It is important to note that literature examining neural correlates or predictors of youth offending is rarely situated within biopsychosocial or bioecological frameworks. For example, associations have been made between youth offending and factors such as processing of socioemotional stimuli (Aghajani et al., 2021), executive dysfunction (Yoder & Precht, 2020) and emotional regulation (Perino et al., 2019). These factors do not reliably predict behavioural issues or offending on their own. Rather, these should be situated within the context of the young person's social and psychological environment. Studies aiming to better understand the risk of offending in adolescence have found a relatively high rate of success in identifying risk patterns of reoffending when incorporating biological (e.g., cortisol, heart rate variability), psychological (e.g., affective and behavioural issues) and social measures (e.g., whether peers engage in crime, familial relationships, etc.) (de Ruigh et al., 2021). Overall, it is important to consider that the antecedents and consequences of neural and developmental factors are one part of a larger system encompassing children's wider social worlds. This again reinforces the importance of viewing the child in a holistic manner, in line with the rights-based approach.

The Multi-faceted Nature of Young People's Involvement in Offending

The literature highlights that the circumstances and factors in young people's lives that can lead to involvement in criminal behaviour can be multi-faceted, and that children in contact with the justice system often have high levels of complex need (Case & Browning, 2021). Scholars have highlighted that young people who face challenges or 'risk factors' associated with offending often do so in multiple domains, and individual factors, such as attitudes to offending and impulsivity, often overlap with broader issues such as parenting styles, attendance at school where involvement in criminal activity is a significant problem and low socio-economic status (Farrington, 2015; Freeman, 2008; Jolliffe et al., 2017; Junger-Tas et al., 2004). The interplay between multiple adverse circumstances in a child's life is a common theme (Lay et al., 2005). Studies have found that the sum and accumulation of psychosocial burdens in the child's environment is the most important factor associated with offending behaviour (Van der Laan et al., 2009). In other words, while there are biological, psychological and socio-cultural risks during development, it is the wider life experiences of the child that will inform or mediate the risk of future offending (Dodge & Pettit, 2003). This coheres with the rights-based approach, as set out in the Convention on the Rights of the Child, which recognises that each child is worthy of dignity and respect in their own right, while their diverse circumstances require an individualised approach in the fulfilment of their rights (Committee on the Rights of the Child, 2019, para. 18).

Cause and effect are notoriously difficult to establish in relation to factors influencing children's offending, and it is important to bear in mind that while a myriad of personal, family and community factors can help to explain why certain young people come into conflict with the law, they are not necessarily determinative. Although previously framed as an approach susceptible to a process of 'risk management' (Farrington et al., 2016), it is now better understood that young people are not 'fated' to come into conflict with the law (Haines & Case, 2008; Kemshall, 2008). Instead, policymakers need to consider the particular challenges faced by young people in their families, and in their communities, and ensure that they have access to appropriate resources at the right time in order to minimise any contact with the law and the harm that may result.

In relation to the complexity of child and adolescent development, there are two frameworks that may be especially helpful in understanding involvement in offending—Engel's biopsychosocial model (Engel, 1977) and Bronfenbrenner's bioecological model of human development (Bronfenbrenner & Morris, 2007). While these theories are distinct from one another, they share some commonalities which aid in understanding how the child's development, behaviour and life trajectories are formed from a systems theory perspective. For instance, at the core of both models is the notion that individual development is situated within the wider context of their environment, including the impact of physical, emotional, family, education, situational, cultural or political factors (Bronfenbrenner,

1999). In other words, while each of these domains may provide opportunities for risk and resilience, the risks can be considered as a cumulative process within an inter-connected system of development (Evans et al., 2013). Billingham's and Irwin-Rogers' recently developed theoretical framework, which couches the psychosocial theory of 'mattering' within these factors, seems particularly pertinent in trying to understand youth violence (Billingham & Irwin-Rogers, 2022).

Research that seeks to contextualise the complexity of young people's offending behaviour further emphasises the necessity to understand the interplay between cultural, political, economic and social factors which contribute to understanding why young people engage in violence. Within the context of youth justice, this is critical in understanding how a young person may first come into contact with police, how they may react to the experience, or how likely they are to reoffend (Snyder & Duchschere, 2022). It also reinforces the need for child-appropriate service provision and a developmentally informed approach (Case & Browning, 2021). The Committee on the Rights of the Child, in line with this, recommends that early intervention and prevention efforts should take into account both the multiple psychosocial causes of offending and factors which promote resilience (Committee on the Rights of the Child, 2019, para. 11).

Non-discrimination and Disproportionate Contact

Article 2 of the CRC prohibits discrimination in the enjoyment of children's rights on all grounds, including gender, and ethnic and racial origin. To implement this provision in the context of youth justice, the Committee on the Rights of the Child has emphasised that safeguards against discrimination are needed from the earliest stages of contact with the youth justice system, and that training should be provided to professionals on the potential disparities affecting marginalised groups of children (Committee on the Rights of the Child, 2019, paras. 40 and 112). Despite these standards, however, certain cohorts of children are over-represented in youth justice systems globally including, in particular, Black and Minority Ethnic children backgrounds, children with disabilities and children with care experience. The sections that follow detail the literature documenting these issues.

Race and Ethnicity

The over-representation of children from culturally and ethnically diverse groups racial ethnic backgrounds has been identified as a major issue in many countries in literature seeking to document children's involvement with the criminal justice system. It is well documented that people from such groups are at increased risk for social exclusion and the negative sequela that follows such as: reduced opportunities for education and employment and consequent risks for increased mental health issues and involvement with the criminal justice system (Priest et al., 2013). In countries such as the UK, Australia, the US, Canada, New Zealand and elsewhere, the disproportionate representation of children from Black, indigenous and minority backgrounds is a dominant and intractable feature of the youth justice landscape (Abrams et al., 2021; Bishop, 2005, Goldson et al., 2021; Lynch & Liefaard, 2020; van den Brink et al., 2022). This raises serious questions about discriminatory treatment of children in these over-represented groups. The use of discriminatory policing practices has been strongly associated with bringing a disproportionate number of these young people into contact with the criminal justice system in literature examining this issue (Goldson et al., 2021). Disparate treatment has been noted at court stage decision-making too, where less favourable decisions are made in relation to minority or marginalised children with regard to transfer to adult court and sentencing (Lynch & Liefaard, 2020; van den Brink, 2022; van den Brink et al., 2022). The disproportionate number of young people from black, indigenous and minority backgrounds deprived of their liberty has also been raised as a persistent issue in a number of countries across the globe (Nowak, 2019).

There is thus a significant problem documented in the literature with regard to children's right to non-discrimination with respect to contact with the justice system. It has been noted in the UK context, for example, how state responses to youth violence disproportionately target young Black men in marginalised communities (Billingham & Irwin-Rogers, 2022). Other research has highlighted that religious minorities are also subject to discriminatory practices, with studies indicating that children from Muslim backgrounds in Australia and England and Wales facing higher risks of being drawn into contact with the criminal justice system (Goldson et al., 2021). A study comparing juvenile court interventions in Florida showed that minority youth and in particular Black males are more likely to receive punitive sanctions and less rehabilitative opportunities (Cochran & Mears, 2015) whereas in Europe, migrant and minority ethnic children and young people—exacerbating their existing vulnerability due to their migrant and low socio-economic status—are found to be especially vulnerable to criminalisation through racialisation (Hunter, 2022; Webster, 2019). In some countries, this has been found to result in higher rates of pre-trial detention for children from migrant communities (Lynch & Liefaard, 2020; van den Brink, 2022; van den Brink et al., 2022). Separately, studies have demonstrated how children from indigenous backgrounds Ireland, Australia, New Zealand and Canada have been found to be subject to racialised decision-making leading to their increased contact with the justice system (Goldson et al., 2021; Joyce et al., 2022; Lynch & Liefaard, 2020; van den Brink et al., 2022). These studies highlight the significant role played by race and ethnic background with regard to children who come into conflict with the law, and the prevalence of breaches of children's rights to non-discrimination in this regard in youth justice systems across the world. Policies that reduce systemic discrimination and increase participation in protective factors are required to assist this cohort (Joyce et al., 2022; Priest et al., 2013).

Gender

Gender is also an important factor in this context with many studies noting that being male is associated with higher levels of involvement in offending behaviour (Junger-Tas et al., 2004; McAra & McVie, 2022; Rocque et al., 2015; Seddig & Reinecke, 2017). Being male was found in one study to be a moderate predictor of involvement in prolonged, intensive forms of offending (Fagan et al., 2007), while in another, gender was highlighted as a relevant factor in the context of decision-making about pre-trial detention (van den Brink et al., 2022). It has been suggested that this may be attributable to a combination of boys experiencing simultaneously more risk and less protection than girls (Fagan et al., 2007). Additionally, literature on young people's mental health suggests that boys are more prone to externalising behaviours whereas girls are more likely to internalise mental distress (Campbell, 2006).

Other studies have highlighted that gender can be a dimension which impacts decision-making within the justice system, impacting children's level of continued contact with legal authorities. For example, it has been highlighted that gender can interact with factors like race, socio-economic status and mental health considerations to impact sentencing decisions (van den Brink et al., 2022). Other studies have highlighted that boys tend to be deprived of their liberty at significantly higher rates than girls, while girls may be vulnerable within the youth justice system due to experiences of trafficking or institutionalised care (Nowak, 2019).

In comparing girls' and boys' trajectories, longitudinal research has highlighted a relatively low level of offending among girls, with offending behaviour peaking in middle or late adolescence, and with desistance generally occurring in late adolescence (Jennings et al., 2018). Studies have also highlighted that no significant gender differences appear in correlates of offending, suggesting that there is no need for radically different explanations of offending in boys and girls (Junger-Tas et al., 2004). Broad societal assumptions about girls' behaviour can also have negative impacts, with girls having particular experience of both the advantages and the disadvantages of welfare-based responses to offending (Gelsthorpe & Worrall, 2009).

Research across various disciplines propose multiple theories that attempt to explain gender disparities in delinquent behaviour (Pusch & Holtfreter, 2018). Risk factors for offending behaviour are largely similar across genders and include factors such as attachment, educational attainment, relationships, community environment and experiences of adversity/trauma. However, the degree to which males and females are exposed to these risk factors and the way in which they respond/are impacted by them differs. For example, research indicates a stronger relationship between maltreatment and delinquent behaviour in female adolescents, compared to males (Zahn et al., 2010), and it has been suggested that girls may experience more 'risk factors' than boys before they become involved in offending (Reef et al., 2011). Moreover, the prevalence of child sexual violence is greater in females than males (Chesney-Lind & Irwin, 2007).

While boys and girls may rely on different factors to help them avoid involvement in criminal behaviour and to foster resilience, what is important for both is an accumulation of protective factors (Hartman et al., 2009). In efforts to help young people avoid coming into conflict with the law, it is therefore important to give attention to gender-specific issues. It is necessary to consider research relating to masculinities in relation to the over-representation of boys in the youth justice system (Dowd, 2006–2007); however, in a system in which boys are pre-dominant, there is also a need to ensure that interventions within that system are appropriate and suitable for the needs of girls in conflict with the law (Goodfellow, 2017). Both aspects are essential to secure greater protection for all children's rights in this regard.

Children with Care Experience

Children with experience of alternative or state care have been found to be vastly over-represented in youth justice systems, in many different jurisdictions and contexts (Baidawi & Ball, 2023a; Gerard et al., 2019; Malvaso et al., 2017; McFarlane, 2018; Smith & McVie, 2003; Youth Justice Board/Ministry of Justice, 2020), with experiences that are marked by placement instability, precarious relationships leading to involvement in offending behaviour (Baidawi & Ball, 2023a; Gerard et al., 2019; Goodkind et al., 2013; Jansen, 2010). While many children have positive experiences in residential care (Baidawi & Ball, 2023b; Malvaso et al., 2017; McFarlane, 2018), many young people in state care have experienced multiple forms of loss, abuse, neglect and violence (McFarlane, 2018). Conversely, more positive outcomes among children living in well-run residential care settings (Taylor, 2003) highlights the value of addressing the distinctive needs of children in residential care (Baidawi & Ball, 2023b).

Stigma and negative attitudes towards young people in care are also relevant to their contact with the justice system. For instance, Canadian studies have highlighted how police profiling and racial discrimination have influenced the pathways of young people who have been in state care into the criminal justice system (Boyd et al., 2016). Research indicates that actions and interactions of state stakeholders can heighten this exposure, for example through antagonism between different actors, increased surveillance and over-reliance by residential care workers on police interventions to address behavioural (Gerard et al., 2019; Taylor, 2003). Lack of adequate support mechanisms for children in state care, like the lack of proper aftercare support, can lead to further association with negative behaviours such as drug use and further involvement with the criminal justice system (Boyd et al., 2016; Taylor, 2003).

This disadvantage has been further emphasised by findings from the Edinburgh Study of Youth Transitions and Crime, which found that outcomes for care-experienced people in their cohort were the most negative, experiencing continued disadvantage across multiple domains; where contact with agencies made a positive difference in young people's lives, this was attributed to strong relationships with individual care workers (McAra & McVie, 2022). Additionally, the transition for young people from state care into adulthood can be an especially challenging time, and without proper support and aftercare, this can be experienced as a time of instability and tumult (Boddy et al., 2020). Recent research in Ireland on the time-limited aftercare supports for young people, coupled with an unstable housing market, has highlighted that these factors often leave young people leaving care feeling abandoned by the state and in distress, with their autonomy undermined and their future opportunities hampered (Glynn & Mayock, 2023). This highlights the importance of continuous care planning and interagency work for young people in the care system (Taylor, 2003). Conversely, research shows that while young people in care are at elevated risk of experiencing mental health issues, having strong social support is highly effective in improving later life outcomes (Evans et al., 2022).

Children with Disabilities

Children's rights standards acknowledge the particular vulnerability of children with disabilities in the justice system, although the link between disability and coming into conflict with the law is not well developed. Research suggests that children with disabilities are over-represented within youth justice systems globally and while precise figures are not available, it is considered to lie somewhere between 15 and 50% (Hughes et al., 2012; Reising et al., 2019). Children with disabilities have been found to be particularly over-represented at the 'deeper' end of criminal justice system contact, in contexts where children are deprived of their liberty (Nowak, 2019). In particular, cognitive, intellectual, and other neurodevelopmental factors increase the risk that a young person will come into contact with the law.

Typically, the term 'neurodevelopmental disorders' refers to any number of several conditions wherein the typical development of the brain is disrupted during gestation and/or sensitive periods of development in childhood and infancy (Thapar et al., 2017). While the exact definition of 'neurodevelopmental disorders' differs across studies, commonly it includes presentations such as wider intellectual disabilities, speech and language disabilities, epilepsy, motor disorders, Autism and Attention Deficit Hyperreactivity Disorder (Thapar et al., 2017). It is important to note, however, that there is a movement within psychology and wider adolescent well-being research to consider many of these as normal variations of human development. In other words, it is recognised that excessive focus on cure and prevention can be both unhelpful and indeed harmful to young people and that instead, a strengths-based approach should be adopted to facilitate full participation of children experiencing these difficulties in society (Kirby, 2021). What is certain is that young people with disabilities or who are neurodiverse are at an increased risk of coming into contact with youth justice compared to other young people. For instance, young people with traumatic brain injury (Nkoana et al., 2020), Foetal Alcohol Spectrum Disorder (Pedruzzi et al., 2021), intellectual and cognitive impairments (Christensen & Baker, 2020) and speech and language difficulties (Cronin & Addo, 2021; Day, 2022) are disproportionately represented within the justice system. However, this should be considered in the wider context of the child's environment and social context, given the relationship between disability, maltreatment, mental health and offending behaviour. For instance, different types of disabilities will be associated with different patterns of offending (Shandra & Hogan, 2012) and the risk of offending is far greater when there is comorbidity of maltreatment or mental health issues (Mallett, 2014).

Overall, the evidence from a large body of literature demonstrates that there is a significant over-representation of certain cohorts of children—specifically boys, Black and Minority Ethnic children from racial and ethnic minority groups, children with experience of state care and children with disabilities—in the justice system, a situation at odds with the general principle of the CRC that children are entitled to enjoy their rights—including prevention from contact with the justice system—without discrimination. The research demonstrates equally the range of measures to be taken to ensure that this right is implemented for each child.

Marginalisation of Children and the Right to Be Heard

The right of all children to be heard in matters affecting them is set out in Article 12 of the CRC and associated instruments, as explained in Chapter 2. While this right has particular relevance in the context of the due process rights children enjoy when involved in the justice system, as explained in Chapter 4, it also resonates with the fact that children at the margins of society, who are less frequently heard, are more likely to end up in the justice system. Conversely, and as the research indicates, ensuring such children are heard and their views taken into account can act as a preventive or protective measure, minimising the disengagement that pushes such children to the marginalised fringes of society with negative implications for their contact with the justice system. This section presents some of the emerging literature in this area, highlighting the link between preventing children from such contact and their avoidance of marginalisation.

It is well established in the research that poverty and low socio-economic status can lead to the marginalisation and exclusion of children within their local neighbourhoods and communities (Hamilton, 2021). Moreover, studies have highlighted the negative impact of young people's marginalisation within their communities—young people are often negatively perceived by adults and have limitations placed on them by parents on where they are able to go in their communities or because of the need to avoid danger (Neary et al., 2013; Nichols, 2017). This type of exclusionary practice not only impacts on children's right to be heard, it can also have negative impacts both on self-perception and indeed, on their contact with the criminal justice system. Studies have documented young people feeling that they were labelled as a result of where they lived and went to school (Nichols, 2017). This type of labelling, in particular those that assign risk to young people, is experienced as a form of alienation, stigmatisation and further marginalisation (Deakin et al., 2022). This cycle of risk-labelling also impacts on young people's self-concept, self-value and their own belief in their capacity to change behaviour (Tyler & Slater, 2018). These patterns are difficult to break within punitive systems and are often only aided by a strengthening of important relationships within the life of the young person (Matos et al., 2023). In other words, although experiences of marginalisation and poverty create an elevated level of risk of being drawn into contact with the justice system, this risk is further exacerbated when young people are treated as an 'at-risk' person.

Article 12 of the CRC highlights the importance of ensuring that children have a right to be heard in all matters affecting them. Findings in relation to the marginalisation of young people in their communities highlight that an absence of meaningful youth voice can shape young people's experience of exclusion, which in turn can impact on the likelihood of their involvement in offending behaviour (Nichols, 2017).

For example, where children have negative contact with police during childhood—particularly for children who are already marginalised or over-policed—there can be further long-term negative outcomes (Testa et al., 2022). This is further evidenced by the relationship between community policing and in particular, violent youth crimes, where community policing can be an effective strategy to reducing rates of violent behaviour (Paez & Dierenfeldt, 2020).

This is also confirmed by Billingham's and Irwin-Roger's (2022) recent application of the concept of 'mattering' as both an explanatory and a preventative factor in understanding and preventing violence among and by young people. They suggest that youth violence can be explained by a cultural and societal lack of recognition and solidarity with young people, resulting in young people feeling that they do not 'matter' in their communities and adult society in general. They argue that investing in young people's lives, particularly those from marginalised communities, is of utmost importance in preventing youth violence. In this regard, Deuchar's study of young people and gangs highlights the scope for positive outcomes when children are engaged and offered opportunities to build social capital through sport and civic participation (Deuchar, 2009). Young people's well-being needs to be addressed holistically so that their sense of 'mattering' is increased, contributing to the reduction of violence (Billingham & Irwin-Rogers, 2022). Conversely, it has also been suggested that enabling young people to participate in their communities, and fostering greater social inclusion (Case & Browning, 2021)—reflective of Article 12 of the CRC—may be effective in helping to reduce anti-social behaviour (Neary et al., 2013), creating a place where young people feel they belong and a sense of social capital (Magson et al., 2016). This highlights clearly the relationship between the literature on youth engagement and the imperative of the rights-based approach to child participation under the CRC (Kilkelly, 2023).

The Role of Health and Access to Healthcare

As the international standards set out in Chapter 2 indicate, there are multiple aspects to the child's right to health that have the effect of preventing children from coming into conflict with the law. They include protection of a child's mental and emotional health, physical health and avoiding the harms related to substance use (Committee on the Rights of the Child, 2013). Such health issues can be especially acute during adolescence—a period of additional vulnerability particular challenge for children—requiring that the right to optimum health be promoted during adolescence, with particular attention required in relation to health risks at this time (Committee on the Rights of the Child, 2016). In this regard, studies have demonstrated that children who are in contact with the justice system experience a number of challenges in relation to full enjoyment of their right to health; issues related to substance use and poor mental health have been specifically highlighted as factors which can contribute to involvement in offending. Several factors related to health can increase risk for young people being involved in criminal behaviour (e.g., mental health, brain injury and substance dependence) and these issues can be compounded where there is social exclusion and marginalisation preventing access to relevant services and supports. Additionally, involvement in criminal activity also increases risk for poor health outcomes such as accident, illness and injury (Siponen et al., 2023). The next section will address mental health and the related issue of substance use in more detail.

Mental Health

Scholarship that considers children's pathways to involvement in offending frequently cites mental health issues as a common issue, and studies have found that children who are experiencing mental health problems are over-represented in youth justice systems (Goodkind et al., 2013; Graves et al., 2007; Reising et al., 2019). Some have noted that poor mental health may be a factor contributing to persistence in offending among young people (Basto-Pereira & Farrington, 2022). The experience of poor mental health appears to be common, with studies estimating very high prevalence rates for at least one psychiatric disorder among children in conflict with the law (McReynolds et al., 2010). However, the types of mental health problems experienced by young people in these circumstances can take different forms and the directionality of the link between poor mental health and offending is not always clear. In this regard, anxiety and depression have been linked, in the literature, with involvement in delinquent and criminal activity (Fanti et al., 2019). A recent UK study found that young people involved in gangs were vulnerable to mental health difficulties (Frisby-Osman & Wood, 2020), and multiple studies have found that increases in depression and anxiety are often *outcomes* of offending, rather than being clear 'risk factors' for involvement in offending. In this regard, the literature highlights that causal chains linking depression, anxiety and offending remain uncertain and complex (Jolliffe et al., 2019; Reising et al., 2019).

Other types of mental health difficulty have also been linked to the involvement in offending, with several studies documenting a link between mental health difficulties and offending behaviour. One such study, upon controlling for offence level and poverty, attributed a significant proportion of male (15.3%) and female (20.6%) youth offending to mental health disorders (Copeland et al., 2007). Additionally, some of the most socially excluded young people struggle to navigate mental health services and can, as a consequence, have undiagnosed mental health issues (Lambert & Murphy, 2019). In other contexts, it has been noted that young people experience difficulties in accessing appropriate mental health services (Case & Browning, 2021). Overall, given the prevalence of research linking mental health difficulties to children in conflict with the law, and the gaps in current knowledge, this is clearly an aspect of the child's right to health that requires further attention.

The presence of mental health issues may also exacerbate or intensify other behavioural or affective issues. For instance, in a sample of young benzodiazepine users, one of the primary motivations for substance use was the regulation of negative emotions (Murphy et al., 2018). In other words, it is critical to consider mental health as one single part within a system of accumulating factors linked to offending behaviour. Other research has highlighted the high prevalence of behavioural and mental health issues among young people in contact with both the care systems and the justice systems (Baidawi & Ball, 2023a), further drawing attention to the overlapping, multiple needs experienced by many children in the youth justice system. Finally, exposure to crime in the home and neighbourhood is associated with worse mental health (Baranyi et al., 2021), as well as increased likelihood of contact with police (Baskin & Sommers, 2015).

In summary, the link between mental health, substance use and involvement in offending behaviour, while complex, is well established in the research literature, all of which points to the importance of providing strong protection of the child's right to health as a strategy for preventing children from coming into conflict with the law.

Substance Use

One of the factors commonly associated with young people's involvement in offending is the use of alcohol and other drugs or illicit substances (Chan, 2021; Hill et al., 2018; Van der Laan et al., 2009). While the relationship between substance use and involvement in offending is complex, studies have highlighted the role that drug use can play in bringing young people into conflict with the law (Webster et al., 2006). In particular, some research has linked drug use among young people with more serious and frequent forms of offending and has identified it as a potential barrier to desistance from patterns of offending (Basto-Pereira & Farrington, 2022; Gushue & McCuish, 2021; McAra & McVie, 2022). It also frequently intersects with other adverse circumstances such as experience of state care and homelessness; the convergence of these factors can increase marginalisation of young people and the likelihood of criminal justice system contact (Boyd et al., 2016).

Whilst substance use is commonly treated as a criminal issue, it is a health issue with links to mental health concerns, traumatic and/or adverse experiences, developmental issues and stressful life events (particularly those occurring in early childhood and throughout adolescence), including attachment difficulties and adversity within the family and community (Douglas et al., 2010; Lambert et al., 2022; Miley et al., 2020; Misiak et al., 2022; Murphy et al., 2018; Oei et al., 2021). Research indicates that the greater the exposure to psychological trauma, the higher the risk of substance dependence, earlier onset of use, injecting at an earlier age and more treatment attempts (Weber & Lynch, 2021). Taken together, studies across gender, socio-economic status and geographical regions all conclude that people in addiction have higher rates of childhood trauma than individuals with fewer exposures to adversity. While it is now generally accepted that substance dependence is frequently a coping strategy for trauma symptoms, the self-medication of mental distress also increases risk for additional deleterious experiences (Murphy et al., 2018). In this respect, it is important to recall that the Committee on the Rights of the Child emphasises the need to protect children from the negative effects of substance use, while welcoming alternatives to punitive and repressive drug control policies (Committee on the Rights of the Child, 2016, para. 64).

There is thus a direct relationship between the use of illicit substances as an issue relating to children's rights to health and a child's involvement in offending behaviour. Among other variables, it is important to consider the nature of the substance use. For instance, research indicates that substance use patterns are changing, with poly-substance use, or the use of multiple substances, rapidly increasing among young people (Zuckermann et al., 2019). This is important, as young people who engage in poly-substance use are more likely to engage in risky behaviour than non-using and single-substance users (Zuckermann et al., 2020). For young people in conflict with the law, then, the complexity of the relationship between poly-use and later outcomes highlights the need for comprehensive support around educational, psychological, behavioural and social domains (Banks et al., 2019; Gill et al., 2023).

The use of illicit substances by young people can also often overlap with other adverse circumstances such as experience of state care and homelessness, and the convergence of these factors can increase marginalisation of young people and the likelihood of criminal justice system contact (Boyd et al., 2016). Involvement in substance use can serve to increase existing vulnerabilities. For example, studies have highlighted instances where involvement in drug-taking and heavy alcohol use provided the context in which young people experienced violence and assaults during their teenage years, further exacerbating levels of victimisation among this group of young people (McAra & McVie, 2022). Where problematic substance use is treated solely as a criminal justice issue, rather than as a health issue, this can further increase the marginalisation of young people. For example, a recent large-scale Swedish study with young people involved in substance use found that the imposition of criminal sanctions on young people for minor drug use further contributed to their social exclusion, hence leading to adverse outcomes for the young person (Anderberg et al., 2022).

In order to prevent young people coming into conflict with the law, regard must be had to the structural barriers to treatment experienced by some young people. In particular, those with a dual diagnosis of a mental health issue and substance use dependence can find it difficult to access professional supports (Kenny et al., 2006). Historic views of addiction, via the disease model, viewed mental health difficulties as a consequence of problematic drug and alcohol use, and for many years, a chicken and egg debate resulted in services that operated in parallel, rather than an integrated fashion (Cullen & Norton, 2022). The increased understanding of the link between psychological trauma, social exclusion and the development of mental health and addiction issues demonstrates these challenges are most likely a consequence of difficult experiences (Lambert & Murphy, 2019). This literature highlights the need for integrated services and supports for young people experiencing both drug and mental health issues to avoid them falling through the cracks. In order to advance the child's right to health and prevent them coming into conflict with the law, however, research recommends that developmentally appropriate dual diagnosis services are required to meet the needs of young people with the highest levels of risk and exposure to interpersonal and community adverse experiences (Fantuzzi & Mezzina, 2020).

Educational Engagement and the School Environment

Research highlights that the school environment and the level of educational attainment are important factors with regard to whether a young person becomes involved in offending behaviour (Farrington, 2015; Savage & Ellis, 2018; Van der Laan et al., 2009). In light of this, practices which exclude children from school are especially problematic with studies highlighting that the practice can lead to disengagement from education and increased likelihood of involvement in problem drug use, anti-social behaviour and further marginalisation within society as a whole (Baldry et al., 2018; Kemshall et al., 2006; McAra & McVie, 2022; McCrystal et al., 2007; Rocque & Snellings, 2018; Welch, 2018). Truancy and lack of engagement with school have been linked with later involvement in offending, although it is important to consider the reasons for this. For instance, disengagement by young people from education has been linked in some studies to experiences of bullying and problems occasioned by undiagnosed learning disabilities (McAra & McVie, 2022). Some studies suggest that truancy itself was less important than how that time was spent; in particular, where the time not spent in school was spent with offending peers, this was significant (Webster et al., 2006). However, the research is clear that unstructured socialising is not problematic in and of itself; rather, its link to involvement in offending behaviour depends instead on the likelihood of young people and their peers engaging in risky or criminal activity during this time (Gerstner & Oberwittier, 2018).

Disengagement from education at an early stage can lead to longer-term problems for young people and can act as a barrier to accessing third-level education or certain types of employment. Given the strong association in the research between negative educational experiences and educational exclusion and offending, therefore, it seems clear that many children in conflict with the law have experienced failures in relation to their educational rights, as set out under the CRC. It seems clear that inadequate protection for children's educational rights during childhood has multiple negative impacts, which can include later involvement in offending and in the youth justice system.

And yet, the converse is also true—education provides important protection from contact with the justice system. The literature indicates, for instance, that fuller realisation of children's educational rights might be an important tool for prevention of these negative outcomes and research shows that school can be a very important site for preventative efforts (Savage & Ellis, 2018). For instance, the German Crimoc study demonstrated that strong school bonds were negatively correlated with involvement in offending (Seddig & Reinecke, 2017). Furthermore, results from longitudinal studies have found that individual levels of commitment to, and attachment to a young person's school and peers predict lower rates of offending during adolescence (Higgins et al., 2020).

The importance of creating positive school environments emerges particularly strongly from the literature which highlights how school can be an important site for children to learn prosocial norms and attitudes that mitigate against involvement in offending through positive relationship with teachers (Theimann, 2015). Studies have shown that positive school environments, including a positive climate in the school, and positive relationships with and supervision by teachers were highly significant factors for the development of prosocial norms during adolescence (Bors & Reinecke, 2010). In addition, the quality of individual relationships between teachers and students in childhood has been demonstrated to be a protective factor against offending. Conversely, in schools where disciplinary measures are prioritised, it has been observed that the extent to which a school will punish a student may positively predict higher rates of offending behaviour in later adolescence (Mowen et al., 2020). At its most extreme, research indicates that where police are present in schools, it leads directly to increased engagement with law enforcement for children in what has become known as the school to prison pipeline (Nance, 2016). And this is not one direction only—once children move from school to the justice system, despite the established benefits of reenrolment in school, they find it increasingly difficult to find their way back (Feierman et al., 2009).

In light of these studies, the importance of strong protection for children's educational rights and a positive school environment from an early age emerges as a very important protective factor for children. In this regard, it is important that Article 28(2) of the CRC specifically warns against school discipline that undermines a child's dignity or their Convention rights and that the Committee on the Rights of the Child has stated clearly that specific supports should be in place for children who stop attending school or who are excluded from school as a core part of preventing children from coming into conflict with the law (Committee on the Rights of the Child, 2019, para. 9).

Protection from Harm

Given the harms experienced by children who come into conflict with the law, the child's right to protection from harm under Article 19 of the CRC is directly relevant to the justice context. A body of literature shows that children who come into contact with the justice system have often experienced myriad forms of trauma and harm. The overrepresentation of children who have experienced these types of harm in the justice system indicates that breaches of these children's rights in this regard are common, suggesting a link between children who experience violence and who come into conflict with the law.

Adverse Childhood Experiences and Childhood Trauma

One of the key issues emerging from the literature in this area is the fact that many children in contact with the youth justice system have experienced high rates of early childhood trauma. Research consistently highlights the relationship between early childhood adversity and trauma and high rates of offending behaviour and recidivism in young people (Yohros, 2022). The severity and rates of childhood adversity among justice-involved young people are significantly higher than the general population (Malvaso et al., 2022a). One study, which examined the predictive role of trauma in offending and health-risking sexual behaviour in adolescent girls, found that traumatic experiences, such as physical abuse, sexual abuse, parental incarceration and witnessing domestic violence, increased the likelihood of offending behaviour among this cohort (Smith et al., 2006). Notably, the findings suggest that the combination and complex nature of multiple traumatic events (including the personal impact of these experiences on the individual, the degree of loss, the nature/perceived sense of threat of the event(s) and the young person's sense of personal blame) are the strongest predictors of negative outcomes (i.e., trauma-related mental health difficulties) in girls in conflict with the law (Smith et al., 2006). A report on young people involved with diversion services in Ireland found that young people had significantly higher levels of childhood traumas than those of the general public, including much more frequent experiences of loss of a parent due to death or separation; difficulties in processing this type of loss can lead to young people being seen as 'bad' instead of 'sad' (Dermody et al., 2020). Furthermore, within a sample of women engaging with Irish probation services, participants were between two and three times more likely to have experienced domestic violence, physical or sexual abuse, have had a parent with mental health or other substance use issues during their childhood, or have experienced homelessness as children; for most, contact with justice services began in adolescence (Lambert & Dermody, 2021).

Further studies have highlighted the prevalence of trauma and adverse experiences in childhood among young people in contact with the youth justice system. One small-scale study in England and Wales found that 90% of young people in the sample either had a background of various forms of child abuse, or there was partial evidence in files or staff interviews to suggest that this had been the case (Boswell, 1998). Exposure to violence during childhood has been found to have negative effects on young people, including contributing to propensity to violence (Logan-Greene et al., 2011). Bereavement or loss of contact with a parent or significant family member is also a factor (Boswell, 1998). Self-harming behaviour was also associated with offending in the Edinburgh Study of Youth Transitions and Crime (McAra & McVie, 2010; see further Batchelor, 2005).

However, the exact mechanisms through which early childhood trauma/victimisation potentiates offending behaviour remain unclear. Ford et al. proposed a chronological pathway towards delinquency, which posited that trauma victimisation during early childhood activates 'survival coping', a process of escalating emotional dysregulation and social information processing difficulties (presenting as depression, anxiety and conflicted interpersonal relationships), which in turn precipitates persistent and repeated delinquency and covert resistance, through trauma-related reactivity (Ford et al., 2006). It is thus suggested that the relationship between childhood trauma and youth delinquency may result from the interplay of numerous interpersonal and intrapersonal mechanisms.

A framework to understand the relationship between experiences of trauma and future behavioural outcomes is through Adverse Childhood Experiences (ACE) (Felitti et al., 1998). There are ten ACEs, which can be broadly categorised into three domains: Abuse, Household Dysfunction and Neglect (Boullier & Blair, 2018). It is critical to note that ACEs cannot and are not intended to provide an assessment of risk, or to make predictive assumptions about individuals (Anda et al., 2020). Instead, the strength of using ACEs to inform our understanding of youth justice lies in understanding that young people who have experienced traumas in early life are especially vulnerable to several types of negative behavioural, health, psychological, physiological and social outcomes in later life (Baglivio et al., 2014; Bellis et al., 2014; Cole et al., 2022; Scully et al., 2020; Zarse et al., 2019). Again, it is important to note that the experiences of ACEs and later outcomes are not deterministic, but rather one factor within a system. For instance, multiple ACEs have been shown to positively predict poorer mental health, but the interaction of ACEs with parenting style and relationships is associated with rates of internalising, externalising and prosocial behaviour. There can be variations in the definitions of what constitutes an ACE, and some ACE scales limit all aversity to within the family home and fail to recognise the role that social policies such as housing and welfare have in terms of family functioning. There are ACE scales that have a broader view, such as the WHO scale, which also considers exposure to community violence, bullying and experiences of war (World Health Organization, 2013). However, there is no one scale that can capture the broad range of adversities in childhood that have the potential to impact on a child's social, emotional and cognitive development. Considering this, interventions that occur in the absence of addressing systematic issues such as poverty and social exclusion may be limited. It has been well established that poverty is one of the biggest predictors of later life difficulties (Nikulina et al., 2011).

Furthermore, this relationship is also impacted upon by socio-cultural factors. For instance, ethnic minority children from culturally and ethnically diverse groups are disproportionately exposed to ACEs in early life

(Hicks et al., 2021). While experiences of ACEs will happen within the family home, socio-cultural factors, such as access to resources, treatment within mental health systems, victimisation from police, or experiences of discrimination will further increase the risk of behavioural issues in adolescence (Dermody et al., 2020). There are others who argue that there is limited evidence to suggest that trauma symptoms predict offending behaviour (Malvaso et al., 2022b). Overall, it is important to remember that the experiences of trauma, and the ability to protect from the risks associated with these experiences are highly determined by socio-cultural factors.

A number of studies have looked at ACEs as they impact on youth justice system involvement and offending behaviour, noting that accumulated experiences of adversity tend to increase convictions over the life-course (Craig et al., 2017). While there is a clear overlap here with studies that examine experiences of victimisation, and difficult family backgrounds, literature highlights the long-term impact of adverse experiences during childhood. For instance, one US study on the prevalence of ACEs among a cohort of arrested young people showed that over four-fifths of the young people had experienced family violence; this study found that if a young person had been exposed to one ACE, they were significantly more likely to have experienced another (Baglivio & Epps, 2016). Other studies have also documented cohorts of young people who experience multiple types of trauma, including bereavement, domestic violence, emotional and physical abuse, and community violence, among others (Dierkhising et al., 2013; Finkelhor, 2011).

The link between early traumatic experiences and children's involvement in offending is an important children's rights issue. The Committee on the Rights of the Child has highlighted the importance of taking preventive measures to protect the child from violence in order to avoid them coming into contact with the law (Committee on the Rights of the Child, 2019, para. 18). Such preventive efforts should focus in particular on families in vulnerable situations and on the need to reinforce the capacities of parents including promoting their positive social potential (Committee on the Rights of the Child, 2019, paras. 19 and 20). Given that the CRC places a duty on states parties to ensure all children have equal access to their rights (Committee on the Rights of the Child, 2019, para. 18), research has found that the high level of trauma and adverse childhood experiences among children in the youth justice system to be indicative of a series of failures in the provision of care to these children.

It is also important to emphasise here that the distribution of how failures in the provision of care fall on children and their families tends to be highly unequal and is frequently related to social class, inequality and poverty (Currie, 2020; Kramer, 2000; Lister, 2021; White & Cunneen, 2015). The relationship with the non-discrimination principle in Article 2 of the CRC is clear.

Victimisation and Exploitation

A further theme emerging from the literature on preventing children's contact with the law is the experience of victimisation, adversity and exploitation. Research demonstrates that young people in contact with the youth justice system are often themselves the victims of crime. The Edinburgh Study of Youth Transitions and Crime found that involvement in violent behaviour at age 15 was significantly predicted by being a victim of crime at the same age (McAra & McVie, 2010). It also found that for boys, in particular, there was a complex interaction between early experiences of crime victimisation and later experiences of crises within the family that suggested that later involvement in violent offending is predicted by sustained adversity over time (McAra & McVie, 2010). Equally, high rates of victimisation, particularly within the family, were common among one study involving young women in custody in Scotland (Batchelor, 2005). This study found that experiences of violence and abuse could result in anger and aggression, as well as unresolved feelings of grief and rage (Batchelor, 2005).

Research on inter-family conflict, including child-to-parent violence, highlights its gendered nature, often involving violence by a son towards a mother (Armstrong et al., 2018; Condry & Miles, 2014; Ibabe & Jaureguizar, 2010). Daughters who engaged in this type of behaviour were found to have significantly higher levels of direct and multiple forms of victimisation (Armstrong et al., 2018; Condry & Miles, 2014). Prior experience of intra-family violence has been highlighted as a potential factor in child-to-parent violence (Ibabe & Jaureguizar, 2010). Further, it has been suggested that a child's involvement in violence is partly influenced by their perception that the environment is unsafe. For instance, a Canadian study highlighted that being on the street, having criminal peers and using drugs and alcohol influence how young people perceive harm, their willingness to use force to settle a dispute and the routines developed to deal with conflict (Baron et al., 2007). A child's relationship with violence is clearly complex.

Gangs and Criminal Exploitation

Exposure to violence among young people who are members of gangs has also been documented, noting that participation in gangs puts young people at risk of exposure to further violence (Frisby-Osman & Wood, 2020). A German study has suggested that young people may engage in deviant coping strategies as a reaction to victimisation, but the nature of this overlap does not appear to be stable over time and reactions may change over the life-course (Erdmann & Reinecke, 2018). Research findings also highlight that there are links between childhood sexual exploitation and offending, with 40% of participants in one study who had experienced this exploitation being implicated in criminal activities (Cockbain & Brayley, 2012). Being a victim of repeated bullying can also be linked to involvement in offending (Higgins et al., 2012; Staubli & Killias, 2011; Visser et al., 2017).

Some of the literature in this area raises the issue of childhood criminal exploitation or situations where adult offenders involve children in criminal activities, often involving drug running or associated offences. Studies have documented the use of children in drug trafficking and other associated offences such as in the UK's 'county lines', where children are routinely used to carry drugs across different police areas (Windle et al., 2020). These studies have highlighted that the young people who become involved in these activities are often particularly vulnerable and are exposed to a range of ancillary dangers in addition to the dangers of arrest and criminalisation (Windle et al., 2020). Some studies have highlighted how neighbourhood and family networks can play a part in getting children involved in criminal activities, sometimes of a serious nature (Redmond, 2015). However, it is important to highlight that deprived urban neighbourhoods are the result of policy decisions which impact on the lifeworld of urban youth (Armstead et al., 2021; van Lanen, 2018). Youth gang membership is a complex issue bound up in marginalisation, victimisation, mental health and identity at individual, family, peer and community levels (Densley et al., 2020).

Article 19 of the CRC clearly recognises the right of all children to protection from all forms of harm, and the Committee on the Rights of the Child recognises that children who experience such harms are especially vulnerable to exploitation and abuse (Committee on the Rights of the Child, 2019, para. 18). The high prevalence, among children in conflict with the law, of victimisation and criminal exploitation highlights the need to adopt a rights-based and integrated approach to prevent children coming into conflict with the law (Committee on the Rights of the Child, 2019, para. 19). The standards, which focus on the child as an individual, have so far had little to say about gangs, or the treatment of children in drugs or other networks. This appears to be an area where research has yet to have an impact.

Access to an Adequate Standard of Living

Article 27 of the CRC sets out the right to 'a standard of living adequate for the child's physical, mental, spiritual, moral and social development' and the Committee on the Rights of the Child has recognised the link between this right and a child's involvement in criminal activity (Committee on the Rights of the Child, 2019, para. 18). While parents and guardians have primary responsibility for fulfilling children's needs in relation to their development under Articles 5 and 18 of the CRC, states parties also have responsibilities in taking measures to assist parents and in providing appropriate services and programmes to promote their positive development (Kilkelly, 2020).

The Importance of Communities

Beyond families, a large body of research demonstrates the extent to which children in conflict with the law have experienced poverty and lack necessary resources and services within their communities. For example, many studies examine the neighbourhood and communities in which children's offending takes places to understand how young people come into conflict with the law. It is suggested in some of the literature that community factors—including economic disadvantage, the prevalence of danger and violence in the community, and exposure to peer groups involved in offending—can increase the risk of involvement in criminal activity (Ingoldsby & Shaw, 2002). While studies have often associated offending with disadvantaged neighbourhoods, this is not always consistent across studies (Webster et al., 2006).

Access to resources of various kinds within a community is seen as important (Leventhal & Brooks-Gunn, 2000). Lack of having 'something to do' has been linked to involvement in offending behaviour as young people feel a need to seek alternatives to generate excitement (Corr, 2014). Neighbourhood dynamics can also influence the extent to which young people become associated with peers who are involved in offending (Ingoldsby & Shaw, 2002). Equally, the availability, accessibility and affordability of community resources such as schools, medical services, and recreational and social facilities can play an important role (Leventhal & Brooks-Gunn, 2000). Importantly, neighbourhoods can help to shape the expectations that children and young people have about the employment opportunities that may be open to them (Leventhal & Brooks-Gunn, 2000). In this respect, children and young people are particularly affected by 'territorial stigmatisation' (Wacquant, 2008), where communities which have been disinvested from are not in a position to provide them with opportunities and recognition (Billingham & Irwin-Rogers, 2022). The literature in this area therefore highlights the importance of ensuring that young people can access resources in a wide range of areas in order to avoid coming into conflict with the law.

In essence, the relationship between community/neighbourhood and youth involvement in the justice system is strong. The impacts of social and community disadvantage are far-reaching and exacerbate the difficulties presented from early life trauma, family dysfunction, disability status, education, poverty, among many other factors (Hughes et al., 2020). From a children's rights perspective, findings such as these add weight to international guidelines which emphasise that efforts to prevent young people from becoming involved in young offending are best situated in the wider community, through providing appropriate mainstream supports and services for children and their families (Committee on the Rights of the Child, 2019; UN General Assembly, 1990). This recommendation is also bolstered by recent findings from the Edinburgh of Youth Transitions and Crime, which emphasised that an holistic approach, encompassing education, housing, the economy and justice together, and 'which target risk factors across communities rather than risky individuals in childhood and adolescence, are likely to be successful in reducing children's involvement in the justice system across the life-course' (McAra & McVie, 2022).

Poverty and Homelessness

Neighbourhood factors are often exacerbated by the marginalisation of young people within their communities, as well as by experiences of poverty. Family Low Socioeconomic Status (SES) has been identified in the literature as a risk factor for victimisation and offending, although this is interrelated with other factors like race and family structure (Hartinger-Saunders et al., 2011). Haynie et al. suggest that low SES is associated with direct and indirect victimisation, behavioural difficulties and increased offending in adolescence (Haynie et al., 2006).

Marginalisation, poverty and social exclusion also play a strong role in determining access to mental health services. For instance, due to disparities in available resources making mental health resources inaccessible, it has been noted that children from ethnic minority backgrounds often rely on the justice system to access necessary care (Fante-Coleman & Jackson-Best, 2020). Additionally, and linked to the discussion above, factors such as mental health, substance use, bereavement, care burden and lack of affordable housing can exacerbate the impact of poverty and marginalisation, including as significant causes of homelessness (Lambert et al., 2018).

Experiences of marginalisation are also particularly problematic to the extent that cycles of marginalisation and exclusion can become self-perpetuating. In seeking to access legitimate employment or training opportunities, a history of criminal justice system contact can disrupt these attempts, working against reintegration (Corr, 2014). This can be further exacerbated by broader economic factors, which can further increase the risk of offending in unstable neighbourhoods (Webster et al., 2006). For instance, one Irish study indicated how economic marginalisation impacted young people who experienced challenges in accessing employment, and as a result, the drug economy filled a gap for young people without a legitimate means of earning money (Corr, 2014; Hourigan, 2012).

Homelessness is a global problem, and many OECD countries have reported a rise in youth homelessness, with Ireland experiencing the largest increase, an 82% during the period 2014–2018. Denmark experienced a 43% increase between 2011 and 2017, a 20% increase was observed in Australia between 2011 and 2016 and 23% in New Zealand between 2006 and 2013 (OECD, 2020). Youth homelessness in the

US has been described as a significant national challenge, with an estimated 1 in every 30 adolescents with homelessness experience, with intersectional effects for those already marginalised, such as indigenous groups (Morton et al., 2019). Research indicates that the experience of homelessness is detrimental to well-being and linked with increased emotional and behavioural difficulties, substance use, reduced educational attainment and criminal activity (Martijn & Sharpe, 2006). Homelessness is thus viewed both as a risk factor for criminal behaviour and as a consequence of criminal involvement relating to the stigma of criminal conviction (Committee on the Rights of the Child, 2019, para. 78). Studies have also highlighted that young people who live in persistently food insecure households are significantly more likely to be involved in early delinquency and demonstrate lower levels of self-control (Jackson et al., 2018).

The issue of poverty, linked to living standards and housing, is clearly a matter of children's rights that requires urgent attention in order to prevent children from coming into conflict with the law. In this respect, the Committee on the Rights of the Child reminds states parties of the obligation to provide assistance to families through investment in childhood care and education as part of a strategy to prevent children from becoming involved in offending (Committee on the Rights of the Child, 2019, para. 10). It also considers it important that states adopt comprehensive national strategies addressing individual, family and community factors, in order to prevent children coming into conflict with the law (Committee on the Rights of the Child, 2019, para. 19).

The Importance of Family Care

There is significant emphasis throughout the CRC on the important role that parents and family play in children's development and in protecting children's rights (e.g., Articles 5 and 18). In the context of children in conflict with the law, the Committee on the Rights of the Child has emphasised the important role of the family in providing guidance to the child, and preventive programmes are also recommended to be family-based (Kilkelly, 2020). While the positive influence of the family is recognised in the research, studies also point to the fact that such relationships can be problematic for children in the event that families are insufficiently supportive or their guidance inappropriate.

Adverse family conditions, including parental conflict, have been noted to correlate with children's involvement in offending (Farrington, 2015; Lay et al., 2005; McAra & McVie, 2022; Smith & McVie, 2003; Vazsonyi et al., 2016). The Edinburgh of Youth Transitions and Crime found that growing up in less stable family environments was associated with early involvement in serious offending, and that family turbulence and deprivation could be particularly problematic for girls (Manly et al., 2013; McAra & McVie, 2010; Thijs et al., 2015). Parental drug use (Bright & Jonson-Reid, 2010) and parental involvement in criminal behaviour have also been associated with children's involvement in offending (Connolly et al., 2018). However, the Cambridge Study on Delinquent Development further suggested that family-based prevention programmes such as parent education and parent management training could be offered to all fathers with a conviction, regardless of whether their own offending has been sporadic or chronic in nature, as a means of supporting more positive outcomes for children (Besemer & Farrington, 2012). Further, some studies have suggested that the negative impact of parental criminal history may be mitigated by ensuring the accessibility of education (Ramakers et al., 2011).

The levels of support available for children within the family seem to be an important factor, linked to whether children will come into conflict with the law. Poor parental monitoring has been identified as a significant factor linked to involvement in offending (McAra & McVie, 2010; Salmi & Kivivuori, 2006; Smith & McVie, 2003; Van der Laan et al., 2009), and low levels of parental support are similarly linked. Some studies suggest that some single parent families experience greater difficulties meeting a child's needs while attending to the competing demands of the single parent household, with increased likelihood that the child may become involved in offending (McNulty & Bellair, 2003). This appears consistent with other research, whose findings suggest that such parental absence is associated with increased delinquency in adolescents (Demuth & Brown, 2004). The findings suggest that reduced parental monitoring, supervision, involvement and closeness, as a result of parental absence, may account for this. However, this association appears less evident in more recent studies, with research now indicating a small, however, temporary, relationship between parental divorce/separation and delinquency in adolescence (Boccio & Beaver, 2019). Finally, many studies have examined the relationship between attachment and delinquency, and one meta-analytic review suggested a small to moderate association between poor attachment to parents and increased offending behaviour (Hoeve et al., 2012). This had a stronger effect if the child and parent were of the same sex and the influence of the attachment relationship weakened as the child became older.

In line with the emphasis placed on promoting positive family relationships in the international children's rights standards in this area (Committee on the Rights of the Child, 2019), the literature emphasises the importance of the quality of parenting. Several studies have shown that factors such as parental warmth (Klatt & Kliem, 2021), parental harshness (Bosk et al., 2021), parental control (Walters, 2021) and the quality of relationships (Liu et al., 2020) influence the relationship between risk factors and youth offending. In other words, the type of parenting a young person receives can either ameliorate or exacerbate the risk of offending presented by other challenges during a child's development.

Crucially, therefore, while the influence can be negative, the family can also be a protective environment, helping young people to avoid coming into conflict with the law. Positive attachments to parents, and the child-rearing methods practised by parents to support child development and build up resilience and internal inhibitions against offending, are important factors in the literature in this area (Farrington, 2015; Hill et al., 2018). Support from parents was considered to be a significant protective factor in helping children to avoid coming into conflict with the law (Farrington et al., 2016; Hill et al., 2018; Svensson et al., 2017).

Importantly, high parental interest in education has been found to operate as an important protective factor (Meinert & Reinecke, 2018). Parents can also have a positive influence on self- control in early and mid-adolescence; however, this influence gradually decreases during mid-adolescence (Gunnar et al., 2019; Reid et al., 2021). This research evidence further recommends that appropriate supports should be provided to parents and caregivers to enhance parenting capacity, providing programmes designed to strengthen parent–child relationships (Committee on the Rights of the Child, 2019, para. 19). All these approaches find favour with the rights-based approach in the CRC (Kilkelly, 2020).

Rest, Leisure and the Role of Peers

Article 31 of the CRC recognises the right of all children to play, rest and leisure. Given the strong link in the literature between unsupervised leisure time with peers who exert a negative influence and offending, the realisation of children's rights under Article 31 merits particular attention here. The research on children's pathways into conflict with the law makes a strong link between offending and association with peers who are already involved in such behaviour (Defoe et al., 2021; McAra & McVie, 2010; Megens & Weerman, 2010; Rocque et al., 2015; Seddig & Reinecke, 2017; Smith & Ecob, 2013; Smith & McVie, 2003). However, some studies cast doubt on whether this association is as straightforward as it may seem at first glance. For example, one Dutch study has suggested that associations with offending peers increase the risk of offending only where friends live in close proximity, and where there are regular contact and strong attachments (Rokven et al., 2017).

Peer social attachments can be particularly important in relation to the development of attitudes and values that facilitate involvement in offending behaviour. Association with peers who are involved in offending is considered to be a potential source of the development of pro-offending attitudes and beliefs, particularly for young people considered to have hedonistic tendencies (Bors & Reinecke, 2010; Defoe et al., 2021; Seddig & Reinecke, 2017; Svensson et al., 2017). Co-offending with peers has been linked to the development of offending trajectories (Seddig, 2014). Acceptance of pro-violent norms and violent behaviour can facilitate the development and maintenance of offending cycles (Seddig, 2014). Peer groups can also support learning criminal behaviour through imitation, and learning of context-specific criminal behaviour, such as theft (Beier, 2014; Rokven et al., 2017).

Group dynamics within peer groups are also a possible source of explanation for involvement in offending during teenage years (Bors & Reinecke, 2010*)* and peer dynamics can be—but are not always (see for example Hill et al., 2018)—an important factor in sustaining involvement in offending behaviour (Seddig & Reinecke, 2017). A Dutch study found that peer group dynamics were less important during emerging adulthood than they were during adolescence (Webster et al., 2006), and others have highlighted that friendships can act as a protective factor in helping young people avoid pathways into drug use and crime (Maclure & Sotelo, 2014).

Conversely, findings from a large-scale longitudinal study suggest that young people who spend more time with prosocial peers were less likely to engage in future offending behaviour or drug use (Walters, 2020). Another study, in seeking to disentangle the relationship between peer association, offending behaviour and low empathy, found that positive peer associations moderated the effect of these factors on offending behaviour (Walters, 2020). For some interviewees in the Edinburgh Study, desistance from offending in adulthood was linked with cutting ties with friends associated with their previous offending during their teenage years (McAra & McVie, 2022).

One of the key factors relevant to relationships with offending peers is that social networks often tend to become smaller over time; this can operate to restrict long-term opportunities to access wider networks for education, training and employment (Webster et al., 2006). Drug use can further limit these networks, and these factors can operate against desistance (Webster et al., 2006). Studies highlight that in contexts characterised by a lack of opportunity, social capital may be gained from friendship bonds, but yield limited opportunities for social mobility or access to other forms of capital (Maclure & Sotelo, 2014). The ability of young people to change their social setting and to form new relationships has been highlighted as being important to support the desistance process (Smith & Ecob, 2013). These findings highlight the importance of how young people spend their leisure time in relation to their potential involvement in offending behaviour, and suggest that ensuring that young people have positive outlets and environments in which to spend their leisure time is important in avoiding coming into conflict with the law. Providing programmes to promote positive peer association and involvement in positive cultural and leisure activities has been recommended as part of prevention strategies by the UN Committee on the Rights of the Child (Committee on the Rights of the Child, 2019, para. 10).

Conclusion

This chapter set out to explore the themes in the contemporary literature relating to preventing children from coming into conflict with the law. It highlighted that dominant in the lives of children in conflict with the law are a range of complex and inter-connected factors including mental health, substance use, marginalisation, educational disadvantage, poverty and adverse personal and family circumstances, including experience of harm and exploitation. It also highlighted that, in line with the children's rights standards, it is important to ensure the child has access to good healthcare, inclusive education and strong family and community supports in order to prevent the child coming into conflict with the law. In these respects, the children's rights approach aligns well with the findings from the research literature. However, there are some themes from the literature that are not sufficiently addressed in the international children's rights standards. In particular, disproportionate minority contact, especially racial discrimination, is a dominant theme of the youth justice literature, but it is not adequately covered in the international standards meaning that they offer little explicit guidance on how such contact is to be prevented, from a children's rights perspective. Other elements are also missing including children's involvement in gangs, the important role played by peers, in both directions, and the connection between exploitation, marginalisation and criminal networks. The significance of exposure to state care and to harm and trauma—including children's complex relationship with violence—have also yet to be sufficiently addressed in the international standards. The impact of marginalisation—and the wider role that can be played by ensuring children are involved in matters that affect them—also requires greater attention in the context of preventing children from coming into conflict with the law. In order to ensure the standards remain relevant and informed by the leading research evidence, therefore, consideration should be given to ensure these gaps are addressed.

Bibliography

Abrams, L. S., Mizel, M. L., & Barnert, E. S. (2021). The criminalization of young children and overrepresentation of Black youth in the juvenile justice system. *Race and Social Problems, 13*, 73–84. https://doi.org/10.1007/s12552-021-09314-7

Aebi, M., Giger, J., Plattner, B., Metzke, C. W., & Steinhausen, H. C. (2014). Problem coping skills, psychosocial adversities and mental health problems in children and adolescents as predictors of criminal outcomes in young adulthood. *European Child & Adolescent Psychiatry, 23*(5), 283–293. https://doi.org/10.1007/s00787-013-0458-y

Aghajani, M., Klapwijk, E. T., Andershed, H., Fanti, K. A., van der Wee, N. J., Vermeiren, R. R., & Colins, O. F. (2021). Neural processing of socioemotional content in conduct-disordered juvenile offenders with limited prosocial emotions. *Progress in Neuro-Psychopharmacology and Biological Psychiatry, 105*, 110045. https://doi.org/10.1016/j.pnpbp.2020.110045

Anda, R. F., Porter, L. E., & Brown, D. W. (2020). Inside the adverse childhood experience score: Strengths, limitations, and misapplications. *American Journal of Preventive Medicine, 59*(2), 293–295. https://doi.org/10.1016/j.amepre.2020.01.009

Anderberg, M., Dahlberg, M., & Wennberg, P. (2022). Criminality among young people with substance use problems in Sweden: A one-year follow-up study. *Journal of Drug Issues, 52*(3), 406–420. https://doi.org/10.1177/00220426211046596

Armstead, T. L., Wilkins, N., & Nation, M. (2021). Structural and social determinants of inequities in violence risk: A review of indicators. *Journal of Community Psychology, 49*(4), 878–906. https://doi.org/10.1002/jcop.22232

Armstrong, G. S., Cain, C. M., Wylie, L. E., Muftic, L. R., & Bouffard, L. A. (2018). Risk factor profile of youth incarcerated for child to parent violence: A representative sample. *Journal of Criminal Justice, 58*(1), 1–9. https://doi.org/10.1016/j.jcrimjus.2018.06.002

Baglivio, M. T., Epps, N., Swartz, K., Huq, M. S., Sheer, A., & Hardt, N. S. (2014). The prevalence of adverse childhood experiences (ACE) in the lives of juvenile offenders. *Journal of Juvenile Justice, 3*(2), 1–23.

Baglivio, M. T., & Epps, N. (2016). The interrelatedness of adverse childhood experiences among high-risk juvenile offenders. *Youth Violence and Juvenile Justice, 14*(3), 179–198. https://doi.org/10.1177/1541204014566286

Baidawi, S., & Ball, R. (2023a). Child protection and youth offending: Differences in youth criminal court-involved children by dual system involvement. *Children and Youth Services Review, 144*, 106736. https://doi.org/10.1016/j.childyouth.2022.106736

Baidawi, S., & Ball, R. (2023b). Multi-system factors impacting youth justice involvement of children in residential out-of-home care. *Child & Family Social Work, 28*(1), 53–64. https://doi.org/10.1111/cfs.12940

Baldry, E., Briggs, D. B., Goldson, B., & Russell, S. (2018). 'Cruel and unusual punishment': An inter-jurisdictional study of the criminalisation of young people with complex support needs. *Journal of Youth Studies, 21*(5), 636–652. https://doi.org/10.1080/13676261.2017.1406072

Banks, D. E., Hershberger, A. R., Pemberton, T., Clifton, R. L., Aalsma, M. C., & Zapolski, T. C. (2019). Poly-use of cannabis and other substances among juvenile-justice involved youth: Variations in psychological and substance-related problems by typology. *The American Journal of Drug and Alcohol Abuse, 45*(3), 313–322. https://doi.org/10.1080/00952990.2018.1558450

Baranyi, G., Di Marco, M. H., Russ, T. C., Dibben, C., & Pearce, J. (2021). The impact of neighbourhood crime on mental health: A systematic review and meta-analysis. *Social Science & Medicine, 282*, 114106. https://doi.org/10.1016/j.socscimed.2021.114106

Baron, S. W., Forde, D. R., & Kennedy, L. W. (2007). Disputatiousness, aggressiveness, and victimization among street youths. *Youth Violence and Juvenile Justice, 5*(4), 411–425. https://doi.org/10.1177/1541204077299582

Baskin, D., & Sommers, I. (2015). Trajectories of exposure to community violence and mental health symptoms among serious adolescent offenders. *Criminal Justice and Behavior, 42*(6), 587–609. https://doi.org/10.1177/0093854814556882

Basto-Pereira, M., & Farrington, D. P. (2022). Developmental predictors of offending and persistence in crime: A systematic review of meta-analyses. *Aggression and Violent Behaviour, 65*, 101761. https://doi.org/10.1016/j.avb.2022.101761

Batchelor, S. (2005). 'Prove me the bam!': Victimization and agency in the lives of young women who commit violent offences. *Probation Journal, 52*(4), 358–375. https://doi.org/10.1177/0264550505058034

Beier, H. (2014). Peer effects in offending behaviour across contexts: Disentangling selection, opportunity and learning processes. *European Journal of Criminology, 11*(1), 73–90. https://doi.org/10.1177/1477370813486865

Bellis, M. A., Hughes, K., Leckenby, N., Jones, L., Baban, A., Kachaeva, M., Povilaitis, R., Pudule, I., Qirjako, G., Ulukol, B., Raleva, M., & Terzic, N. (2014). Adverse childhood experiences and associations with health-harming behaviours in young adults: Surveys in eight eastern European countries. *Bulletin of the World Health Organisation, 92*(9), 641–655. https://doi.org/10.2471/BLT.13.129247

Besemer, S., & Farrington, D. P. (2012). Intergenerational transmission of criminal behaviour: Conviction trajectories of fathers and their children. *European Journal of Criminology, 9*(2), 120–141. https://doi.org/10.1177/1477370811422801

Billingham, L., & Irwin-Rogers, K. (2022). *Against youth violence: A social harm perspective*. Bristol University Press.

Bishop, D. M. (2005). The role of race and ethnicity in juvenile justice processing. In D. F. Hawkins & K. Kempf-Leonard (Eds.), *Our children, their children: Confronting racial and ethnic differences in American juvenile justice* (pp. 23–82). University of Chicago Press.

Blankenstein, N. E., Telzer, E. H., Do, K. T., Van Duijvenvoorde, A. C., & Crone, E. A. (2020). Behavioral and neural pathways supporting the development of prosocial and risk-taking behavior across adolescence. *Child Development, 91*(3), 665–681. https://doi.org/10.1111/cdev.13292

Boccio, C. M., & Beaver, K. M. (2019). The influence of family structure on delinquent behavior. *Youth Violence and Juvenile Justice, 17*(1), 88–106. https://doi.org/10.1177/1541204017727836

Boddy, J., Bakketeig, E., & Østergaard, J. (2020). Navigating precarious times? The experience of young adults who have been in care in Norway, Denmark and England. *Journal of Youth Studies, 23*(3), 291–306. https://doi.org/10.1080/13676261.2019.1599102

Bors, K., & Reinecke, J. (2010). Explaining the development of adolescent violent delinquency. *European Journal of Criminology, 7*(6), 499–520. https://doi.org/10.1177/1477370810376572

Bosk, E. A., Anthony, W. L., Folk, J. B., & Williams-Butler, A. (2021). All in the family: Parental substance misuse, harsh parenting, and youth substance misuse among juvenile justice-involved youth. *Addictive Behaviors, 119*, 106888. https://doi.org/10.1016/j.addbeh.2021.106888

Boswell, G. R. (1998). Criminal justice and violent young offenders. *The Howard Journal of Crime and Justice, 37*(2), 148–160. https://doi.org/10.1111/1468-2311.00087

Boullier, M., & Blair, M. (2018). Adverse childhood experiences. *Paediatrics and Child Health, 28*(3), 132–137. https://doi.org/10.1016/j.paed.2017.12.008

Boyd, J., Fast, D., & Small, W. (2016). Pathways to criminalization for street-involved youth who use illicit substances. *Critical Public Health, 26*(5), 530–554. https://doi.org/10.1080/09581596.2015.1110564

Bright, C., & Jonson-Reid, M. (2010). Young adult outcomes of juvenile court-involved girls. *Journal of Social Service Research, 36*(2), 94–106. https://doi.org/10.1080/01488370903577993

Bronfenbrenner, U. (1999). Environments in developmental perspective: Theoretical and operational models. In S. L. Friedman & T. D. Wachs (Eds.), *Measuring environment across the life span: Emerging methods and concepts* (pp. 3–28). American Psychological Association. https://doi.org/10.1037/10317-001

Bronfenbrenner, U., & Morris, P. A. (2007). The bioecological model of human development. In R. M. Lerner & W. Damon (Eds.), *Handbook of child psychology: Theoretical models of human development* (pp. 793–828). Wiley. https://doi.org/10.1002/9780470147658.chpsy0114

Campbell, S. B. (2006). *Behavior problems in preschool children, second edition: Clinical and developmental issues*. Guilford Publications.

Case, S., & Browning, A. (2021). *Child first justice: The research evidence-base* [full Report]. Loughborough University. https://hdl.handle.net/2134/14152040.v1

Chan, H. C. (Oliver). (2021). Violent offending, nonviolent offending, and general delinquency: Exploring the criminogenic risk factors of Hong Kong male and female adolescents. *International Journal of Offender Therapy and Comparative Criminology, 65*(9), 975–998. https://doi.org/10.1177/0306624X19881917

Chesney-Lind, M., & Irwin, K. (2007). *Beyond bad girls: Gender, violence and hype*. Routledge.

Christensen, L., & Baker, B. L. (2020). Risk-taking and delinquent behaviors among youth with and without intellectual disabilities. *Journal of Mental Health Research in Intellectual Disabilities, 13*(1), 1–24. https://doi.org/10.1080/19315864.2019.1710786

Cochran, J. C., & Mears, D. P. (2015). Race, ethnic, and gender divides in juvenile court sanctioning and rehabilitative intervention. *Journal of Research in Crime and Delinquency, 52*(2), 181–212. https://doi.org/10.1177/0022427814560574

Cockbain, E., & Brayley, H. (2012). Child sexual exploitation and youth offending: A research note. *European Journal of Criminology, 9*(6), 689–700. https://doi.org/10.1177/1477370812453401

Cohen, A. (2016). When is an adolescent an adult? Assessing cognitive control in emotional and nonemotional contexts. *Psychological Science, 27*(4), 549–562. https://doi.org/10.1177/0956797615627625

Cole, A. B., Armstrong, C. M., Giano, Z. D., & Hubach, R. D. (2022). An update on ACEs domain frequencies across race/ethnicity and sex in a nationally representative sample. *Child Abuse & Neglect, 129*, 105686. https://doi.org/10.1016/j.chiabu.2022.105686

Committee on the Rights of the Child. (2013). *General comment No. 15 (2013) on the right of the child to the enjoyment of the highest attainable standard of health (art. 24)*, 17 April 2013, CRC/C/GC/15.

Committee on the Rights of the Child. (2016). *General comment No. 20 (2016) on the implementation of the rights of the child during adolescence*, 06 December 2016, CRC/C/GC/20.

Committee on the Rights of the Child. (2019). *General comment No. 24 (2019) on children's rights in the child justice system*, 19 September 2019, CRC/C/GC/24.

Condry, R., & Miles, C. (2014). Adolescent to parent violence: Framing and mapping a hidden problem. *Criminology & Criminal Justice, 14*(3), 257–275. https://doi.org/10.1177/1748895813500155

Connolly, E. J., Schwartz, J. A., Jackson, D. B., & Beaver, K. M. (2018). How far does the apple fall from the tree? Maternal delinquency and sex-specific patterns of offspring delinquent behaviour. *Journal of Criminal Justice, 54*, 50–61. https://doi.org/10.1016/j.jcrimjus.2017.12.004

Cooke, E. M., Connolly, E. J., Boisvert, D. L., Armstrong, T. A., Lewis, R. H., Kavish, N., Woeckener, M., Wells, J., & Harper, J. (2020). Examining how testosterone and cortisol influence the relationship between strain, negative emotions, and antisocial behavior: A gendered analysis. *Crime & Delinquency, 66*(10), 1470–1501. https://doi.org/10.1177/0011128720903047

Copeland, W., Miller-Johnson, S., Keeler, G., Angold, A., & Costello, E. J. (2007). Childhood psychiatric disorders and young adult crime: A prospective, population-based study. *American Journal of Psychiatry, 164*(11), 1668–1675. https://doi.org/10.1176/appi.ajp.2007.06122026

Corr, M.-L. (2014). Young people's offending careers and criminal justice contact: A case for social justice. *Youth Justice, 14*(3), 255–268. https://doi.org/10.1177/1473225414549695

Craig, J. M., Piquero, A. R., Farrington, D. P., & Ttofi, M. M. (2017). A little early risk goes a long bad way: Adverse childhood experiences and life-course offending in the Cambridge study. *Journal of Criminal Justice, 53*, 34–45. https://doi.org/10.1016/j.jcrimjus.2017.09.005

Cronin, P., & Addo, R. (2021). Interactions with youth justice and associated costs for young people with speech, language and communication needs. *International Journal of Language & Communication Disorders, 56*(4), 797–811. https://doi.org/10.1111/1460-6984.12628

Cullen, O. J., & Norton, M. J. (2022). Chicken or egg: A dual diagnosis narrative. *Journal of Psychiatric and Mental Health Nursing, 29*(4), 507–511. https://doi.org/10.1111/jpm.12801

Currie, J. (2020). Child health as human capital. *Health Economics, 29*(4), 452–463. https://doi.org/10.1002/hec.3995

Day, A. M. (2022). Disabling and criminalising systems? Understanding the experiences and challenges facing justice experienced, neurodiverse children in the education and youth justice systems. *Forensic Science International: Mind and Law, 3*(100101), 1–9. https://doi.org/10.1016/j.fsiml.2022.100102

Deakin, J., Fox, C., & Matos, R. (2022). Labelled as 'risky' in an era of control: How young people experience and respond to the stigma of criminalized identities. *European Journal of Criminology, 19*(4), 653–673. https://doi.org/10.1177/1477370820916728

Defoe, I. N., van Gelder, J.-L., Ribeaud, D., & Eisner, M. (2021). The co-development of friends' delinquency with adolescents' delinquency and short-term mindsets: The moderating role of co-offending. *Journal of Youth and Adolescence, 50*, 1601–1615. https://doi.org/10.1007/s10964-021-01417-z

Demuth, S., & Brown, S. L. (2004). Family structure, family processes, and adolescent delinquency: The significance of parental absence versus parental gender. *Journal of Research in Crime and Delinquency, 41*(1), 58–81. https://doi.org/10.1177/0022427803256236

Densley, J., Deuchar, R., & Harding, S. (2020). An introduction to gangs and serious youth violence in the united kingdom. *Youth Justice, 20*(1–2), 3–10. https://doi.org/10.1177/1473225420902848

Dermody A., Lambert S., Rackow, A., Garcia J., & Gardner C. (2020). *An exploration of early life trauma and its implications for garda youth diversion projects*. Youthrise/Quality Matters.

de Ruigh, E. L., Bouwmeester, S., Popma, A., Vermeiren, R. R. J. M., van Domburgh, L., & Jansen, L. M. C. (2021). Using the biopsychosocial model for identifying subgroups of detained juveniles at different risk of re-offending in practice: A latent class regression analysis approach. *Child and Adolescent Psychiatry and Mental Health, 15*(33), 1–15. https://doi.org/10.1186/s13034-021-00379-1

Deuchar, R. (2009). *Gangs, marginalised youth and social capital*. Trentham Books.

Dierkhising, C., Ko, S., Woods-Jaeger, B., Briggs, E., Lee, R., & Pynoos, R. (2013). Trauma histories among justice-involved youth: Findings from the National Child Traumatic Stress Network. *European Journal of Psychotraumatology, 4*(1), 20274. https://doi.org/10.3402/ejpt.v4i0.20274

Dodge, K. A., & Pettit, G. S. (2003). A biopsychosocial model of the development of chronic conduct problems in adolescence. *Developmental Psychology, 39*(2), 349–371. https://doi.org/10.1037/0012-1649.39.2.349

Douglas, K. R., Chan, G., Gelernter, J., Arias, A. J., Anton, R. F., Weiss, R. D., Brady, K., Poling, J., Farrer, L., & Kranzler, H. R. (2010). Adverse childhood events as risk factors for substance dependence: Partial mediation by mood and anxiety disorders. *Addictive Behaviors, 35*(1), 7–13. https://doi.org/10.1016/j.addbeh.2009.07.004

Dowd, N. E. (2006–2007). Boys, masculinities and juvenile justice. *Journal of Korean Law, 6*(2).

Duell, N., Steinberg, L., Icenogle, G., Chein, J., Chaudhary, N., Di Giunta, L., Dodge, K. A., Fanti, K. A., Lansford, J. E., Oburu, P., Pastorelli, C., Skinner, A. T., Sorbring, E., Tapanya, S., Uribe Tirado, L. M., Alampay, L. P., Al-Hassan, S. M., Takash, H. M. S., Bacchini, D., & Chang, L. (2018). Age patterns in risk taking across the world. *Youth Adolescence, 47*, 1052–1072. https://doi.org/10.1007/s10964-017-0752-y

Engel, G. L. (1977). The need for a new medical model: A challenge for biomedicine. *Science, 196*(4286), 129–136. https://doi.org/10.1126/science.847460

Erdmann, A., & Reinecke, J. (2018). Youth violence in Germany: Examining the victim-offender overlap during the transition from adolescence to early adulthood. *Criminal Justice Review, 43*(3), 325–344. https://doi.org/10.1177/0734016818761529

Evans, G. W., Li, D., & Whipple, S. S. (2013). Cumulative risk and child development. *Psychological Bulletin, 139*(6), 1342–1396. https://doi.org/10.1037/a0031808

Evans, R., Katz, C. C., Fulginiti, A., & Taussig, H. (2022). Sources and types of social supports and their association with mental health symptoms and life satisfaction among young adults with a history of out-of-home care. *Children, 9*(4), 520. https://doi.org/10.3390/children9040520

Fagan, A. A., Van Horn, M. L., Hawkins, J. D., & Arthur, M. W. (2007). Gender similarities and differences in the association between risk and protective factors and self-reported serious delinquency. *Prevention Science, 8*, 115–124. https://doi.org/10.1007/s11121-006-0062-1

Fante-Coleman, T., & Jackson-Best, F. (2020). Barriers and facilitators to accessing mental healthcare in Canada for Black youth: A scoping review. *Adolescent Research Review, 5*(2), 115–136. https://doi.org/10.1007/s40894-020-00133-2

Fanti, K. A., Colins, O. F., & Andershed, H. (2019). Unraveling the longitudinal reciprocal associations between anxiety, delinquency and depression from early to middle adolescence. *Journal of Criminal Justice, 62*, 29–34. https://doi.org/10.1016/j.jcrimjus.2018.09.004

Fantuzzi, C., & Mezzina, R. (2020). Dual diagnosis: A systematic review of the organization of community health services. *International Journal of Social Psychiatry, 66*(3), 300–310. https://doi.org/10.1177/0020764019899975

Farrington, D. P. (1986). Age and crime. *Crime and Justice, 7*, 189–250. http://www.jstor.org/stable/1147518

Farrington, D. P. (2015). Cross-national comparative research on criminal careers, risk factors, crime and punishment. *European Journal of Criminology, 12*(4), 386–399. https://doi.org/10.1177/1477370815584262

Farrington, D. P., Ttofi, M. M., & Piquero, A. R. (2016). Risk, promotive and protective factors in youth offending: Results from the Cambridge study in delinquent development. *Journal of Criminal Justice, 45*, 63–70. https://doi.org/10.1016/j.jcrimjus.2016.02.014

Feierman, J., Levick, M., & Mody, A. (2009). The school-to-prison pipeline... and back: Obstacles and remedies for the re-enrollment of adjudicated youth. *New York Law School Law Review, 54*, 1115.

Felitti, V. J., Anda, R. F., Nordenberg, D., Williamson, D. F., Spitz, A. M., Edwards, V., Koss, M. P., & Marks, J. S. (1998). Relationship of childhood abuse and household dysfunction to many of the leading causes of death in adults: The Adverse Childhood Experiences (ACE) study. *American Journal of Preventive Medicine, 14*(4), 245–258. https://doi.org/10.1016/S0749-3797(98)00017-8

Figueiredo, P., Ramiao, E., Azeredo, A., Moreira, D., Barroso, R., & Barbosa, F. (2020). Relation between basal cortisol and reactivity cortisol with externalizing problems: A systematic review. *Physiology & Behavior, 225*, 113088. https://doi.org/10.1016/j.physbeh.2020.113088

Finkelhor, D. (2011). Prevalence of child victimization, abuse, crime, and violence exposure. In J. W. White, M. P. Koss, & A. E. Kazdin (Eds.), *Violence against women and children: Mapping the terrain* (pp. 9–29). American Psychological Association.

Ford, J. D., Chapman, J., Mack, J. M., & Pearson, G. (2006). Pathways from traumatic child victimization to delinquency: Implications for juvenile and permanency court proceedings and decisions. *Juvenile and Family Court Journal, 57*(1), 13–26. https://doi.org/10.1111/j.1755-6988.2006.tb00111.x

Freeman, S. (2008). The experience of young people remanded in custody: A case for bail support and supervision schemes. *Irish Probation Journal, 5*, 91–102.

Frisby-Osman, S., & Wood, J. L. (2020). Rethinking how we view gang members: An examination into affective, behavioral, and mental health predictors of UK gang-involved youth. *Youth Justice, 20*(1–2), 93–112. https://doi.org/10.1177/1473225419893779

Gelsthorpe, L., & Worrall, A. (2009). Looking for trouble: A recent history of girls, young women and youth justice. *Youth Justice, 9*(3), 209–223. https://doi.org/10.1177/1473225409345100

Gerard, A., McGrath, A., Colvin, E., & McFarlane, K. (2019). 'I'm not getting out of bed!' The criminalisation of young people in residential care. *Australian & New Zealand Journal of Criminology, 52*(1), 76–93. https://doi.org/10.1177/0004865818778739

Gerstner, D., & Oberwittier, D. (2018). Who's hanging out and what's happening? A look at the interplay between unstructured socialising, crime propensity and delinquent peers using social network data. *European Journal of Criminology, 15*(1), 111–129. https://doi.org/10.1177/1477370817732194

Gill, A., Felker-Kantor, E., Cunningham-Myrie, C., Greene, L. G., Lyew-Ayee, P., Atkinson, U., Wendel, A., Anderson, S. G., & Theall, K. P. (2023). Neighborhoods and adolescent polysubstance use in Jamaica. *PeerJ, 11*, e14297. https://doi.org/10.7717/peerj.14297

Glynn, N., & Mayock, P. (2023). Housing after care: Understanding security and stability in the transition out of care through the lenses of liminality, recognition and precarity. *Journal of Youth Studies, 26*(1), 80–97. https://doi.org/10.1080/13676261.2021.1981838

Goldson, B., Cunneen, C., Russell, S., Brown, D., Baldry, E., Schwartz, M., & Briggs, D. (2021). *Youth justice and penalty in a comparative context*. Routledge.

Goodfellow, P. (2017). *Outnumbered, locked up and over-looked? The use of penal custody for girls in England and Wales*. Griffins Society. https://www.thegriffinssociety.org/system/files/papers/fullreport/griffins_research_paper_2017-02_-_full_paper.pdf

Goodkind, S., Shook, J. J., Kim, K. H., Pohlig, R. T., & Herring, D. J. (2013). From child welfare to juvenile justice: Race, gender, and system experiences. *Youth Violence and Juvenile Justice, 11*(3), 249–272. https://doi.org/10.1177/1541204012463409

Graves, K. N., Frabutt, J. M., & Shelton, T. L. (2007). Factors associated with mental health and juvenile justice involvement among children with severe emotional disturbance. *Youth Violence and Juvenile Justice, 5*(2), 147–167. https://doi.org/10.1177/1541204006292870

Gunnar, M. R., DePasquale, C. E., Reid, B. M., Donzella, B., & Miller, B. S. (2019). Pubertal stress recalibration reverses the effects of early life stress in postinstitutionalized children. *Proceedings of the National Academy of Sciences, 116*(48), 23984–23988. https://doi.org/10.1073/pnas.1909699116

Gushue, K., & McCuish, E. (2021). Incarcerated girls' early life experiences and their influence on serious offending in emerging adulthood. *Canadian Journal of Criminology and Criminal Justice, 63*(3), 112–134.

Haines, K., & Case, S. (2008). The rhetoric and reality of the "risk factor prevention paradigm" approach to preventing and reducing youth offending. *Youth Justice, 8*(1), 5–20. https://doi.org/10.1177/1473225407087039

Hamilton, P. (2021). *Diversity and marginalisation in childhood: A guide for inclusive thinking 0-11* (pp. 1–272). Sage.

Hartinger-Saunders, R. M., Rittner, B., Wieczorek, W., Nochajski, T., Rine, C. M., & Welte, J. (2011). Victimization, psychological distress and subsequent offending among youth. *Children and Youth Services Review, 33*(11), 2375–2385. https://doi.org/10.1016/j.childyouth.2011.08.009

Hartman, J. L., Turner, M. G., Daigle, L. E., Exum, M. L., & Cullen, F. T. (2009). Exploring the gender differences in protective factors: Implications for understanding resiliency. *International Journal of Offender Therapy and Comparative Criminology, 53*(3), 249–277. https://doi.org/10.1177/0306624X08326910

Haynie, D., Silver, E., & Teasdale, B. (2006). Neighborhood characteristics, peer networks, and adolescent violence. *Journal of Quantitative Criminology, 22*(2), 147–169. https://doi.org/10.1007/s10940-006-9006-y

Hicks, M. R., Kernsmith, P., & Smith-Darden, J. (2021). The effects of adverse childhood experiences on internalizing and externalizing behaviors among Black children and youth. *Journal of Child & Adolescent Trauma, 14*, 115–122. https://doi.org/10.1007/s40653-020-00316-y

Higgins, G. E., Khey, D. N., Dawson-Edwards, B. C., & Marcum, C. D. (2012). Examining the link between being a victim of bullying and delinquency trajectories among an African American sample. *International Criminal Justice Review, 22*(2), 110–122. https://doi.org/10.1177/1057567712443965

Higgins, K., Perra, O., Jordan, J. A., O'Neill, T., & McCann, M. (2020). School bonding and ethos in trajectories of offending: Results from the Belfast Youth

Development Study. *British Journal of Educational Psychology, 90*(2), 424–448. https://doi.org/10.1111/bjep.12303

Hill, J. M., Blokland, A. A. J., & van der Geest, V. R. (2018). Risk factors for self-reported delinquency in emerging adulthood. *European Journal of Criminology, 15*(5), 544–566. https://doi.org/10.1177/1477370817749495

Hoeve, M., Stams, G. J. J., Van der Put, C. E., Dubas, J. S., Van der Laan, P. H., & Gerris, J. R. (2012). A meta-analysis of attachment to parents and delinquency. *Journal of Abnormal Child Psychology, 40*(5), 771–785. https://doi.org/10.1007/s10802-011-9608-1

Hourigan, N. (2012). Juvenile justice, crime and early intervention: Key challenges from the Limerick context. *Irish Probation Journal, 9*, 63–73.

Hughes, N., Ungar, M., Fagan, A., Murray, J., Atilola, O., Nichols, K., Garcia, J., & Kinner, S. (2020). Health determinants of adolescent criminalisation. *The Lancet Child & Adolescent Health, 4*(2), 151–162. https://doi.org/10.1016/S2352-4642(19)30347-5

Hughes, N., Williams, W., Chitsabesan, P., Walesby, R., & Mounce, L. (2012). *Nobody made the connection: Neurodisability in the youth justice system*. Office of the Children's Commissioner for England.

Hunter, K. (2022). 'Out of place': The criminalisation of black and minority ethnic looked after children in England and Wales. *Prison Service Journal, 258*, 13–18.

Ibabe, I., & Jaureguizar, J. (2010). Child-to-parent violence: Profile of abusive adolescents and their families. *Journal of Criminal Justice, 38*(4), 616–624. https://doi.org/10.1016/j.jcrimjus.2010.04.034

Icenogle, G., Steinberg, L., Duell, N., Chein, J., Chang, L., Chaudhary, N., Di Giunta, L., Dodge, K. A., Fanti, K. A., Lansford, J. E., Oburu, P., Pastorelli, C., Skinner, A. T., Sorbring, E., Tapanya, S., Uribe Tirado, L. M., Alampay, L. P., Al-Hassan, S. M., Takash, H. M. S., & Bacchini, D. (2019). Adolescents' cognitive capacity reaches adult levels prior to their psychosocial maturity: Evidence for a "maturity gap" in a multinational, cross-sectional sample. *Law and Human Behavior, 43*(1), 69–85. https://doi.org/10.1037/lhb0000315

Ingoldsby, E. M., & Shaw, D. S. (2002). Neighborhood contextual factors and early-starting antisocial pathways. *Clinical Child and Family Psychology Review, 5*(1), 21–55. https://doi.org/10.1023/A:1014521724498

Jackson, D. B., Newsome, J., Vaughan, M. G., & Johnson, K. R. (2018). Considering the role of food insecurity in low self-control and early delinquency. *Journal of Criminal Justice, 56*, 127–139. https://doi.org/10.1016/j.jcrimjus.2017.07.002

Jansen, A. (2010). Victim or troublemaker? Young people in residential care. *Journal of Youth Studies, 13*(4), 423–437. https://doi.org/10.1080/13676261003801770

Jennings, W. G., Loeber, R., Ahonen, L., Piquero, A. R., & Farrington, D. P. (2018). An examination of developmental patterns of chronic offending from self-report records and official data: Evidence from the Pittsburgh Girls Study (PGS). *Journal of Criminal Justice, 55*, 71–79.

Jolliffe, D., Farrington, D. P., Brunton-Smith, I., Loeber, R., Ahonen, L., & Palacios, A. P. (2019). Depression, anxiety and delinquency: Results from the Pittsburgh Youth Study. *Journal of Criminal Justice, 62*, 42–49. https://doi.org/10.1016/j.jcrimjus.2018.08.004

Jolliffe, D., Farrington, D. P., Piquero, A. R., Loeber, R., & Hill, K. G. (2017). Systematic review of early risk factors for life-course-persistent, adolescence limited, and late-onset offenders in prospective longitudinal studies. *Aggression and Violent Behavior, 33*, 15–23. https://doi.org/10.1016/j.avb.2017.01.009

Joyce, S., O'Reilly, O., O'Brien, M., Joyce, D., Schweppe, J., & Haynes, A. (2022). Irish Travellers' access to justice. *Report, European Centre for the Study of Hate, Limerick.*

Junger-Tas, J., Ribeaud, D., & Cruyff, M. J. L. F. (2004). Juvenile delinquency and gender. *European Journal of Criminology, 1*(3), 333–375. https://doi.org/10.1177/1477370804044007

Kemshall, H. (2008). Risks, rights and justice: Understanding and responding to youth risk. *Youth Justice, 8*(1), 21–37. https://doi.org/10.1177/1473225407087040

Kemshall, H., Marsland, L., & Boeck, T. (2006). Young people, pathways and crime: Beyond risk factors. *Australian & New Zealand Journal of Criminology, 39*(3), 354–370. https://doi.org/10.1375/acri.39.3.354

Kenny, A., Kidd, S., Tuena, J., Jarvis, M., & Roberston, A. (2006). Falling through the cracks: Supporting young people with dual diagnosis in rural and regional Victoria. *Australian Journal of Primary Health, 12*(3), 12–19.

Kilkelly, U. (2020). "Evolving capacities" and "parental guidance" in the context of youth justice. *The International Journal of Children's Rights, 28*(3), 500–520. https://doi.org/10.1163/15718182-02803004

Kilkelly, U. (2023). Child first and children's rights: An opportunity to advance rights-based youth justice. In S. Case & N. Hazel (Eds.), *Child first. Developing a new youth justice system* (pp. 109–133). Palgrave Macmillan.

Kirby, A. (2021). *Neurodiversity—A whole-child approach for youth justice.* Academic Insights 2021/08.

Klatt, T., & Kliem, S. (2021). The influence of harsh parenting and parental warmth during childhood on later involvement in prison misconduct. *Journal of Interpersonal Violence, 36*(13–14), 6838–6858. https://doi.org/10.1177/0886260518820675

Kolk, S. M., & Rakic, P. (2022). Development of prefrontal cortex. *Neuropsychopharmacol, 47*, 41–57. https://doi.org/10.1038/s41386-021-01137-9

Kramer, R. C. (2000). Poverty, inequality, and youth violence. *The Annals of the American Academy of Political and Social Science, 567*(1), 123–139. https://doi.org/10.1177/000271620056700109

Lambert, S., & Dermody, A. (2021, October). Applying trauma research to service design and delivery. *Eolas*. https://www.eolasmagazine.ie/applying-trauma-research-to-service-design-and-delivery/

Lambert, S., & Murphy, R. (2019). The role of trauma in dual diagnosis. *Forum: Journal of the Irish College of General Practitioners*, 1–10. https://hdl.handle.net/10468/11435

Lambert, S., Murphy, R., Gill-Emerson, G., Horan, A., & Naughton, A. (2022). Adverse childhood experiences in a cohort of adults experiencing homelessness. *The Irish Psychologist, 48*(2), 40–45.

Lambert, S., O'Callaghan, D., & Jump, O. (2018). *Young families in the homeless crisis: Challenges and solutions*. Focus Ireland.

Lay, B., Ihle, W., Esser, G., & Schmidt, M. H. (2005). Juvenile-episodic, continued or adult-onset delinquency? Risk conditions analysed in a cohort of children followed up to the age of 25 years. *European Journal of Criminology, 2*(1), 39–66. https://doi.org/10.1177/1477370805048629

Leather, N. C. (2009). Risk-taking behaviour in adolescence: A literature review. *Journal of Child Health Care, 13*(3), 295–304. https://doi.org/10.1177/1367493509337443

Leventhal, T., & Brooks-Gunn, J. (2000). The neighbourhoods they live in: The effects of neighbourhood residence on child and adolescent outcomes. *Psychological Bulletin, 126*(2), 309–337. https://doi.org/10.1037/0033-2909.126.2.309

Lister, R. (2021). *Poverty* (2nd ed.). Wiley.

Liu, F., Chui, H., & Chung, M. C. (2020). The effect of parent–adolescent relationship quality on deviant peer affiliation: The mediating role of self-control and friendship quality. *Journal of Social and Personal Relationships, 37*(10–11), 2714–2736. https://doi.org/10.1177/0265407520937358

Loeber, R., Menting, B., Lynam, D. R., Moffitt, T. E., Stouthamer-Loeber, M., Stallings, R., Farrington, D. P., & Pardini, D. (2012). Findings from the Pittsburgh Youth Study: Cognitive impulsivity and intelligence as predictors of the age-crime curve. *Journal of the American Academy of Child & Adolescent Psychiatry, 51*(11), 1136–1149.

Logan-Greene, P., Nurius, P. S., Herting, J. R., Hooven, C. L., Walsh, E., & Adams Thomson, E. (2011). Multi-domain risk and protective factor predictors of violent behaviour among at-risk youth. *Journal of Youth Studies, 14*(4), 413–429. https://doi.org/10.1080/13676261.2010.538044

Lynch, N., & Liefaard, T. (2020). What is left in the "too hard basket"? Developments and challenges for the rights of children in conflict with the law. *The*

International Journal of Children's Rights, 28(1), 89–110. https://doi.org/10.1163/15718182-02801007

Maclure, R., & Sotelo, M. (2014). Youth social capital formation in Nicaragua. *The International Journal of Children's Rights, 22*(2), 385–413. https://doi.org/10.1163/15718182-02202003

Magson, N. R., Crave, R. G., Munns, E., & Yeung, A. S. (2016). It is risky business: Can social capital reduce risk-taking behaviours among disadvantaged youth? *Journal of Youth Studies, 19*(5), 569–592. https://doi.org/10.1080/13676261.2015.1098776

Mallett, C. A. (2014). Youthful offending and delinquency: The comorbid impact of maltreatment, mental health problems, and learning disabilities. *Child and Adolescent Social Work Journal, 31*, 369–392. https://doi.org/10.1007/s10560-013-0323-3

Malvaso, C. G., Cale, J., Whitten, T., Day, A., Singh, S., Hackett, L., Delfabbro, P. H., & Ross, S. (2022a). Associations between adverse childhood experiences and trauma among young people who offend: A systematic literature review. *Trauma, Violence, & Abuse, 23*(5), 1677–1694. https://doi.org/10.1177/15248380211013132

Malvaso, C. G., Day, A., Hackett, L., Cale, J., Delfabbro, P., & Ross, S. (2022b). Adverse childhood experiences and trauma among young people in the youth justice system. *Trends and Issues in Crime and Criminal Justice, 651*, 1–19. https://doi.org/10.52922/ti78610

Malvaso, C. G., Delfabbro, P., & Day, A. (2017). Child maltreatment and criminal convictions in youth: The role of gender, ethnicity and placement experiences in an Australian population. *Children and Youth Services Review, 73*(1), 57–73. https://doi.org/10.1016/j.childyouth.2016.12.001

Manly, J. T., Oshri, A., Lynch, M., Herzog, M., & Wortel, S. (2013). Child neglect and the development of externalizing behavior problems: Associations with maternal drug dependence and neighborhood crime. *Child Maltreatment, 18*(1), 17–29. https://doi.org/10.1177/1077559512464119

Martijn, C., & Sharpe, L. (2006). Pathways to youth homelessness. *Social Science & Medicine, 62*(1), 1–12. https://doi.org/10.1016/j.socscimed.2005.05.007

Matos, R., Campos, L., Martins, F., Deakin, J., Carneiro, A., Fox, C., & Markina, A. (2023). At the 'risky' end of things: Labelling, self-concept and the role of supportive relationships in young lives. *Journal of Youth Studies, 26*(3), 313–330. https://doi.org/10.1080/13676261.2023.2174007

McAra, L., & McVie, S. (2010). Youth crime and justice: Key messages from the Edinburgh Study of Youth Transitions and Crime. *Criminology & Criminal Justice, 10*(2), 179–209. https://doi.org/10.1177/1748895809360971

McAra, L., & McVie, S. (2022). *Cause and impacts of offending and criminal justice pathways: Follow-up of the Edinburgh cohort at age 35*. The University of Edinburgh.

McCrystal, P., Percy, A., & Higgins, K. (2007). Exclusion and marginalisation in adolescence: The experience of school exclusion on drug use and antisocial behaviour. *Journal of Youth Studies, 10*(1), 35–54. https://doi.org/10.1080/13676260701196103

McFarlane, K. (2018). Care-criminalisation: The involvement of children in out-of-home care in the New South Wales criminal justice system. *Australian & New Zealand Journal of Criminology, 51*(3), 412–433. https://doi.org/10.1177/0004865817723954

McNulty, T. L., & Bellair, P. E. (2003). Explaining racial and ethnic differences in adolescent violence: Structural disadvantage, family well-being, and social capital. *Justice Quarterly, 20*(1), 1–31. https://doi.org/10.1080/07418820300095441

McReynolds, L. S., Schwalbe, C. S., & Wasserman, G. A. (2010). The contribution of psychiatric disorder to juvenile recidivism. *Criminal Justice and Behavior, 37*(2), 204–216. https://doi.org/10.1177/0093854809354961

Megens, K. C. I. M., & Weerman, F. M. (2010). Attitudes, delinquency and peers: The role of social norms in attitude-behaviour inconsistency. *European Journal of Criminology, 7*(4), 299–316. https://doi.org/10.1177/1477370810365023

Meinert, J., & Reinecke, J. (2018). Self-control during adolescence: Examining the stability of low self-control and the effects of parental social controls. *European Journal of Criminology, 15*(5), 523–543. https://doi.org/10.1177/1477370817749180

Miley, L. N., Fox, B., Muniz, C. N., Perkins, R., & DeLisi, M. (2020). Does childhood victimization for specific adolescent offending? An analysis of generality versus specificity in the victim-offender overlap. *Child Abuse & Neglect, 101*, 104328. https://doi.org/10.1016/j.chiabu.2019.104328

Misiak, B., Stańczykiewicz, B., Pawlak, A., Szewczuk-Bogusławska, M., Samochowiec, J., Samochowiec, A., Tyburski, E., & Juster, R.P. (2022). Adverse childhood experiences and low socioeconomic status with respect to allostatic load in adulthood: A systematic review. *Psychoneuroendocrinology, 136*, 105602. https://psycnet.apa.org/doi/10.1016/j.psyneuen.2021.105602

Moffitt, T. E. (1993). Adolescence-limited and life-course-persistent antisocial behavior: A developmental taxonomy. *Psychological Review, 100*, 674–701.

Morton, M. H., Chávez, R., & Moore, K. (2019). Prevalence and correlates of homelessness among American Indian and Alaska native youth. *The Journal of Primary Prevention, 40*(6), 643–660. https://doi.org/10.1007/s10935-019-00571-2

Mowen, T. J., Brent, J. J., & Boman, J. H., IV. (2020). The effect of school discipline on offending across time. *Justice Quarterly, 37*(4), 739–760. https://doi.org/10.1080/07418825.2019.1625428

Murphy, K. D., Lambert, S., McCarthy, S., Sahm, L. J., & Byrne, S. (2018). "You don't feel": The experience of youth benzodiazepine misuse in Ireland. *Journal of Psychoactive Drugs, 50*(2), 121–128. https://doi.org/10.1080/02791072.2017.1371365

Nance, J. (2016). Students, police, and the school-to-prison pipeline. *Washington Law Review, 93.* http://scholarship.law.ufl.edu/facultypub/766

Neary, J., Egan, M., Keenan, P. J., Lawson, L., & Bond, L. (2013). Damned if they do, damned if they don't: Negotiating the tricky context of anti-social behaviour and keeping safe in disadvantaged urban neighbourhoods. *Journal of Youth Studies, 16*(1), 118–134. https://doi.org/10.1080/13676261.2012.710745

Nichols, N. (2017). Technologies of evidence: An institutional ethnography from the standpoints of 'youth-at-risk.' *Critical Social Policy, 37*(4), 604–624. https://doi.org/10.1177/0261018317690664

Nikulina, V., Widom, C. S., & Czaja, S. (2011). The role of childhood neglect and childhood poverty in predicting mental health, academic achievement and crime in adulthood. *American Journal of Community Psychology, 48*, 309–321.

Nkoana, W., Williams, H., Steenkamp, N., Clasby, B., Knowler, H., & Schrieff, L. (2020). Understanding the educational needs of young offenders: A prevalence study of traumatic brain injury and learning disabilities. *International Journal of Educational Development, 78*, 102261. https://doi.org/10.1016/j.ijedudev.2020.102261

Nowak, M. (2019). *Global study on children deprived of liberty*, A/74/136.

OECD. (2020). *HC3.1. Homeless population.* OECD Affordable Housing Database. Retrieved April 3, 2023, from https://www.oecd.org/els/family/HC3-1-Homeless-population.pdf

Oei, A., Chu, C. M., Li, D., Ng, N., Yeo, C., & Ruby, K. (2021). Relationship between adverse childhood experiences and substance use in youth offenders in Singapore. *Child Abuse & Neglect, 117*, 105072. https://doi.org/10.1016/j.chiabu.2021.105072

Ozkan, T. (2016). Reoffending among serious juvenile offenders: A developmental perspective. *Journal of Criminal Justice, 46*, 18–31. https://doi.org/10.1016/j.jcrimjus.2016.02.017

Paez, R. A., & Dierenfeldt, R. (2020). Community policing and youth offending: A comparison of large and small jurisdictions in the United States. *International Journal of Adolescence and Youth, 25*(1), 140–153.

Pedruzzi, R. A., Hamilton, O., Hodgson, H. H. A., Connor, E., Johnson, E., & Fitzpatrick, J. (2021). Navigating complexity to support justice-involved

youth with FASD and other neurodevelopmental disabilities: Needs and challenges of a regional workforce. *Health Justice, 9*(8). https://doi.org/10.1186/s40352-021-00132-y
Perino, M. T., Guassi Moreira, J. F., McCormick, E. M., & Telzer, E. H. (2019). Apples to apples? Neural correlates of emotion regulation differences between high-and low-risk adolescents. *Social Cognitive and Affective Neuroscience, 14*(8), 827–836. https://doi.org/10.1080/02673843.2019.1601115
Priest, N., Paradies, Y., Trenerry, B., Truong, M., Karlsen, S., & Kelly, Y. (2013). A systematic review of studies examining the relationship between reported racism and health and wellbeing for children and young people. *Social Science & Medicine, 95*, 115–127.
Pusch, N., & Holtfreter, K. (2018). Gender and risk assessment in juvenile offenders: A meta-analysis. *Criminal Justice and Behavior, 45*(1), 56–81.
Ramakers, A. A., Bijleveld, C., & Ruiter, S. (2011). Escaping the family tradition: A multi-generation study of occupational status and criminal behaviour. *The British Journal of Criminology, 51*(5), 856–874. https://doi.org/10.1093/bjc/azr039
Redmond, S. (2015). The Greentown crime networks: Introducing its cast of principle (sic) actors. *Irish Probation Journal, 12*, 205–228.
Reef, J., Donker, A. G., Van Meurs, I., Verhulst, F. C., & Van Der Ende, J. (2011). Predicting adult violent delinquency: Gender differences regarding the role of childhood behaviour. *European Journal of Criminology, 8*(3), 187–197. https://doi.org/10.1177/1477370811403444
Reid, B. M., DePasquale, C. E., Donzella, B., Leneman, K. B., Taylor, H., & Gunnar, M. R. (2021). Pubertal transition with current life stress and support alters longitudinal diurnal cortisol patterns in adolescents exposed to early life adversity. *Developmental Psychobiology, 63*(6), e22146. https://doi.org/10.1002/dev.22146
Reising, K., Ttofi, M. M., Farrington, D. P., & Piquero, A. R. (2019). Depression and anxiety outcomes of offending trajectories: A systematic review of prospective longitudinal studies. *Journal of Criminal Justice, 62*, 3–15. https://psycnet.apa.org/doi/10.1016/j.jcrimjus.2018.05.002
Rocque, M., Posick, C., Marshall, I. H., & Piquero, A. R. (2015). A comparative, cross-cultural criminal career analysis. *European Journal of Criminology, 12*(4), 400–419. https://doi.org/10.1177/1477370815579951
Rocque, M., & Snellings, Q. (2018). The new disciplinology: Research, theory and remaining puzzles on the school-to- prison pipeline. *Journal of Criminal Justice, 59*, 3–18. https://doi.org/10.1016/j.jcrimjus.2017.05.002
Rokven, J. J., de Boer, G., Tolsma, J., & Ruiter, S. (2017). How friends' involvement in crime affects the risk of offending and victimization. *European Journal of Criminology, 14*(6), 697–719. https://doi.org/10.1177/1477370816684150

Salmi, V., & Kivivuori, J. (2006). The association between social capital and juvenile crime: The role of individual and structural factors. *European Journal of Criminology, 3*(2), 123–148. https://doi.org/10.1177/1477370806061967

Savage, J., & Ellis, S. (2018). Academic achievement, school attachment, and school problems in the differential etiology of violence. *Journal of Developmental and Life-Course Criminology, 5*, 243–265. https://doi.org/10.1007/s40865-018-0090-0

Schmidt, E. P., & Skelton, A. (2022). A developmental perspective on children who commit serious violent offences. In N. Lynch, Y. van den Brink, & L. Forde (Eds.), *Responses to serious offending by children. Principles, practice and global perspectives*. Routledge.

Scott, E. (2013). "Children are different": Constitutional values and justice policy. *OHIO State Journal of Criminal Law, 11*, 71–105.

Scully, C., McLaughlin, J., & Fitzgerald, A. (2020). The relationship between adverse childhood experiences, family functioning, and mental health problems among children and adolescents: A systematic review. *Journal of Family Therapy, 42*(2), 291–316. https://doi.org/10.1111/1467-6427.12263

Seddig, D. (2014). Peer group association, the acceptance of norms and violent behaviour: A longitudinal analysis of reciprocal effects. *European Journal of Criminology, 11*(3), 319–339. https://doi.org/10.1177/1477370813496704

Seddig, D., & Reinecke, J. (2017). Exploration and explanation of adolescent self-reported delinquency trajectories in the Crimoc study. In A. Blokland & V. van de Geest (Eds.), *The Routledge international handbook of life-course criminology* (pp. 159–178). Routledge.

Shandra, C. L., & Hogan, D. P. (2012). Delinquency among adolescents with disabilities. *Child Indicators Research, 5*, 771–788. https://doi.org/10.1007/s12187-012-9135-9

Siponen, R., Andersson, A., Oskarsson, S., Garcia-Argibay, M., Beckley, A. L., Långström, N., Fazel, S., Chang, Z., Larsson, H., Evans, B., & Tuvblad, C. (2023). A population-based study of unintentional injury and premature death among non-imprisoned and imprisoned youth offenders. *Journal of Criminal Justice, 84*, 102009.

Smith, D. J., & Ecob, R. (2013). The influence of friends on teenage offending: How long does it last? *European Journal of Criminology, 10*(1), 40–58. https://doi.org/10.1177/1477370812456345

Smith, D. J., & McVie, S. (2003). Theory and method in the Edinburgh study of youth transitions and crime. *British Journal of Criminology, 43*(1), 169–195. https://doi.org/10.1093/bjc/43.1.169

Smith, D. K., Leve, L. D., & Chamberlain, P. (2006). Adolescent girls' offending and health-risking sexual behavior: The predictive role of trauma.

Child Maltreatment, 11(4), 346–353. https://doi.org/10.1177/107755950 6291950

Snyder, S. E., & Duchschere, J. E. (2022). Revisiting ecological systems theory: Practice implications for juvenile justice youth. *Translational Issues in Psychological Science, 8*(2), 234–245. https://psycnet.apa.org/doi/10.1037/tps000 0324

Staubli, S., & Killias, M. (2011). Long-term outcomes of passive bullying during childhood: Suicide attempts, victimization and offending. *European Journal of Criminology, 8*(5), 377–385. https://doi.org/10.1177/1477370811415761

Steinberg, L. (2017). Adolescent brain science and juvenile justice policymaking. *Psychology, Public Policy, and Law, 23*(4), 410–420. https://doi.org/10. 1037/law0000128

Steinberg, L., Icenogle, G., Shulman, E. P., Breiner, K., Chein, J., Bacchini, D., Chang, L., Chaudhary, N., Di Giunta, L., Dodge, K. A., Fanti, K. A., Lansford, J. E., Malone, P. S., Oburu, P., Pastorelli, C., Skinner, A. T., Sorbring, E., Tapanya, S., Uribe Tirado, L. M., … Takash, H. M. S. (2018). Around the world, adolescence is a time of heightened sensation seeking and immature self-regulation. *Developmental Science, 21*(2), e12532. https://doi.org/ 10.1111/desc.12532

Svensson, R., Pauwels, L. J. R., Weerman, F. M., & Bruinsma, G. J. N. (2017). Explaining individual changes in moral values and moral emotions among adolescent boys and girls: A fixed-effects analysis. *European Journal of Criminology, 14*(3), 290–308. https://doi.org/10.1177/147737081664 9626

Taylor, C. (2003). Justice for looked after children? *Probation Journal, 50*(3), 239–251. https://doi.org/10.1177/0264550503503005

Taylor-Cavelier, S. J., Micol, V. J., Roberts, A. G., Geiss, E. G., & Lopez-Duran, N. (2021). DHEA moderates the impact of childhood trauma on the HPA axis in adolescence. *Neuropsychobiology, 80*(4), 299–312. https://doi.org/10. 1159/000511629

Testa, A., Turney, K., Jackson, D. B., & Jaynes, C. M. (2022). Police contact and future orientation from adolescence to young adulthood: Findings from the pathways to desistance study. *Criminology, 60*(2), 263–290. https://doi. org/10.1111/1745-9125.12297

Thapar, A., Cooper, M., & Rutter, M. (2017). Neurodevelopmental disorders. *The Lancet Psychiatry, 4*, 339–346. https://doi.org/10.1016/S2215-0366(16)30376-5

Theimann, M. (2015). School as a space of socialization and prevention. *European Journal of Criminology, 13*(1), 67–91. https://doi.org/10.1177/147 7370815597254

Thijs, P. E., van Dijk, I. K., Stoof, R., & Notten, N. (2015). Adolescent problem behaviour: The gender gap in European perspective. *European*

Journal of Criminology, 12(5), 598–615. https://doi.org/10.1177/1477370815578195

Tyler, I., & Slater, T. (2018). Rethinking the sociology of stigma. *The Sociological Review, 66*(4), 721–743. https://doi.org/10.1177/0038026118777425

UN General Assembly. (1990). *United Nations guidelines for the prevention of juvenile delinquency (The Riyadh Guidelines)*, 14 December 1990, 45/112.

van den Brink, Y. (2022). Equality in the youth court: Meaning, perceptions and implications of the principle of equality in youth justice. *Youth Justice, 22*(3), 245–271. https://doi.org/10.1177/14732254211013420

van den Brink, Y., Forde, L., Burghout, P., & Beljaars, D. (2022). Disparities in responses to children who commit serious offences. In N. Lynch, Y. van den Brink, & L. Forde (Eds.), *Responses to serious offending by children*. Routledge.

van der Laan, A. M., Blom, M., & Kleemans, E. R. (2009). Exploring long-term and short-term risk factors for serious delinquency. *European Journal of Criminology, 6*(5), 419–438. https://doi.org/10.1177/1477370809337882

Van Lanen, S. (2018). Encountering austerity in deprived urban neighbourhoods: Local geographies and the emergence of austerity in the lifeworld of urban youth. *Geoforum, 110*, 220–231.

Vazsonyi, A. T., Jiskrova, G. K., Ksinan, A. J., & Blatný, M. (2016). An empirical test of self-control theory in Roma adolescents. *Journal of Criminal Justice, 44*, 66–76. https://doi.org/10.1016/j.jcrimjus.2015.12.004

Visser, K., Sichling, F., & Chaskin, R. J. (2017). Hot times, hot places: Youths' risk perceptions and risk management in Chicago and Rotterdam. *Journal of Youth Studies, 20*(60), 763–779. https://doi.org/10.1080/13676261.2016.1273511

Wacquant, L. (2008). *Urban outcasts: A comparative sociology of advanced marginality*. Polity.

Walters, G. D. (2020). Prosocial peers as risk, protective, and promotive factors for the prevention of delinquency and drug use. *Journal of Youth and Adolescence, 49*, 618–630. https://doi.org/10.1007/s10964-019-01058-3

Walters, G. D. (2021). Parental control as a stimulus for youth control: Mediating the parental knowledge-child delinquency relationship with cognitive impulsivity. *Crime & Delinquency, 67*(5), 717–736. https://doi.org/10.1177/0011128720962449

Weber, S., & Lynch, S. (2021). Understanding the relations among adverse childhood experiences (ACE), substance use, and reoffending among detained youth. *Child Abuse & Neglect, 120*, 105211. https://doi.org/10.1016/j.chiabu.2021.105211

Webster, C. (2019). 'Race', ethnicity and social class. In B. Goldson (Ed.), *Juvenile justice in Europe: Past, present and future* (pp. 148–161). Routledge.

Webster, C., MacDonald, R., & Simpson, M. (2006). Predicting criminality? Risk factors, neighbourhood influence and desistance. *Youth Justice, 6*(1), 7–22. https://doi.org/10.1177/1473225406063449

Welch, K. (2018). The effect of minority threat on risk management and the 'new disciplinology' in schools. *Journal of Criminal Justice, 59*, 12–17. https://doi.org/10.1016/j.jcrimjus.2017.05.006

White, R., & Cunneen, C. (2015). Social class, youth crime and youth justice. In B. Goldson & J. Muncie (Eds.), *Youth crime and justice* (2nd ed., pp. 17–30). Sage.

Windle, J., Moyle, L., & Coomber, R. (2020). 'Vulnerable' kids going country: Children and young people's involvement in county lines drug dealing. *Youth Justice, 20*(1–2), 64–78. https://doi.org/10.1177/1473225420902840

World Health Organization. (2013). *Adverse childhood experiences international questionnaire (ACE-IQ)* [Internet]. Geneva. http://www.who.int/violence_injury_prevention/violence/activities/adverse_childhood_experiences/en/

Yoder, J., & Precht, M. (2020). Victimization experiences and executive dysfunction as discriminating risk indicators for youth offender typologies. *International Journal of Offender Therapy and Comparative Criminology, 64*(1), 63–82. https://doi.org/10.1177/0306624X19865185

Yohros, A. (2022). Examining the relationship between adverse childhood experiences and juvenile recidivism: A systematic review and meta-analysis. *Trauma, Violence, & Abuse, 24*(3). https://doi.org/10.1177/15248380211073846

Youth Justice Board/Ministry of Justice. (2020). *Assessing the needs of sentenced children in the Youth Justice System 2018/19*. https://assets.publishing.service.gov.uk/government/uploads/system/uploads/attachment_data/file/887644/assessing-needs-of-sentenced-children-youth-justice-system.pdf

Zahn, M. A., Agnew, R., Fishbein, D., Miller, S., Winn, D. M., Dakoff, G., & Chesney-Lind, M. (2010). *Causes and correlates of girl's delinquency*. U.S. Department of Justice, Office of Justice Programs, Office of Juvenile Justice and Delinquency Prevention.

Zarse, E. M., Neff, M. R., Yoder, R., Hulvershorn, L., Chambers, J. E., & Chambers, R. A. (2019). The adverse childhood experiences questionnaire: Two decades of research on childhood trauma as a primary cause of adult mental illness, addiction, and medical diseases. *Cogent Medicine, 6*(1), 1581447. https://doi.org/10.1080/2331205X.2019.1581447

Zuckermann, A. M., Williams, G. C., Battista, K., de Groh, M., Jiang, Y., & Leatherdale, S. T. (2019). Trends of poly-substance use among Canadian youth. *Addictive Behaviors Reports, 10*, 100189. https://doi.org/10.1016/j.abrep.2019.100189

Zuckermann, A. M., Williams, G. C., Battista, K., Jiang, Y., de Groh, M., & Leatherdale, S. T. (2020). Prevalence and correlates of youth poly-substance use in the COMPASS study. *Addictive Behaviors, 107*, 106400. https://doi.org/10.1016/j.addbeh.2020.106400

CHAPTER 4

Diversion and Justice

Abstract While there is a direct link between children's rights—to education, to health and to protection from harm—and measures that prevent children coming into conflict with the law, children do not always benefit from such rights protections. Thus, when they come into conflict with the law, they are entitled to specific rights protections that both seek to minimise the harm through diversion and ensure their procedural rights are protected while within the justice system. This chapter proposes that these two rights fall into two categories: 'Diversion' rights and 'Justice' rights. This chapter will first focus on the literature relating to state efforts to prevent children's contact with formal justice processes, through both prevention and early intervention efforts, and through diversion efforts in situations where children may otherwise be subject to criminal prosecution. It will then explain the literature related to the procedural rights that children must enjoy when they are in contact with the justice system, drawing attention to the ways in which breaches of children's rights can occur, and the steps needed to ensure greater protection of children's rights in this area.

Keywords Children rights · Children in conflict with the law · Diversion · Early intervention · Due process · Procedural rights · Police

U. Kilkelly et al., *Children in Conflict with the Law*, Palgrave Critical Studies in Human Rights and Criminology, https://doi.org/10.1007/978-3-031-36652-9_4

Introduction

International children's rights standards make clear that all children are entitled to enjoy their rights without discrimination, and as Chapter 2 set out, the instruments have particular resonance with children who come into conflict with the law, providing specific protection against the harms of the justice system. As Chapter 3 explains, there is a direct link between children's rights—to education, health, family care and protection from harm—and measures that prevent children coming into conflict with the law. In reality, however, children do not always benefit from such rights protections and when they do come into conflict with the law, they are entitled to very specific rights protections that both seek to minimise the harm it can cause by both diverting them out of the system and alternatively, ensuring their procedural rights are protected while within it. This chapter proposes that these two rights fall into two categories. First, Diversion rights provide that children who come into conflict with the law are entitled to be diverted away from the justice system in order to prevent them from further offending and from getting deeper into the system. Second, Justice rights provide that children who come into the justice system are entitled to have procedural and due process rights protected, through an adapted and child-friendly justice system. The aim of this chapter is to present the research behind these aspects of the rights-based approach, specifically addressing the principles of diversion and due process, respectively.

The principle of diversion is explicitly recognised in the CRC which expresses a strong preference for ensuring children have minimal contact with the formal justice system. In particular, Article 40 (3) requires states parties to use diversionary approaches wherever appropriate and desirable as long as the minimum threshold of rights protections is not breached. As part of this approach, Article 40 (3)(a) of the CRC prescribes that states parties must set a minimum age of criminal responsibility, below which children will be presumed not to have the capacity to infringe the criminal law. Although the CRC is silent on the preferred minimum age, the Committee on the Rights of the Child has recommended that it should not be lower than 14 years (Committee on the Rights of the Child, 2019, para. 21). Early intervention measures, focused on family and universal supports, offer vital protection to children below the minimum age who are involved in behaviour that would otherwise amount to a criminal offence (Committee on the Rights of the Child, 2019, paras. 9–12).

Efforts at both early intervention to avoid children coming into conflict with the law and diversion to minimise children's contact with the formal justice system are thus clearly aligned with the children's rights approach. Significantly, these principles are also broadly in line with the large body of literature in this area, as demonstrated below.

For children who come into contact with the justice system, the international standards require that procedural safeguards should be in place in recognition of the vulnerability of children in this situation and their lesser maturity and capacity. Article 40 (2) of the CRC sets out the rights to which children are entitled throughout their contact with the justice system, and states are urged to ensure higher standards in practice (Committee on the Rights of the Child, 2019, para. 38). These procedural protections are crucial, both in terms of supporting children both to navigate complex legal processes which can have potentially far-reaching consequences for their lives and also to achieve the goal of reintegration into society. Research also demonstrates the importance of children's rights being protected in the justice system, highlighting the synergies that exist between children's rights standards and the evidence that underpins them.

In light of the international standards, this chapter sets out the literature regarding the application of these important children's rights provisions to children who come into contact with the justice system. The first section presents the research on measures to prevent children's contact with formal justice processes, including both prevention and early intervention efforts, and diversion from criminal prosecution. While Chapter 3 has already considered the breaches of children's rights that can lead to children coming into conflict with the law, and how greater respect for children's rights can act as a protective factor, this chapter focuses on the literature which considers interventions by the state to promote early intervention and diversion when such contact takes place. The second part of the chapter then goes on to explain the research related to the procedural rights that children must enjoy when they are in contact with the justice system, drawing attention to the ways in which breaches of children's rights can occur, and the steps needed to ensure greater protection of children's rights in this area.

Diversion

Prevention and Early Intervention

The international standards stress the importance of prevention and early intervention as core aspects of any youth justice policy (Committee on the Rights of the Child, 2019, para. 6). In line with the literature presented in Chapter 3, the Committee on the Rights of the Child has emphasised that children's physical and psychological development must form the basis for understanding their involvement in offending, including their lesser culpability; this requires that a different approach must be taken when responding to this behaviour in order to limit the potential harm to children caused by exposure to the criminal justice system (Committee on the Rights of the Child, 2019, para. 2). As demonstrated in Chapter 3, there is extensive research to demonstrate the relevance of children's rights—to health, education, family life, rest and leisure, protection from harm—to children in conflict with the law, making it clear that prevention efforts must build respect for children's rights across these multiple domains. In line with this, international research supports the view that prevention efforts must be rooted in community- and family-based programmes that reduce the risk of children coming into the justice system, as well as investing in early childhood care and education that increases protective factors that strengthen children's resilience (Committee on the Rights of the Child, 2019, paras. 9–11).

The international literature supports this general view, with some scholars highlighting the importance of positive influences and strong integration during adolescence as a means of helping children to avoid contact with the youth justice system (Case & Browning, 2021; Smith & McVie, 2003). Scholarship exploring children's pathways into the justice system highlights protective factors which can help young people avoid involvement in offending behaviour. This emphasises that the broader social context in which children find themselves, in addition to individual and personal factors, can help children to avoid coming into conflict with the law. Some studies have indicated that personal factors, such as low levels of hyperactivity, 'troublesomeness' and higher levels of nervousness, can predict lower levels of involvement in offending (Craig et al., 2020; Farrington et al., 2016). The literature also suggests that interventions that seek to prevent young people from becoming involved in offending should address problems in multiple domains, including individual, family, and peer and school environments (Logan-Greene et al., 2011). The role of developing positive relationships with both peers and adults has also been highlighted as a key component of preventative practice (Case & Browning, 2021; Kern et al., 2016), as has ensuring a strengths-based and inclusive approach to targeted prevention programmes (Case & Browning, 2021). This is in line with the rights-based approaches that aim to prevent children coming into conflict with the law (Kilkelly, 2023), while also requiring decision-makers to regard the child's best interests as a primary consideration (Committee on the Rights of the Child, 2013).

The Riyadh Guidelines recommend that approaches to early intervention should include both mainstream initiatives to ensure that young people and their families have access to a range of social services in the community, and targeted interventions for young people who have particular needs (UN General Assembly, 1990); both aspects are considered vital for a comprehensive early intervention strategy. The Committee on the Rights of the Child has further recommended that prevention and early intervention programmes should be focused on support for families, adopt a systemic approach that includes closing pathways into contact with the youth justice system, as well as child-friendly and multidisciplinary approaches based on a comprehensive assessment of the child's needs (Committee on the Rights of the Child, 2019, paras. 9–12). It is important to note that within the context of any intervention, the identification of needs should be considered as the basis for providing any intervention (De Nike et al., 2019).

It is clear that in efforts to prevent children coming into conflict with the law, states are required to take positive steps in relation to prevention generally and early intervention in particular, where children appear to have additional needs. However, while there are a variety of approaches to early intervention and prevention across jurisdictions, not all such approaches are equally effective, and some concerns have been raised in the literature about programmes which target early intervention efforts on the basis of perceived risk (Haines & Case, 2008). For instance, the traditional Nordic model of child welfare was based on the strict separation of criminal justice and social welfare systems, the prioritisation of minimum intervention and a preference for using social welfare measures (Harrikari, 2013). However, this model has been changed by the introduction of initiatives focused on local crime prevention through directing early intervention at criminogenic risk factors such as a poor home environment and poor parental skills, targeted primarily at those who were considered in danger of marginalisation (Harrikari, 2013). Some have raised concerns that programmes such as these—based on concepts of concern, risk and intervention—are reflective of a tougher climate of regulation and control directed almost exclusively at children (Harrikari, 2013). Programmes focused on targeting risk have also been introduced in other jurisdictions, including Northern Ireland, where these programmes have equated 'risk of offending' to other types of vulnerability and social marginalisation, with the result that those tasked with implementing the programmes struggle to disentangle these factors (Haydon, 2014).

Risk assessment tools, although controversial for their net-widening effects, arguably have their place in minimising the intrusiveness of the justice system as long as they are appropriately, consistently and ethically used (Olver et al., 2009). However, concerns have been raised about the potential for targeted early intervention programmes to stigmatise young people who are already marginalised, even where participation in these programmes may have some positive outcomes for young people (Kelly, 2012). The Edinburgh Study of Youth Transitions and Crime has indicated that some early intervention programmes, rather than reducing the number of offence referrals, can have the opposite effect and draw young people into repeated cycles of contact with the system (McAra & McVie, 2007). This has recently been affirmed by a follow-up study which found early and intensive formal system contact, including care experience, to be strongly associated with later contact with the justice system and other negative outcomes (McAra & McVie, 2022). Similarly, in an Australian sample from the Better Evidence Better Outcomes Linked Data (BEBOLD), early contact with youth justice was shown to result in greater economic disadvantage, more frequent serious child protection contact (e.g., care), more related hospitalisations and more serious youth offending patterns later on (Magann, 2021). A particular difficulty with early intervention programmes focused on targeting risks lies in the fact that this strategy may legitimise unnecessary intervention in the lives of young people who would not have been otherwise involved in or convicted of offending; this may be counter-productive by increasing system contact, leading to damaging long-term effects (Haydon, 2014). In the same vein, scholars have found that early intervention can result in net-widening and the increased criminalisation of some young people; this contrasts with the view that early intervention can be an effective way to avoid more serious intervention later on (Kelly, 2012; Olver et al., 2009). The proportionality between the severity of the offending behaviour and the nature of the intervention is clearly important.

Conversely, prevention and early intervention efforts which focus on providing child-centred, mainstreamed and non-stigmatising supports are more likely to be effective. This reinforces the message from the international standards in relation to the importance of community- and family-centred supports, and fulfilment of state obligations to provide adequate assistance to parents in carrying out their duties under Articles 18 and 27 of the Convention (Committee on the Rights of the Child, 2019, paras. 10–11). In line with this view, the recent follow-up to the Edinburgh Study of Youth Transitions and Crime has highlighted that there should be strong support for prevention and early intervention policies which are spread across policy portfolios, and which include 'health, education, housing, policies which focus on communities and economy' as well as justice (McAra & McVie, 2022). This suggestion is strengthened by research evidence on prevention programmes which promoted positive behaviours across domains related to education, employment, family and citizenship, and which aims to promote positive views of children engaged with these programmes (Case & Browning, 2021; Case & Haines, 2015). Further studies have shown the positive outcomes of early intervention and prevention programmes which bear the hallmarks of child-centred and rights-respecting approaches. For instance, in the UK's 'Positive Futures' initiative, it was found that young people valued the social interactions, fun, enjoyment, developing relationships with coaches and the opportunities to volunteer or access training as positive elements of their engagement with the programme (Kelly, 2012). Other early intervention projects highlight the importance of family support in reducing the likelihood of involvement in the criminal justice system (Haydon, 2014).

Studies point to the importance of social inclusion in prevention efforts (Case & Browning, 2021; Shen, 2016). For instance, one UK study of early intervention projects found that helping young people return to education may not automatically lead to them gaining sustainable employment, such efforts being hampered by broader societal exclusionary processes (Kelly, 2012). Other studies have also drawn attention to the importance of social inclusion—drawing on surveys of young people in the UK, one study highlighted young people's view that having greater access to things to do in the community and places to go could help to reduce their involvement in anti-social behaviour (Crawford, 2009). Research on engagement with gang members has also demonstrated the positive effects of developing social capital and participation (Deuchar, 2009).

Research provides support for the use of preventive measures that target particular issues, such as young people reporting with Adverse Childhood Experiences (ACEs) (Kowalski, 2019). Here, too, however, caution is required in relation to the means by which this is delivered. Some studies, for example, indicate that targeted interventions, in and of themselves, may not be enough to prevent offending (Shen, 2016) and those that occur in the absence of addressing systematic issues such as poverty and social exclusion may be limited. It has been well established that poverty is one of the biggest predictors of later life difficulties (Hoff & Laursen, 2019; Johnston et al., 2016), and therefore, targeted interventions should be situated in the broader social context of the child's life.

It is important to note that there is no universal agreement on effective early intervention. What is known, however, is that interventions which employ interagency collaboration, skill building, mental health supports, restorative justice and strengths-based frameworks are more effective than programmes that are centred around discipline or deterrence (Lipsey et al., 2010). While there are many potential reasons for this, it is relevant that factors such as self-concept, self-efficacy and self-value are all critical components of behaviour change (Michie & Johnston, 2012). This highlights the significance of strengths-based, comprehensive intervention supports, suggesting that interventions that move away from the traditional criminal justice focus, and instead implement characteristics of psychological and behavioural health theory, may be more effective in promoting prosocial behaviour (Cunningham et al., 2023). Findings such as these which emphasise the importance of child-centred, holistic approaches which stretch across policy portfolios resonate with international standards which emphasise the importance of community-based, mainstreamed supports which promote access to services for children and their families and bolster family capacity to care for children as critical components of prevention and early intervention policies (Committee on the Rights of the Child, 2019, paras. 9–11; UN General Assembly, 1990). Ensuring greater respect for children's rights in all aspects of their lives, as discussed in Chapter 3, emerges from the literature therefore as a key feature of successful early intervention and prevention programmes.

Diversion

The importance of diverting children from the justice system and from offending is reflected in the inclusion of diversion as a general principle in the international children's rights standards. In this regard, it is recalled that diversion is set out in Article 40 (3)(b) of the CRC, requiring states parties to respond to offending by young people without resorting to judicial proceedings, so long as children's procedural rights are adequately respected. The Committee on the Rights of the Child has noted the importance of ensuring multiple opportunities for diverting young people in conflict with the law, further reinforcing the desirability of minimising formal system contact (Committee on the Rights of the Child, 2019). Diversion is therefore a fundamental aspect of any rights-respecting approach to responding to children in conflict with the law (Committee on the Rights of the Child, 2019, para 24; Forde, 2021). Diversionary approaches are particularly desirable, given that they can help young people avoid the negative and stigmatising effects of formal criminal justice contact and can also impact on custody rates (Bateman, 2012; NeMoyer et al., 2020; Wilson & Hoge, 2013).

Approaches to Diversion

The research literature shows that approaches to diversion vary from jurisdiction to jurisdiction, and the term is not always consistently applied. What 'diversion' means in practice can vary, and it can be understood to mean different things in different contexts (NeMoyer et al., 2020; Richards, 2014). This being said, many countries have embedded formal systems of diversion into their youth justice systems and provide for different types of measures and mechanisms to remove children from contact with more formal justice processes, particularly prosecution before the courts. Diversion programmes can take a wide variety of forms (Kretschmar et al., 2018; NeMoyer et al., 2020; Seroczynski, 2016; Wong et al., 2016). Research in this area has suggested that similar to early intervention and prevention strategies, effective diversion programmes and efforts should be based around young people's individual needs (Case & Browning, 2021; Case).

Some diversionary approaches attempt to target a range of factors considered to be important in influencing children's pathways into and out of contact with the youth justice system. These encompass family, health and educational domains. Rather than focusing solely on the young person, family-based treatment programmes are used to address both risk and protective factors within the young person's family (Kretschmar et al., 2018). Other programmes focus on young people's needs for treatment for mental health challenges or to address behavioural difficulties, with an emphasis on community-based treatment and alternatives to arrest and imprisonment (Jeong et al., 2014). These programmes can use a variety of types of interventions, including task-centred case management, parent management training and cognitive behavioural therapy approaches (Gearing et al., 2017). Additionally, these programmes may focus on building the individual competency and skills of the young person and facilitate them to develop positive prosocial relationships (Williams et al., 2021). Further to this, it has been noted that juvenile diversion programmes benefit from adopting a risk-needs perspective when working with young people (Wylie et al., 2019).

Impact of Diversion

In some of the literature in this area, there is a focus on attempting to measure diversion programmes' outcomes with regard to children's involvement in offending, with studies that evaluate the impact of diversion programmes on recidivism producing varying results (Wilson & Hoge, 2013; Wong et al., 2016; Wylie et al., 2019). A meta-analysis of 73 diversion programmes based either on a non-interventionist 'caution' approach or on diverting young people to specific interventions in Canada found that both types of diversionary programmes were significantly more effective in reducing rates of reoffending among young people than the traditional criminal justice system (Wilson & Hoge, 2013). Notwithstanding concerns about net-widening (Griffin, 2007) and legitimate concerns about the dilution of due process guarantees (Brennan, 2012; Campbell, 2005), diversion is considered to be one of the key strengths of the youth justice system in Ireland too (Kilkelly, 2011). According to the Garda Síochána Analysis Unit from 2013 to 2017, 64% of young people who received a formal or an informal caution as a first warning had not reoffended by the end of 2017 (An Garda Síochána, 2017). However, others have shown more limited impacts on recidivism rates. For example, a study synthesising experimental research evaluations of diversion programmes published between 1980 and 2011 found that formal diversion programmes did not prevent recidivism rates any better than 'warn-and-release' models or formal court processing, although evidence-based interventions were not routinely used as central components of the diversion programmes studies (Schwalbe et al., 2012). In a US study of 72 diversion programmes, the programmes were found to enjoy varying levels of success in reducing recidivism, a variation that could be related either to the level of risk among young people involved in these programmes in the first instance, or to specific factors related to service delivery that made them more or less effective (Sullivan & Latessa, 2011).

Aside from effects on recidivism, however, these programmes may produce other effects that are not immediately or clearly related to rates of reoffending within the study follow-up period or at all. In particular, there is potential for diversion programmes to promote greater respect for children's rights across a number of the domains discussed in Chapter 3 and to have less tangible but no less important outcomes for children. This, in turn, may help to produce better long-term outcomes. For instance, mental health interventions may impact positively on mental health outcomes, as well as recidivism rates (Gearing et al., 2017), providing support for children's right to health as well as removing them from contact with the formal justice system outcomes. After-school programmes can help to keep young people from experiencing homelessness, having diversionary benefits outside of the school setting as well as within school (Fader et al., 2015). In addition, programmes that adopt a therapeutic approach can aim to address young people's needs and behaviours through empowering, strengths-based interventions that are focused on setting goals and helping young people to attain those goals (Belciug et al., 2016). Engagement with diversion programmes may also encourage better service utilisation in young people (Barrett et al., 2022).

All of these positive impacts are significant as they have the potential to reduce the risk of reoffending associated with many behavioural, mental health and social difficulties associated with young people who have engaged with the criminal justice system, and where their rights have often not been adequately realised previously. Similarly, where concerns around young people's involvement in offending are related to their educational engagement, diversion programmes sometimes aim to provide wraparound services to young people, including tutoring, mentoring, attendance checks, inclusion in after-school programmes and daily check-ins with programme staff (Fader et al., 2015; Sullivan et al., 2010). In the US, success has been achieved in reducing the number of referrals to the youth justice system for school-based offences through the introduction of civil citation (non-criminal) programmes which identify appropriate community service operations and assess the young person's need for further assessment or services (Sullivan et al., 2010). Efforts to increase children's engagement with education and strengthen more positive relationships and engagement with the school environment may be in line with helping to secure greater respect for children's educational rights, in addition to reducing their contact with the damaging impact of the justice system.

Diversion as a Means of Supporting Positive Outcomes for Children
The importance of interventions and approaches that take an individualised and holistic approach to young people has also been emphasised in the literature in this area, further reinforcing the overall message of the Convention, set out in Chapter 2, of the need to take an individualised and age-appropriate approach in the response taken to children who come into conflict with the law. There is a need to consider whether diversion programmes work in terms of connecting young people to the services they need through an individualised approach to diversion planning, rather than focusing solely on effectiveness in terms of recidivism (Wylie et al., 2019). Studies of diversionary interventions have demonstrated that programmes should consider the major needs of the young people they work with, provide suitable treatment based on these needs and ensure follow-up at a later date to assess the effectiveness of the programme (Sullivan et al., 2007). Some studies have found that diversion schemes focused on mental health issues had some success in referring children to more appropriate services, including mental health services (Case & Browning, 2021; Haines et al., 2012). There is a strong case for ensuring that such responses are trauma informed, regardless of gender (Brown et al., 2021).

While diversion programmes vary in focus and effectiveness, some studies have indicated elements that are particularly important in supporting positive outcomes for children. In particular, scholarship suggests that interventions focused on young people's strengths by building on their solution-building competencies can be an important component in diversionary practice (Belciug et al., 2016). The development of personal relationships between young people and mentors or facilitators in the context of diversionary interventions has also been considered important (Belciug et al., 2016; O'Dwyer, 2019; Seroczynski, 2016). The need for relationships to support positive outcomes is a particularly significant finding and chimes with the strong emphasis placed by the Committee on the Rights of the Child on ensuring that all professionals within the justice system receive multidisciplinary training on the content and meaning of the Convention (Committee on the Rights of the Child, 2019, para. 112).

Diversionary practices include restorative justice programmes (Wong et al., 2016), which have been highlighted by the Committee on the Rights of the Child as an approach with the potential to protect children's rights (Committee on the Rights of the Child, 2019). Such practices can be incorporated in a range of different ways. As young people are often unfairly treated within systems such as the justice system or education system, it is necessary for these systems to facilitate restorative practice (Velez et al., 2020). Police diversion schemes—involving an informal or formal caution—have been proven to incorporate restorative elements in an effective manner (Kilkelly, 2011; Smith, 2014). In this regard, a meta-analysis of restorative justice diversion programmes implemented in the US, Australia, New Zealand and Europe found that diversion programmes often have a beneficial impact in terms of reduced recidivism (Wong et al., 2016). Studies have also shown the potential of interventions that offer a direct psychosocial intervention, such as family-based interventions or behavioural components which offer opportunities for restorative justice approaches (including family group conferences or victim-offender mediation to be developed further) (Schwalbe et al., 2012). Overall, there is good evidence for the effectiveness of restorative justice programmes (Kimbrell et al., 2022).

However, while restorative justice can be an important tool to help divert children successfully, scholars have raised a note of caution about whether this is always a rights-respecting approach, highlighting the extent to which positive outcomes can depend on the implementation of these techniques in practice (Lynch, 2010). A number of factors may impact the extent to which restorative practice supports children's rights and promotes better outcomes for children. For example, while restorative justice approaches have been found to be promising in terms of combating recidivism, motivation on the part of young people to engage in and fulfil requirements relating to victim and community reparation may be important in achieving successful outcomes (Wong et al., 2016). Aside from impacting on reoffending rates, however, it is important to recognise that other positive outcomes can emerge from restorative justice approaches, including remorse on the part of offenders, improved perceptions of the fairness of the processes involved and victim satisfaction with the process (Earle et al., 2002; Wong et al., 2016). In practice, however, much of the success of restorative justice approaches can depend on the approach of the facilitator, and restorative justice approaches also carry risks for the rights of individuals involved (Lynch, 2010). This means that significant attention must be paid to how particular approaches are implemented in practice, and the training and skill of facilitators tasked with doing so.

Conversely, the literature has also drawn attention to the factors in some diversion programmes that have impacted negatively on the young people participating in them. For example, where young people had to meet multiple requirements in order to satisfactorily complete the programme, this was found, proportionately, to decrease the likelihood of the young person successfully completing the programme (NeMoyer et al., 2020). It has also been suggested that where diversion programmes contain a number of requirements to allow charges to be dismissed, those that offer services based on risk and needs (but where a young person is not required to necessarily complete those services as a condition of their charge being dismissed) may be preferable (Wylie et al., 2019). Further, inconsistency in delivery of diversion services across different geographical areas, ambiguity in what is meant by 'diversion' and lack of sufficient funding have been identified as barriers to more positive practices (Case & Browning, 2021).

Despite the potential benefits of diversion, there are risks attached to diversion where instead of 'diverting from' offending, a young person is effectively 'diverted to' another initiative leading to problems of system contact and stigmatisation (Richards, 2014). There can be substantial differences in practice with a system that prioritises diversion from court processes based on the assumption that a young person will grow out of offending as part of their routine development, and a system which presupposes that without some form of more active intervention, a young person will inevitably engage in further offending behaviour (Nelken, 2006). There is thus a need to ensure that diversion from the youth justice system is promoted along with diversion to forms of intervention that enhance the well-being of young people and promote their social inclusion (Smith, 2014).

The Edinburgh Study of Youth Transitions and Crime has highlighted the importance of minimal intervention and maximum diversion in responses to young people in conflict with the law in order to prevent young people from being drawn into cycles of contact with the criminal justice system (McAra & McVie, 2007). Some studies of the effectiveness of diversionary programmes have supported this approach based on minimum intervention and the promotion of diversion (Corr, 2014; Smith, 2014; Wilson & Hoge, 2013). Approaches to youth justice based on 'children first, offenders second' principles, for example, have emphasised the need for diversion to be a core objective of the youth justice system, based on principles relating to minimum intervention, the needs of children and restorative principles (Case & Haines, 2015, 2018; Haines & Case, 2015; Smith, 2014). It has been suggested that these interventions, based on principles of prevention, diversion and minimal intervention, are key to supporting more positive outcomes for young people in conflict with the law, and promoting more child-centred and developmentally-aware approaches in response to offending by children (Case & Browning, 2021). The link to a rights-based approach, as part of the Child First policy approach in England and Wales, is evident here too (Kilkelly, 2023).

Some studies have highlighted the importance of considering systems which regulate access to diversion. It has been suggested that it is particularly important to consider the socio-cultural components of diversion, as there can be implicit bias in the selection of those who are granted diversion (Samuels-Wortley, 2022). In light of the importance of diversion and the avoidance of formal system contact for young people coming into conflict with the law, it is important that while legal safeguards and appropriate thresholds should be maintained, these requirements should not be so stringent as to have the effect of acting as a barrier to accessing the benefits of diversion, with the result that young people are processed through formal criminal justice systems unnecessarily. In this regard, it has been noted that legal requirements around admission can act as a barrier to young people accessing the benefits of diversion (Cushing, 2014). This emphasises the importance, in line with the edict set out in Article 40 (3) of the Convention, that diversion should only be preferred where procedural safeguards are adequately protected. Children's perceived legitimacy of a police intervention is also a critical factor, with interventions that respect children's right to a say in the decision-making process having most positive impact (Hinds, 2007).

Justice

As illustrated in Chapter 2, the international children's rights standards recognise the importance of children in conflict with the law enjoying procedural and legal safeguards including due process guarantees and the principles of child-friendly justice. Children's lack of maturity and development can frustrate their full enjoyment of these legal safeguards meaning they are ill-equipped to safely navigate the complexity of the criminal justice system (Gooch & von Berg, 2019). Article 40 (2) of the CRC sets out a long list of due process rights that children are entitled to enjoy when in contact with the justice system. These include the right to information, the right to legal or other appropriate assistance, and to have their privacy respected throughout the proceedings. The child also has a right to be heard under Article 12 of the CRC, a right which encompasses a right to 'effective participation' in the justice process (Committee on the Rights of the Child, 2019), a concept taken from European Court of Human Rights jurisprudence on the rights of child defendants (Liefaard, 2016). Regardless of its source, the procedural rights to which young people are entitled are of paramount importance in ensuring that children's engagement with the courts and the wider criminal justice system reflects their entitlement to adapted and child-appropriate justice.

Within the international standards, focus has shifted to children's experience of the justice process with a strong and deliberate move towards adapted child justice processes that respect, protect and fulfil the rights of the child. This is exemplified by the adoption by the Council of Europe of the Guidelines on Child-friendly Justice (Committee of Ministers, 2010), a movement that has gathered momentum in Europe (Liefaard & Kilkelly, 2018) and around the world (Liefaard, 2016). Within all aspects of the youth justice system, international standards require a developmentally informed approach focused on the best interests of the child. This is true of children's procedural rights, as well as in relation to provisions setting out to the overall goals of the justice system and the treatment that children receive when they are subject to sanctions and measures in the justice system. Article 40 (4) of the CRC requires that a range of measures should be available within the youth justice system 'to ensure that children are dealt with in a manner appropriate to their well-being and proportionate both to their circumstances and the offence'. Indeed, the focus on well-being, individual circumstances and proportionality—in relation to both the offence and the circumstances of the child—are core components of rights-based youth justice. While research in this area reinforces the importance of these rights, it also reflects the material challenge that exists in ensuring these rights are implemented (Kilkelly, 2008; Liefaard, 2019; Rap, 2016; Taylor, 2016; Zimring et al., 2017).

Police Investigation

From the beginning of their contact with the youth justice system, from the earliest stages of police investigation, children should enjoy their procedural rights and be supported to exercise their right to participate meaningfully in the process (Hinds, 2007). However, research in this area indicates that children are often particularly vulnerable in this context and experience breaches of their rights (Cleary, 2014; Feld, 2013; Gooch & von Berg, 2019; Kilkelly & Forde, 2020; Parry, 2006). Children's lack of power in the face of police questioning is associated with suggestibility, resulting in potential susceptibility to make false confessions (Cleary, 2014; Feld, 2013; Redlich & Goodman, 2003) as well as impacting on the inter-generational relationship with the police (Hinds, 2007). Children's heightened vulnerability in such situations reinforces the importance of their right to enjoy procedural safeguards and guarantees (Dehaghani, 2017).

Fundamental to children's effective participation in police decision-making is receiving adequate information (Radic, 2018; Stalford et al., 2017). Studies have demonstrated the difficulties children can experience understanding information provided to them by the authorities or by the police and misunderstanding the information or its consequences for them may happen as a result (Feld, 2006; Kilkelly & Forde, 2020; Zelle et al., 2015). Factors like stress and intoxication can inhibit children's ability to take in and process information given to them (Kilkelly & Forde, 2020) and professionals, such as lawyers, have expressed doubt about how well children understand information they receive (Kilkelly & Forde, 2020; Ministry of Justice, 2011). Police officers can play an important role in facilitating better communication and understanding with children, particularly where interactions are based on mutual respect and trust with young people (Lount et al., 2018). This reinforces the need for specialised training for all professionals in the criminal justice system, including police (Committee on the Rights of the Child, 2019), so that their methods can support the realisation of children's procedural rights.

Article 40 (2) of the CRC sets out children's right to access 'legal or other appropriate assistance', and the importance of adequate legal assistance is further reinforced by the European Guidelines on Child-friendly Justice, as set out in Chapter 2 (Liefaard, 2016). Although assistance from a lawyer can play an important role in helping children to navigate their contact with the criminal justice system from the earliest interaction, studies have found that young people often opt not to exercise their right to legal assistance even where they are advised of it, for a variety of reasons (Cleary, 2014; Feld, 2006; Forde & Kilkelly, 2023; Kemp et al., 2011). In this regard, lawyers need to receive specialised training in order to effectively support children to access their rights (A'Court & Arthur, 2020; Forde & Kilkelly, 2023).

Research has found that adequate support from other adults, such as parents or other 'appropriate adults', can play an important role in helping children to access their procedural rights in their interactions with police. Supportive adults, including parents, can provide emotional support and aid children to access their rights (Broeking & Peterson-Badali, 2010). However, where a parent is not supportive, does not understand aspects of the procedure or is conflicted with regard to what is in the child's best interests, their impact can be less than positive (Burke et al., 2014; Cavanagh & Cauffman, 2017; Cleary & Warner, 2017; Cohen, 2020). In such instances, specially-trained and independent 'appropriate adults' should be introduced to the process, although the literature has highlighted the need for such roles to be clearly established and defined, and the parties themselves appropriately trained (Pierpoint, 2000).

The Court Process

Ensuring that child defendants can participate effectively in criminal proceedings is a very real challenge (Forde, 2018). Courts are highly formalised spaces in which adult-centred procedures pre-dominate in the determination of complex legal questions; children often do not have the capacity to engage successfully within this context (Grisso et al., 2003; Rap, 2016). Studies have demonstrated that children experience significant difficulties in communicating and reasoning effectively in this setting (Weijers, 2004) not least due to the routine use of legal language and formality by professionals familiar with the courtroom environment (Kilkelly, 2008; Ministry of Justice, 2011; Piacentini & Walters, 2006; Weijers, 2004; Weijers & Hokwerda, 2003). Legal jargon has been shown to frustrate young people's understanding of the criminal process, increasing their levels of anxiety and stress (Rap & Weijers, 2014). It can also serve to marginalise the child within the process (Fernández-Molina et al., 2021; Kilkelly, 2008), increasing the disengagement of the child (Ministry of Justice, 2011). Lack of understanding can also have legal and long-term consequences for the child; where a young person does not fully understand the bail conditions or other requirements imposed on them by the court, for example, there is a greater chance of breach, which may lead to further entanglement in criminal justice processes (Allan et al., 2005; Bailey, 2009; Freeman, 2008; Kilkelly, 2008; Richards & Renshaw, 2013). The gravity of this is clear from Canadian research that found that the imposition of bail conditions actually had the unintended consequence of young people accumulating further criminal charges (Sprott & Myers, 2011). Moreover, research has found that where young people do not understand reasonings behind their placement in detention, this can lead to feelings of injustice and incomprehension (Dalbert & Filke, 2007; Freeman, 2009; Sykes, 1958), increasing the likelihood of experiencing coping difficulties in prison. By contrast, a focus on communication between court professionals and the young person, and improved communication between legal professionals within the courtroom, can improve the process from the child's point of view (Ministry of Justice, 2011; Weijers, 2004).

Enhancing Children's Participation in Court Processes

The international standards stress the need for to the court envrionment and the legal process for children (Committee on the Rights of the Child, 2007, 2019, para. 46). However, studies have shown that even in youth courts, children can experience challenges participating effectively, particularly in relation to understanding legal language and procedure (Brown & Vaswani, 2023; Forde, 2018; Kilkelly, 2008; Ministry of Justice, 2011; Weijers, 2004). Research has linked understanding of the legal process to the experience of procedural fairness both generally (Hinds, 2007; Tyler, 1988) and with regard to children and the court process (Saunders et al., 2020). In this respect, an important factor is the degree to which children are encouraged to engage directly with the court. One approach aimed at enhancing participation is to provide the child with the opportunity to present their own story to the court (Weijers, 2004), and in this regard, a case has been made for promoting pedagogical dialogue between the court and the young person in order to bring about a more effective process of engagement (Rap & Weijers, 2014). However, the extent to which this happens in practice can vary. For instance, research in Ireland's Children Court showed limited or no direct engagement of any kind between the court and the young person in a substantial number of cases (Kilkelly, 2008; Saunders et al., 2020). In light of difficulties such as these, research has questioned the competency of children to stand trial (Cleland, 2016b; Cooper, 1997) as well as adjudicative competency more generally (O'Donnell & Gross, 2012; Redding & Frost, 2001). This also highlights the importance of creating developmentally appropriate adjudication models, with court personnel who understand the factors—trauma, disability and immaturity—that may be impacting on a child's behaviour both in court and generally (Beyer, 2005).

Research has established that children need significant additional supports in order to participate meaningfully in court procedures (Arthur, 2016; Cooper, 1997; Kilkelly, 2010; Liefaard et al., 2016; Rap, 2016). Some research has indicated that hearing parents' views in court and encouraging parents' participation can be important elements of positive practice (Rap & Weijers, 2014; Saunders et al., 2020). Parents can also be an important source of emotional support for young people and can enhance their ability to participate effectively in the court proceedings (Liefaard, 2016; Rap, 2016). However, some studies of youth courts have highlighted that a significant number of children may attend court without the presence of one or both parents (Kilkelly, 2008), reflecting the challenges of family engagement in such processes (Saunders et al., 2020) including their failure to adopt culturally appropriate approaches (Suaalii-Sauni et al., 2018).

Right to Information and Legal Advice

Research also underlines the importance to young people of receiving appropriate information and adequate preparation prior to attending court (Brown & Vaswani, 2023; Cleghorn et al., 2010; Flin et al., 1989; Plotnikoff & Woolfson, 2002; Rap, 2016), highlighting the lack of understanding among young people of what to expect before going to court (Plotnikoff & Woolfson, 2002). A review of the experiences of young people, professionals and their families attending Youth Court in New Zealand found that young people and families did not feel that they had received sufficient information before coming to court; not only did this lack of information impact young people's understanding, it also prevented family members of young people from assisting them as effectively as they might otherwise have done (Ministry of Justice, 2011). These decisions are particularly important in helping children make important decisions regarding whether or not to make a plea, for instance, or in appreciating the legal consequences of these proceedings (Cleland, 2016a). Despite the important role played by families in this context, developing a model for family involvement in such processes can be challenging for a variety of reasons (Burke et al., 2014).

Access to legal assistance and representation from legal professionals, in particular lawyers, can be particularly important in shaping children's experiences especially given their vulnerability and lack of familiarity with the legal process. However, young people do not always have the benefit of adequate legal assistance, with some US studies finding that young people facing delinquency charges choose to waive their right to legal counsel (Scali, 2019). The literature in this area reinforces the fact that lawyers can have a significant impact on children's experience of court processes and on the outcomes for children. One Australian study highlighted that lawyers can have an important bearing on whether or not children choose to plead guilty to a charge they are facing before the court (Cunneen et al., 2015). US studies have indicated that young people without legal representation were more likely to receive out-of-home placements than young people with legal assistance (Feld, 1989). Literature on bail and remand for young people in Australia identified a lack of access to adequate legal representation as a factor contributing to lengthy remand periods for young people (Mazerolle & Sanderson, 2008; Richards & Renshaw, 2013; Tresidder & Putt, 2005; UnitingCare Burnside, 2009). Some US studies have, however, found the opposite effect, finding that in delinquency proceedings where children are represented by a lawyer, they tend to receive harsher outcomes than children who are not represented; however, the reasons for this were not always clear (Feld, 1989; Kokkalera et al., 2021). Legal assistance can play a crucial role in facilitating children's participation. Lawyers can be a particularly important source of information for children appearing in court (Daly & Rap, 2019; Rap and Weijers, 2004). However, engaging with children effectively is not without challenges, from the perspective of legal professionals; some research has shown practitioner experiences of trying to ensure children are adequately prepared for court can be made more difficult where children are emotionally impacted by other problems or difficulties in their personal lives (Ministry of Justice, 2011). Other studies have highlighted that the time available to consult with young people prior to court appearances is often very short; while the time available for this task will vary between different contexts, studies have noted practitioner concerns that having only 10–15 minutes to consult with a young person prior to a court appearance was not sufficient (Cleland, 2016a).

The Role of the Judge
Some studies have also highlighted, however, that effective communication from judges and legal professionals can play an important role in improving children's access to their rights (Forde, 2018; Kilkelly, 2010; Daly & Rap, 2019; Ministry of Justice, 2011). Judges are particularly important in this regard. Research indicates that children wish to have the opportunity to speak directly to the judge about the case and their personal life (Daly & Rap, 2019; Kilkelly, 2010). Studies have shown that where judges engage directly with young people in court procedures, inviting them to participate and asking questions, they can have a positive impact on children's engagement (Becroft, 2013; Forde, 2018; Ministry of Justice, 2011). Effective communication on the part of the judge can help young people to understand the consequences of the court processes, and what is required of them (Rap & Weijers, 2014). It can also impact the overall experience of the young person; some studies have contrasted the approach of judges who take a confrontational or negative approach to children appearing before the court with the much more positive reactions engendered when judges take the time to address young people directly and respectfully (Carroll et al., 2007; Kilkelly, 2008). In general, this reflects the complex and specialist role of the youth court judge in ensuring the child's procedural rights are protected during the court process (Kilkelly, 2008). Training and specialism for judges dealing with children's cases is critical in this context (Buffington et al., 2010) as well is the importance of understanding the developmental frameworks that impact on children's behaviour, as discussed in Chapter 3.

The Physical Environment and Court Design
The importance of the physical environment from the research, with the courtroom and its processes often considered alien to young people (Cunneen et al., 2015). At a basic level, children should be separated from adults when they are in court (Committee on the Rights of the Child, 2019, para. 92). However, in some contexts, arrangements to

facilitate this separation have not been implemented, with studies finding that children mix with adults waiting to appear before other courts in waiting areas in court buildings (Daly & Rap, 2019; Kilkelly, 2008; Rap, 2013). Some studies have highlighted that children and their families can experience feelings of boredom, frustration or intimidation in court waiting rooms (Brown & Vaswani, 2023; Ministry of Justice, 2011), which are frequently a moment of tension for children (Birckhead, 2010; Fernández-Molina et al., 2021). These physical surroundings can also have significant consequences for a young person's ability to participate effectively in the proceedings (Kilkelly, 2008).

Other factors related to the environment and procedural arrangements can also impact on children's experiences. Some studies have indicated that a negative environment, such as lack of organisation or displays of negative or unprofessional behaviour on the part of court and legal officials can contribute to a negative environment which prevents children from participating (Greene et al., 2010; Rap & Weijers, 2014). Issues with delay and poor case management can increase waiting times for children and their families and contribute to more negative experiences of the process overall (Kilkelly, 2008; Kilkelly et al., 2021). Delay can also increase the length of time for which the child must satisfy conditions imposed by the court, and lead to stress and frustration if there is a lack of certainty about the final outcome (Ministry of Justice, 2011).

Consideration should also be given to the layout and design of courtrooms, and how they affect a child's ability to participate. At a basic level, seating arrangements need to allow the key participants in the court process to hear properly (Kilkelly, 2008; Rap & Weijers, 2014). Equally, large courtrooms have been found to make it more difficult for children to hear, understand and become involved meaningfully in the proceedings as compared to smaller courtrooms (Crofts et al., 2008; Kilkelly, 2008). While the formal nature of the physical environment has been recognised to be an impediment in some contexts, other studies have suggested that both the formal environment and rituals associated with court processes can reinforce the seriousness of the matter under consideration for young people (Rap & Weijers, 2014).

The Importance of Child-Centred Courts

Research in this area points to the need for youth courts to maintain a separate character, distinct from adult systems of justice and tailored specifically to the needs of children. One of the fundamental reasons put forward to support this idea is the 'pedagogical task' of the youth court, when compared to adult courts (Weijers, 2004). This is paired with the need for specialised procedures and supports, which take into account the developmental needs of the child, in order to enable children to participate effectively and navigate the legal landscape in which they find themselves (Rap, 2016; Rap & Weijers, 2014). Some studies have indicated that it may be beneficial for professionals, including lawyers, to adopt a less adversarial approach which takes greater account of the overall best interests of the child, in cases where there is a lack of dispute over the facts of the case; however, this may bring a strict view of protection of due process rights into conflict with what is considered in children's overall best interests (Cleland, 2016a). Studies have suggested, however, that a less formalised approach which encourages a dialogue between the court and the child may help children both to appreciate the broader impact of their crimes on their victims and to assist the court in reaching an appropriate sentence is important (Rap & Weijers, 2014).

Alternatives to traditional, formalised court procedures have been used in some countries to try to ensure that court processes are more child-friendly. In some countries, therapeutic or problem-solving approaches to adapting youth court procedures have been said to have potential for increasing consistency of approach and facilitating access to services for children (Becroft & Norrie, 2015). Further, Family Group Conferences—based on restorative justice principles—have been introduced in some countries, and it has been suggested that they may hold significant potential to further enhance participation by children (Henwood & Stratford, 2014). However, the extent to which the use of alternative procedures such as this facilitates greater protection for children's due process right in reality—and in particular the extent to which it enhances their participation—has been questioned, given that much depends on the approach taken to implementation in practice (Cleland, 2016a; Forde, 2018; Lynch, 2007–2008; 2008).

Trial in Adult Court

Children who commit serious crimes often face particular challenges when it comes to their procedural rights (Lynch et al., 2022). In many countries around the world, even those with progressive youth justice approaches, children are transferred from specialised youth courts to the adult court system, either by mandatory process or waiver, where they experience significant additional challenges in navigating procedures and accessing their rights (Christiaens & Nuytiens, 2009; Cleland, 2016b; Deuchar & Sapouna, 2016; Lynch, 2018). In adult court, where more punitive sanctions are available, children frequently experience a justice system ill adapted to their needs and circumstances. While justified politically with regard to the serious nature of their offending (Cauffman et al., 2007), some studies have indicated that this practice does not have a significant deterrent effect or impact on reducing violent crimes committed by children, or that the deterrent effect is unproven (Liwanga & Ibe, 2021; Steiner et al., 2006). In some instances, it can lead to the imposition of the most punitive form of sanction—life without parole, once described by Feld as 'a slower form of death' (Feld, 2008). Significantly, although the US Supreme Court has begun to moderate its position on life sentences without parole for children in recognition of the impact of the child's development on their culpability (Levick, 2019), the lasting impact of this position is not clear (Hoesterey, 2017; Hritz, 2020).

In some countries, waiver to adult court can lead to the imposition of sanctions served in adult corrective facilities, which can increase the vulnerability and victimisation of children (Steiner et al., 2006). In addition to impacting outcomes for children, there are also serious consequences for children's procedural rights in this context. Studies have found that children often experience these procedures as being particularly harsh and reported having difficulties in understanding procedures and participating in them (Nolan et al., 2018). Although a number of countries have attempted to make changes to procedural rules to make court processes more suitable for children, some scholars have noted the significant challenges in making processes designed for adults appropriate for children (Lynch, 2018; Taylor, 2016). It has been argued that existing, specialised youth courts should continue to be used for the trial of more serious offences, rather than transferring children to inherently unsuitable adult courts (Lynch, 2018).

Both in court and in the police questioning process, difficulties in effectively accessing and exercising procedural rights are compounded further for children who experience communication difficulties (Anderson et al., 2016; Ellem & Richards, 2018), or who have experienced trauma (Crane, 2017). These factors raise additional complexity, which needs to be taken into account in line with the due process rights to be enjoyed by all children, including through appropriate judicial training (Buffington et al., 2010). This is particularly critical given that research consistently shows that children with communication difficulties and other cognitive impairments are disproportionally represented in the justice system (Baidawi & Piquero, 2021; Bryan et al., 2007; Johnston et al., 2016; Vaswani, 2014; Winstanley et al., 2019). Interestingly, the Committee on the Rights of the Child has strongly suggested that these children should not be dealt with within the criminal justice system at all, and if they are not automatically excluded, there should be in place a process to individually assess these children so that their needs can be met (Committee on the Rights of the Child, 2019, para. 28).

In addition to communication difficulties, studies have found that children with more limited education and mental health difficulties can also find it difficult understand information given to them (Ministry of Justice, 2011). Where specific measures are put in place to address these vulnerabilities, they can go some way to enhancing respect for children's rights; for example, the introduction of communication assistants for children in New Zealand has been found to have positive effects on their ability to participate more meaningfully in proceedings (Howard et al., 2020). However, these procedural difficulties, especially for children who are already particularly vulnerable, raise issues not only in relation to children's procedural rights under Articles 40(2) and 12 of the CRC, but also in relation to the rights of children with disabilities under Article 23 and under the Convention on the Rights of Persons with Disabilities.

Protections for Children's Privacy

Privacy protections are robustly set out Article 40 (2) of the CRC, paragraph 2(vii) of which requires that the child's right to privacy must be fully respected 'at all stages of the proceedings'. This is an important safeguard with respect to protecting children's procedural rights in the court process, while it is also integrally linked to the chances of the child successfully reintegrating into society on release (Joyce, 2011). While lax practice can lead to the names of child defendants becoming known around the courthouse setting (Kilkelly, 2008), strict legal requirements can be important in preventing publication of the child's identity in line with reintegration goals (Joyce, 2011). However, notwithstanding that privacy protections exist for child defendants in many countries, exceptions are sometimes used to dispense with these requirements in cases where this is deemed to be in the public interest, particularly in cases of serious crime (Fitz-Gibbon & O'Brien, 2017; Hart, 2014; Kilkelly & Liefaard, 2022). This can have significant consequences for a child, including the risk of harm through lack of privacy, creating significant barriers to reintegration; these risks are often exacerbated through the role of social media (Hart, 2014). The publication of children's identities can have lifelong consequences, particularly in relation to their access to employment later in life, where information about past criminal involvement is freely available online (Siddiky, 2011). It has been argued that permanent and robust name-suppression and protections for children's privacy, even in cases where they commit serious crimes, are in the long-term public interest because of the important role this plays in rehabilitation and facilitating the assumption of a non-offending, positive identity in the future (Hart, 2014; Lynch, 2018). This approach is clearly in line with international children's rights protections.

Conclusion

This chapter presented the key messages from the research literature under the two rights themes of Diversion and Justice, relating to protecting the rights of the child from the harsh impacts of the justice system. It demonstrated that the children's rights principle of diversion is underpinned by a strong and consistent body of research, reinforcing the need for early intervention and frequent and meaningful opportunities to divert the child away from the formal justice system. Similarly, while the importance of due process rights is widely acknowledged, the chapter presented a view from the literature that echoes the integral nature of specially adapted legal safeguards to the child's experience of the justice system as fair and legitimate. While the synergies between the children's rights standards and the research literature are particularly strong here, there are clear challenges with implementation, even in more progressive jurisdictions. Particularly important here is the application of such Diversion and Justice approaches to children involved in offending of a more serious nature. While the emotive, political and moral response to serious youth crime is a difficult narrative to counter, the strength of the research adds important weight to the case for a clear and consistent children's rights approach to all these issues, for advocates and decision-makers alike. Again it is important to reinforce the universal nature of the rights-based approach—all children, all rights, in all circumstances.

Bibliography

A'Court, B., & Arthur, R. (2020). The role of lawyers in supporting young people in the criminal justice system: Balancing economic survival and children's rights. *Journal of Social Welfare and Family Law, 42*(4), 498–515. https://doi.org/10.1080/09649069.2020.1837517

Allan, A., et al. (2005). An observational study of bail decision-making. *Psychiatry, Psychology and Law, 12*(2), 319–333.

An Garda Síochána. (2017). *Annual report of the committee appointed to monitor the effectiveness of the diversion programme 2017*. Garda Youth Diversion and Crime Prevention Bureau.

Anderson, S. S. A., Hawes, D. J., & Snow, P. C. (2016). Language impairments among youth offenders: A systematic review. *Children and Youth Services Review, 65*, 195.

Arthur, R. (2016). Giving effect to young people's right to participate effectively in criminal proceedings. *Child and Family Law Quarterly, 28*(3), 223–238.

Baidawi, S., & Piquero, A. (2021). Neurodisability among children at the nexus of the child welfare and youth justice system. *Journal of Youth and Adolescence, 50*, 803–819.

Bailey, B. (2009). Bail me out: Research report on detention and homelessness. *Parity, 22*(8), 27–28.

Barrett, J. G., Flores, M., Lee, E., Mullin, B., Greenbaum, C., Pruett, E. A., & Cook, B. L. (2022). Diversion as a pathway to improving service utilization among at-risk youth. *Psychology, Public Policy, and Law, 28*(2), 179–187. https://doi.org/10.1037/law0000325

Bateman, T. (2012). Who pulled the plug? Towards an explanation of the fall in child imprisonment in England and Wales. *Youth Justice, 12*(1), 36–52. https://doi.org/10.1177/1473225411435616

Becroft, A. (2013). Access to youth justice in New Zealand: 'The very good, the good, the bad and the ugly.' *Auckland University Law Review, 18*, 23–35.

Becroft, A., & Norrie, S. (2015). The Youth Courts of New Zealand in Ten Years Time: Crystal ball gazing or some realistic goals for the future? https://www.justice.govt.nz/assets/Youth-Court-The-Youth-Courts-of-New-Zealand-in-10-years.pdf

Belciug, C., Franklin, C., Bolton, K. W., Jordan, C., & Lehmann, P. (2016). Effects of goal commitment and solution building on the completion rates for a juvenile diversion program. *Criminal Justice and Behavior, 43*(7), 923–936. https://doi.org/10.1177/0093854815626753

Beyer, M. (2005). Developmentally-sound practice in family and juvenile court. *Nevada Law Journal, 6*, 1215.

Birckhead, T. (2010). Culture clash: The challenge of lawyering across difference in juvenile court. *Rutgers Law Review, 62*(4), 959–991.

Brennan, A. M. (2012). The Garda diversion programme and the juvenile offender: The dilemma of due process rights. *Irish Criminal Law Journal, 22*(2), 46.

Broeking, J., & Peterson-Badali, M. (2010). The extent and nature of parents' involvement in Canadian youth justice proceedings. *Youth Justice, 10*(1), 40–55. https://doi.org/10.1177/1473225409356759

Brown, A., & Vaswani, N. (2023). *Glasgow Youth Court. Full report*. Children and Young People's Centre for Justice & Glasgow City HSCP.

Brown, S. L., Wanamaker, K. A., Greiner, L., Scott, T., & Skilling, T. A. (2021). Complex trauma and criminogenic needs in a youth justice sample: A gender-informed latent profile analysis. *Criminal Justice and Behavior, 48*(2), 175–194.

Bryan, K., Freer, J., & Furlong, C. (2007). Language and communication difficulties in juvenile offenders. *International Journal of Language & Communication Disorders, 42*(5), 505–520. https://doi.org/10.1080/13682820601053977

Buffington, K., Dierkhising, C. B., & Marsh, S. C. (2010). Ten things every juvenile court judge should know about trauma and delinquency. *Juvenile and Family Court Journal, 61*(3), 13–23.

Burke, J. D., Mulvey, E. P., Schubert, C. A., & Garbin, S. R. (2014). The challenge and opportunity of parental involvement in juvenile justice services. *Children and Youth Services Review, 39*, 39–47. https://doi.org/10.1016/j.childyouth.2014.01.007

Campbell, L. (2005). Garda diversion of young offenders: An unreasonable threat to due process rights? *Irish Journal of Applied Social Studies, 6*(1), 13–26.

Carroll, J., Meehan, E., & McPhillips, S. (2007). *The children court: A national study*. Association for Criminal Justice Research and Development.

Case, S., & Haines, K. (2021). Abolishing youth justice systems: Children first, offenders nowhere. *Youth Justice, 21*(1), 3–17. https://doi.org/10.1177/1473225419898754

Case, S. P., & Haines, K. R. (2015). Children first, offenders second: The centrality of engagement in positive youth justice. *The Howard Journal of Criminal Justice, 52*(2), 157–175. https://doi.org/10.1111/hojo.12099

Case, S. P., & Haines, K. R. (2018). Transatlantic 'positive youth justice': Coherent movement or disparate critique? *Crime Prevention and Community Safety, 20*(3), 208–222.

Case, S., & Browning, A. (2021). *Child first justice: The research evidence-base* [full Report]. Loughborough University. https://hdl.handle.net/2134/14152040.v1

Cauffman, E., Piquero, A. R., Kimonis, E., Steinberg, L., Chassin, L., & Fagan, J. (2007). Legal, individual, and environmental predictors of court disposition in a sample of serious adolescent offenders. *Law and Human Behavior, 31*(6), 519–535. https://doi.org/10.1007/s10979-006-9076-2

Cavanagh, C., & Cauffman, E. (2017). What they don't know can hurt them: Mothers' legal knowledge and youth re-offending. *Psychology, Public Policy, and Law, 23*(2), 141–153. https://doi.org/10.1037/law0000112

Christiaens, J., & Nuytiens, A. (2009). Transfer of juvenile offenders to adult court in Belgium: Critical reflections on the reform of a moderate practice. *Youth Justice, 9*(2), 131.

Cleary, H. M. D., & Warner, T. C. (2017). Parents' knowledge and attitudes about youths' interrogation rights. *Psychology, Crime & Law, 23*(8), 777–793.

Cleary, H. M. D. (2014). Police interviewing and interrogation of juvenile suspects: A descriptive examination of actual cases. *Law and Human Behaviour, 38*(3), 271.

Cleghorn, N., Kinsella, R., & McNaughton Nicholls, C. (2010). *Engaging with the views of young people with experience of the youth justice system. Executive Summary*. https://www.phf.org.uk/publications/engaging-views-young-peopleexperience-youth-justice-system-executive-summary/

Cleland, A. (2016a). Will New Zealand's youth justice system take the next step? In T. Liefaard & J. Sloth-Nielsen, J (Eds.), *The United Nations convention on the rights of the child*. Brill | Nijhoff. https://doi.org/10.1163/9789004295056_018

Cleland, A. (2016b). Portrait of the accused as a young man: New Zealand's harsh treatment of young people who commit serious crimes. *The Round Table, 105*(4), 377–387. https://doi.org/10.1080/00358533.2016.1205360

Cohen, L. (2020). When parents are not enough: The case for counsel in juvenile interrogations. *Criminal Justice, 34*(4), 55–56. https://doi.org/10.1080/1068316X.2017.1324030

Committee of Ministers. (2010). *Guidelines of the Committee of Ministers of the Council of Europe on child-friendly justice*. Adopted by the Committee of Ministers of the Council of Europe on 17 November 2010 and explanatory memorandum.

Committee on the Rights of the Child. (2007, April 25). *General Comment No. 10 (2007) Children's rights in juvenile justice*. CRC/C/GC/10.

Committee on the Rights of the Child. (2013, April 17). *General comment No. 15 (2013) on the right of the child to the enjoyment of the highest attainable standard of health (art. 24)*. CRC/C/GC/15.

Committee on the Rights of the Child. (2019, September 19). *General comment No. 24 (2019) on children's rights in the child justice system*. CRC/C/GC/24.

Cooper, D. K. (1997). Juveniles' understanding of trial-related information: Are they competent defendants? *Behavioral Sciences & the Law, 15*(2),

167–180. https://doi.org/10.1002/(sici)1099-0798(199721)15:2%3c167::aid-bsl266%3e3.0.co;2-e. PMID: 9309855.
Corr, M.-L. (2014). Young people's offending careers and criminal justice contact: A case for social justice. *Youth Justice, 14*(3), 255–268. https://doi.org/10.1177/1473225414549695
Craig, J. M., Piquero, A. R., & Farrington, D. P. (2020). Not all at-risk boys have bad outcomes: Predictors of later life success. *Crime & Delinquency, 66*(3), 392–419. https://doi.org/10.1177/0011128719854344
Crane, M. G. (2017). Childhood trauma's lurking presence in the juvenile interrogation room and the need for a trauma-informed voluntariness test for juvenile confessions. *South Dakota Law Review, 62*, 626.
Crawford, A. (2009). Criminalizing sociability through anti-social behaviour legislation: Dispersal powers, young people and the police. *Youth Justice, 9*(1), 5–26. https://doi.org/10.1177/1473225408101429
Crofts, P., Amarasekara, S., Briffa, P., Makari, R., & Remedios, M. (2008). Design and children's courts. *Alternative Law Journal, 33*(4), 229–234. https://doi.org/10.1177/1037969X0803300408
Cunneen, C., White, R., & Richards, K. (2015). *Juvenile justice: Youth and crime in Australia* (5th ed.). Oxford University Press.
Cunningham, K. A., Gubner, N. R., Vick, K., Herting, J. R., & Walker, S. C. (2023). Redesigning juvenile probation to align with behavioral health and positive development principles: A quasi-experimental study. *Criminal Justice and Behavior, 50*(1), 6–21. https://doi.org/10.1177/00938548221082997
Cushing, K. (2014). Diversion from prosecution for young people in England and Wales—Reconsidering the mandatory admission criteria. *Youth Justice, 14*(2), 140–153. https://doi.org/10.1177/1473225414537568
Dalbert, C., & Filke, E. (2007). Belief in a personal just world, justice judgements, and their functions for prisoners. *Criminal Justice and Behaviour, 34*(11), 1516–1527.
Daly, A., & Rap, S. (2019). Children's participation in the justice system. In U. Kilkelly & T. Liefaard (Eds.), *International Human Rights of children. International Human Rights*. Springer. https://doi.org/10.1007/978-981-10-4184-6_14
De Nike, M., Shelden, R., Macallair, D., & Menart, R. (2019). *Collaborating for successful reentry: A practical guide to support justice-involved young people returning to the community*. Center on Juvenile and Criminal Justice.
Dehaghani, R. (2017). 'Vulnerable by law (but not by nature)': Examining perceptions of youth and childhood 'vulnerability' in the context of police custody. *Journal of Social Welfare and Family Law, 39*(4), 454–472. https://doi.org/10.1080/09649069.2017.1390279
Deuchar, R. (2009). *Gangs, marginalised youth and social capital*. Trentham Books.

Deuchar, R., & Sapouna, M. (2016). 'It's harder to go to court yourself because you don't really know what to expect': Reducing the negative effects of court exposure on young people—Findings from an evaluation in Scotland. *Youth Justice, 16*(2), 130–146. https://doi.org/10.1177/1473225415606815

Earle, R., Newburn, T., & Crawford, A. (2002). Referral orders: Some reflections on policy transfer and 'what works.' *Youth Justice, 2*(3), 141–150. https://doi.org/10.1177/147322540200200303

Ellem, K., & Richards, K. (2018). Police contact with young people with cognitive disabilities: Perceptions of procedural (in)justice. *Youth Justice, 18*(3), 230.

Fader, J. J., Lockwood, B., Schall, V. L., & Stokes, B. (2015). A promising approach to narrowing the school-to-prison pipeline: The WISE arrest diversion program. *Youth Violence and Juvenile Justice, 13*(2), 123–142. https://doi.org/10.1177/1541204014521249

Farrington, D. P., Ttofi, M. M., & Piquero, A. R. (2016). Risk, promotive and protective factors in youth offending: Results from the Cambridge study in delinquent development. *Journal of Criminal Justice, 45*, 63–70. https://doi.org/10.1016/j.jcrimjus.2016.02.014

Feld, B. (2006). Police interrogation of juveniles: An empirical study of policy and practice. *The Journal of Criminal Law and Criminology, 97*(1), 219–316.

Feld, B. (2013). Real Interrogation: What actually happens when cops question kids. *Law & Society Review, 47*(1), 1–35.

Feld, B. C. (2008). A slower form of death: Implications of Roper v. Simmons for juveniles sentenced to life without parole. *Notre Dame Journal of Law, Ethics & Public Policy, 22*, 9.

Feld, B. C. (1989). The Right to counsel in juvenile court: An empirical study of when lawyers appear and the difference they make. *The Journal of Criminal Law and Criminology (1973–), 79*(4), 1185–1346.

Fernández-Molina, E., Bermejo, M., & Baz, O. (2021). Observing juvenile courtrooms: Testing the implementation of guidelines on child-friendly justice in Spain. *Youth Justice, 21*(2), 192–209. https://doi-org.ucc.idm.oclc.org/10.1177/1473225420918027

Fitz-Gibbon, K., & O'Brien, W. (2017). The naming of child homicide offenders in England and Wales: The need for a change in law and practice. *The British Journal of Criminology, 57*(5), 1061–1079. https://doi.org/10.1093/bjc/azw042

Flin, R, H., Stevenson, Y., & Davies, G, M. (1989). Children's Knowledge of Court Proceedings. *British Journal of Psychology, 80*, 285–297.

Forde, L. (2018). Realising the right of the child to participate in the criminal process. *Youth Justice, 18*(3), 265–284. https://doi.org/10.1177/1473225418819086

Forde, L. (2021) Welfare, justice, and diverse models of youth justice: A children's rights analysis. *International Journal of Children's Rights, 29*(4), 920–945.

Forde, L., & Kilkelly, U. (2023). Children and police questioning: A rights-based approach. *Criminology and Criminal Justice*, 1–22. https://doi.org/10.1177/17488958231161423

Freeman, S. (2009). *Surviving on remand: A study of how young people cope in remand custody in Ireland*. Doctoral Thesis, Technological University Dublin. https://doi.org/10.21427/D72W2J

Freeman, S. (2008). The experience of young people remanded in custody: A case for bail support and supervision schemes. *Irish Probation Journal, 5*, 91–102.

Gearing, R. E., Schwalbe, C. S., MacKenzie, M. J., Ibrahim, R. W., Bushnaq, S., & Brewer, K. B. (2017). C-FIT adolescent diversion program: A behavioral intervention pilot test for delinquent offenders. *International Social Work, 60*(5), 1111–1125. https://doi.org/10.1177/0020872817695397

Gooch, K., & von Berg, P. (2019). What happens in the beginning, matters in the end: Achieving best evidence with child suspects in the police station. *Youth Justice, 19*(2), 85–101. https://doi.org/10.1177/1473225419868840

Greene, C., Sprott, J. B., Madon, N. S., & June, M. (2010). Punishing processes in Youth Court: Procedural justice, court atmosphere and youths' views of the legitimacy of the justice system. *Canadian Journal of Criminology and Criminal Justice, 52*(5), 527–544.

Griffin, D. (2007). Restorative justice, diversion and social control. In K. Lalor, F. Ryan, M. Seymour, & C. Hamilton (Eds.), *Young people and crime: Research, policy and practice*. Centre for Social and Educational Research.

Grisso, T., Steinberg, L., Woolard, J., Cauffman, E., Scott, E., Graham, S., Lexcen, F., Dickon Reppucci, N., & Schwartz, R. (2003). Juveniles' competence to stand trial: A comparison of adolescents' and adults' capacities as trial defendants. *Law and Human Behaviour, 27*(4), 333.

Haines, A., Goldson, B., Haycox, A., Houten, R., Lane, S., McGuire, J., Nathan, T., Perkins, E., Richards, S., & Whittington, R. (2012) *Evaluation of the Youth Justice Liaison and Diversion (YJLD) pilot scheme. Final Report*. University of Liverpool.

Haines, K., & Case, S. (2008). The rhetoric and reality of the 'risk factor prevention paradigm' approach to preventing and reducing youth offending youth justice. *Youth Justice, 8*(1), 5–20.

Haines, K. R., & Case, S. P. (2015). *Positive youth justice: Children first*. Policy Press.

Harrikari, T. (2013). Securitizing childhood—Childhood and youth in finnish crime prevention programmes. *Youth Justice, 13*(1), 57–72. https://doi.org/10.1177/1365480212474734

Hart. D. (2014). *What's in a name? The identification of children in trouble with the law*. Standing Committee for Youth Justice.

Haydon, D. (2014). Early intervention for the prevention of offending in Northern Ireland. *Youth Justice, 14*(3), 226–240. https://doi.org/10.1177/1473225414549693

Henwood, C., & Stratford, S. (2014). *New Zealand's gift to the world: The youth justice family group conference*. Henwood Trust.

Hinds, L. (2007). Building police-youth relationships: The importance of procedural justice. *Youth Justice, 7*, 195–209.

Hoesterey, A. R. (2017). Confusion in montgomery's wake: State responses, the mandates of montgomery, and why a complete categorical ban on life without parole for juveniles is the only constitutional option. *Fordham Urban Law Journal, 45*, 149.

Hoff, E., & Laursen, B. (2019). Socioeconomic status and parenting. In M. H. Bornstein (Ed.), *Handbook of parenting: Biology and ecology of parenting* (pp. 421–447). Routledge/Taylor & Francis Group.

Howard, K., McCann, C., & Dudley, M. (2020). 'It's really good…why hasn't it happened earlier?' Professionals' perspectives on the benefits of communication assistance in the New Zealand youth justice system. *Australian & New Zealand Journal of Criminology, 53*(2), 265–284. https://doi.org/10.1177/0004865819890377

Hritz, A. C. (2020). Board to death: De facto juvenile life without parole. *American Journal of Criminal Law, 47*, 47.

Jeong, S., Lee, B. H., & Martin, J. H. (2014). Evaluating the effectiveness of a special needs diversionary program in reducing reoffending among mentally Ill youthful offenders. *International Journal of Offender Therapy and Comparative Criminology, 58*(9), 1058–1080. https://doi.org/10.1177/0306624X13492403

Johnston, K., Prentice, K., Whitehead, H., Taylor, L., Watts, R., & Tranah, T. (2016). Assessing effective participation in vulnerable juvenile defendants. *The Journal of Forensic Psychiatry & Psychology, 27*(6), 802–814. https://doi.org/10.1080/14789949.2016.1208264

Joyce, N. (2011). An analysis of the extent of the juvenile offender's right to privacy: Is the child's right to privacy circumvented by public interest? *European Journal of Crime, Criminal Law and Criminal Justice, 19*(2), 113–124. https://doi.org/10.1163/157181711X566335

Kelly, L. (2012). Representing and preventing youth crime and disorder: Intended and unintended consequences of targeted youth programmes in

England. *Youth Justice, 12*(2), 101–117. https://doi.org/10.1177/1473225412447160

Kemp, V., Pleasance, P., & Balmer, N. (2011). Children, young people and requests for police station legal advice: 25 years on from PACE. *Youth Justice, 11*(1), 28.

Kern, M. L., Benson, L., Steinberg, E. A., & Steinberg, L. (2016). The EPOCH measure of adolescent well-being. *Psychological Assessment, 28*(5), 586–597. https://doi.org/10.1037/pas0000201

Kilkelly, U., & Forde, L. (2020). *Children's rights and police questioning: A qualitative study of children's experiences of being interviewed by the Garda Síochána*. Policing Authority/University College Cork.

Kilkelly, U. (2008). Youth courts: The Irish experience. *Youth Justice, 8*, 39.

Kilkelly, U. (2010). *Listening to children about justice: Report of the Council Of Europe Consultation with Children on Child-Friendly Justice*. Council of Europe.

Kilkelly, U. (2011). Policing, young people, diversion and accountability in Ireland. *Crime, Law and Social Change, 55*(2–3), 133–151.

Kilkelly, U. (2023). Child first and children's rights: An opportunity to advance rights-based youth justice. In S. Case & N. Hazel (Eds.), *Child first. Developing a new Youth Justice System* (pp. 109–133). Palgrave Macmillan.

Kilkelly, U., & Liefaard, T. (2022). International children's rights principles and responses to serious offending by children. Recent developments, topical issues and global challenges. In N. Lynch, Y. van den Brink, & L. Forde (Eds.), *Responses to serious offending by children. Principles, practice and global perspectives*. Routledge.

Kilkelly, U., Forde, L., Hurley, E., Lambert, S., Swirak, K., Kelleher, D., & Buckley, S. (2021). *Ensuring the collaborative reform of youth justice in Ireland in line with international research and evidence-based approaches*. Department of Children, Equality, Disability, Integration and Youth.

Kimbrell, C. S., Wilson, D. B., & Olaghere, A. (2022). Restorative justice programs and practices in juvenile justice: An updated systematic review and meta-analysis for effectiveness. *Criminology & Public Policy, 22*(1), 161–195.

Kokkalera, S., Tallas, A., & Goggin, K. (2021). Contextualizing the impact of legal representation on juvenile delinquency outcomes: A review of research and policy. *Juvenile and Family Court Journal, 72*(1), 47–71. https://doi.org/10.1111/jfcj.12192

Kowalski, M. A. (2019). Adverse childhood experiences and justice-involved youth: The effect of trauma and programming on different recidivistic outcomes. *Youth Violence and Juvenile Justice, 17*(4), 354–384. https://doi.org/10.1177/1541204018809836

Kretschmar, J. M., Tossone, K., Butcher, F., & Marsh, B. (2018). Examining the impact of a juvenile justice diversion program for youth with behavioral health concerns on early adulthood recidivism. *Children and Youth Services Review, 91*, 168–176. https://doi.org/10.1016/j.childyouth.2018.06.010

Levick, M. (2019). Kids are different: The United States Supreme Court reforms youth sentencing practices for youth prosecuted in the criminal justice system. *Juvenile and Family Court Journal, 70*(3), 25.

Liefaard, T. (2016). Child-friendly justice: Protection and participation of children in the justice system. *Temple Law Review, 88*, 905–927.

Liefaard, T. (2019). Access to justice for children: Towards a specific research and implementation agenda. *The International Journal of Children's Rights, 27*(2), 195–227. https://doi.org/10.1163/15718182-02702002

Liefaard, T., & Kilkelly, U. (2018). Child-friendly Justice: Past, present and future. In B. Goldson (Ed.), *Juvenile justice in Europe. Past, present and future*. Routledge.

Liefaard, T., Rap, S., & Bolscher, A. (2016). *Can anyone hear me? Participation of children in juvenile justice: A manual on how to make European juvenile justice systems child-friendly*. International Juvenile Justice Observatory.

Lipsey, M. W., Howell, J. C., Kelly, M. R., Chapman, G., & Carver, D. (2010). *Improving the effectiveness of juvenile justice programs*. Center for Juvenile Justice Reform at Georgetown University.

Liwanga, R., & Ibe, P. (2021). Transfer of child offenders to adult criminal courts in the USA: An unnecessary exercise, unconstitutional practice, international law violation, or all of the above? *Georgia Journal of International and Comparative Law, 49*(1), 99–128.

Logan-Greene, P., Nurius, P. S., Herting, J. R., Hooven, C. L., Walsh, E., & Adams Thomson, E. (2011). Multi-domain risk and protective factor predictors of violent behaviour among at-risk youth. *Journal of Youth Studies, 14*(4), 413–429. https://doi.org/10.1080/13676261.2010.538044

Lount, S. A., Hand, L., Purdy, S. C., & France, A. (2018). Tough talk: Youth offenders' perceptions of communicating in the Youth Justice system in New Zealand. *Australian & New Zealand Journal of Criminology, 51*(4), 593–618. https://doi.org/10.1177/0004865817740404

Lynch, N. (2007–2008). Respecting legal rights in the New Zealand youth justice family group conference. *Current Issues in Criminal Justice, 19*(1), 75.

Lynch, N. (2008). Youth justice in New Zealand: A children's rights perspective. *Youth Justice, 8*(3), 215–228.

Lynch, N. (2010). Restorative justice through a children's rights lens. *The International Journal of Children's Rights, 18*(2), 161–183. https://doi.org/10.1163/157181810X12592206285646

Lynch, N. (2018). Towards a principled legal response to children who kill. *Youth Justice, 18*(3), 211–229. https://doi.org/10.1177/1473225418819056

Lynch, N., van den Brink, Y., & Forde, L. (Eds.). (2022). *Responses to serious offending by children*. Routledge.
Magann, M. (2021). *Early versus late contact with the youth justice system: Differences in characteristics measured at birth, child protection system contact and adolescent mental health outcomes*. Doctoral dissertation University of Adelaide.
Mazerolle, P., & Sanderson, J. (2008). *Understanding remand in the juvenile justice system in Queensland*. Griffith University.
McAra, L., & McVie, S. (2007). Youth justice? The impact of system contact on patterns of desistance from offending. *European Journal of Criminology, 4*(3), 315–345. https://doi.org/10.1177/1477370807077186
McAra, L., & McVie, S. (2022). *Cause and impacts of offending and criminal justice pathways: Follow-up of the Edinburgh Cohort at Age 35*. The University of Edinburgh.
Michie, S., & Johnston, M. (2012). Theories and techniques of behaviour change: Developing a cumulative science of behaviour change [Editorial]. *Health Psychology Review, 6*(1), 1–6. https://doi.org/10.1080/17437199.2012.654964
Ministry of Justice. (2011). *Youth Court research: Experiences and views of young people, their families and professionals*. https://thehub.swa.govt.nz/assets/documents/42868_Youth_Court_Research_Report_0.pdf
Nelken, D. (2006). Italian juvenile justice: Tolerance, leniency or indulgence? *Youth Justice, 6*(2), 107–128. https://doi.org/10.1177/1473225406065561
NeMoyer, A., Gale-Bentz, E., Goldstein, N. E. S., & Pema Harvey, L. (2020). Factors associated with successful completion of a community-based, postarrest juvenile diversion program and subsequent rearrest. *Crime & Delinquency, 66*(5), 603–626. https://doi.org/10.1177/0011128719842377
Nolan, D., Dyer, F., & Vaswani, N. (2018). 'Just a wee boy not cut out for prison': Policy and reality in children and young people's journeys through justice in Scotland. *Criminology & Criminal Justice, 18*(5), 533–547. https://doi.org/10.1177/1748895817745347
O'Donnell, P. C., & Gross, B. (2012). Developmental incompetence to stand trial in juvenile courts. *Journal of Forensic Sciences, 57*(4), 989–996.
O'Dwyer, K. (2019). Reducing youth crime: The role of mentoring. *Irish Probation Journal, 16*, 153–167.
Olver, M. E., Stockdale, K. C., & Wormith, J. S. (2009). Risk assessment with young offenders: A meta-analysis of three assessment measures. *Criminal Justice and Behavior, 36*(4), 329–353.
Parry, R. G. (2006). Protecting the juvenile suspect: What exactly is the appropriate adult supposed to do? *Child and Family Law Quarterly, 18*(3), 373–396.

Piacentini, L., & Walters, R. (2006). The politicization of youth crime in Scotland and the rise of the 'Burberry Court.' *Youth Justice, 6*(1), 43–59. https://doi.org/10.1177/1473225406063451

Pierpoint, H. (2000). How appropriate are volunteers as 'appropriate adults' for young suspects? The 'appropriate adult' system and human rights. *Journal of Social Welfare and Family Law, 22*(4), 383–400. https://doi.org/10.1080/014180300750051898

Plotnikoff, J., & Woolfson, R. (2002). *Young defendants pack: Scoping study.*

Radic, I. (2018). Right of the child to information according to the Directive 2016/800/EU on procedural safeguards for children who are suspects or accused persons in criminal proceedings. *EU and Comparative Law Issues and Challenges Series, 2*(2), 468–491.

Rap, S. (2013). *The participation of juvenile defendants in the Youth Court. A comparative study of juvenile justice procedures in Europe*. Pallas Publications.

Rap, S. (2016). A children's rights perspective on the participation of juvenile defendants in the Youth Court. *International Journal of Children's Rights, 24*(1), 93.

Rap, S., & Weijers, I. (2014). *The effective Youth Court: Juvenile justice procedures in Europe*. Eleven International Publishing.

Redding, R. E., & Frost, L. E. (2001). Adjudicative competence in the modern juvenile court. *Virginia Journal of Social Policy & the Law, 9*, 353.

Redlich, A. D., & Goodman, G. S. (2003). Taking responsibility for an act not committed: The influence of age and suggestibility. *Law and Human Behavior, 27*(2), 141–156.

Richards, K. (2014). Blurred lines: Reconsidering the concept of 'diversion' in youth justice systems in Australia. *Youth Justice, 14*(2), 122–139. https://doi.org/10.1177/1473225414526799

Richards, K., & Renshaw, L. (2013). *Bail and remand for young people in Australia: A national research project*. Australian Institute of Criminology.

Samuels-Wortley, K. (2022). Youthful discretion: Police selection bias in access to pre-charge diversion programs in Canada. *Race and Justice, 12*(2), 387–410. https://doi.org/10.1177/2153368719889093

Saunders, B. J., Lansdell, G., & Frederick, J. (2020). Understanding children's court processes and decisions: Perceptions of children and their families. *Youth Justice, 20*(3), 272–292.

Scali, M.-A. (2019). Meeting the mandates of gault: Automatic appointment of counsel in juvenile delinquency proceedings. *Juvenile and Family Court Journal, 70*(3), 7–23.

Schwalbe, C. S., Gearing, R. E., MacKenzie, M. J., Brewer, K. B., & Ibrahim, R. (2012). A meta-analysis of experimental studies of diversion programs for juvenile offenders. *Clinical Psychology Review, 32*(10), 26–33.

Seroczynski, A. D. (2016). Reading for life and adolescent re-arrest: Evaluating a unique juvenile diversion program. *Journal of Policy Analysis and Management, 35*(3), 662–682.
Shen, A. (2016). The role of the study-work school: A Chinese case study on early intervention and child-centred juvenile justice. *Youth Justice, 16*(2), 95–112. https://doi.org/10.1177/1473225415601250
Siddiky, L. R. (2011). Keep the court room doors closed so the doors of opportunity can remain open: An argument for maintaining privacy in the juvenile justice system. *Howard Law Journal, 55*(1), 205–246.
Smith, D. J., & McVie, S. (2003). Theory and method in the Edinburgh study of youth transitions and crime. *British Journal of Criminology, 43*(1), 169–195. https://doi.org/10.1093/bjc/43.1.169
Smith, R. (2014). Re-inventing diversion. *Youth Justice, 14*(2), 109–121. https://doi.org/10.1177/1473225414537567
Sprott, J., & Myers, N. (2011). Set up to fail: The unintended consequences of multiple bail conditions. *Canadian Journal of Criminology and Criminal Justice, 53*(4), 404–423.
Stalford, H., Cairns, L., & Marshall, J. (2017). Achieving child friendly justice through child friendly methods: Let's start with the right to information. *Social Inclusion, 5*(3), 207–218. https://doi.org/10.17645/si.v5i3.1043
Steiner, B., Hemmens, C., & Bell, V. (2006). Legislative waiver reconsidered: General deterrent effects of statutory exclusion laws enacted post-1979. *Justice Quarterly, 23*(1), 34–59. https://doi.org/10.1080/07418820600552444
Suaalii-Sauni, T., Tauri, J., & Webb, R. (2018). Exploring Maori and Samoan youth justice: Aims of an international research study. *Journal of Applied Youth Studies, 2*(5), 29–40. https://search.informit.org/doi/10.3316/informit.974776648942534
Sullivan, C. J., & Latessa, E. (2011). The coproduction of outcomes: An integrated assessment of youth and program effects on recidivism. *Youth Violence and Juvenile Justice, 9*(3), 191–206.
Sullivan, C. J., Dollard, N., Sellers, B., & Mayo, J. (2010). Rebalancing response to school-based offenses: A civil citation program. *Youth Violence and Juvenile Justice, 8*(4), 279–294. https://doi.org/10.1177/1541204009358656
Sullivan, C. J., Veysey, B. M., Hamilton, Z. K., & Grillo, M. (2007). Reducing out-of-community placement and recidivism: Diversion of delinquent youth with mental health and substance use problems from the justice system. *International Journal of Offender Therapy and Comparative Criminology, 51*(5), 555–577. https://doi.org/10.1177/0306624X06296237
Sykes, G. M. (1958). *The society of captives. A study of a maximum security prison.* Princeton University Press.
Taylor, C. (2016). *Review of the youth justice system in England and Wales.* Ministry of Justice.

Tressider, J., & Putt, J. (2005). *Review of data on juvenile remandees in Tasmania: Final report*. Australian Institute of Criminology.

Tyler, T. R. (1988). What is procedural justice? Criteria used by citizens to assess the fairness of legal procedures. *Law & Society Review, 18*, 51–74.

UN General Assembly. (1990, December 14). *United Nations Guidelines for the Prevention of Juvenile Delinquency (The Riyadh Guidelines)*. 45/112.

UnitingCare Burnside. (2009). *Releasing the pressure on remand: Bail support solutions for children and young people in New South Wales*. UnitingCare Burnside. http://www.ncoss.org.au/resources/091028-Releasing-thepressure.pdf

Vaswani, N. (2014). *Speech, language and communication difficulties*. Centre for Youth and Criminal Justice.

Velez, G., Hahn, M., Recchia, H., & Wainryb, C. (2020). Rethinking responses to youth rebellion: Recent growth and development of restorative practices in schools. *Current Opinion in Psychology, 35*, 36–40. https://doi.org/10.1016/j.copsyc.2020.02.011

Weijers, I. (2004). Requirements for communication in the courtroom: A comparative perspective on the Youth Court in England/Wales and The Netherlands. *Youth Justice, 4*(1), 22–31. https://doi.org/10.1177/147322540400400103

Weijers, I., & Hokwerda, Y. M. (2003). Patterns and possibilities for pedagogical communication in juvenile courts: England and Wales and The Netherlands. In F. Dünkel & K. Drenkhahn (Eds.), *Youth violence: New patterns and local responses*. Ernst-Moritz-Arndt-Universität.

Williams, C., Griffin, K. W., Mehta, R. K., & Botvin, G. J. (2021). Testing an evidence-based drug abuse and violence preventive approach adapted for youth in juvenile justice diversionary settings. *Health & Justice, 9*, 1–12. https://doi.org/10.1186/s40352-021-00128-8

Wylie, L. E., Clinkinbeard, S. S., & Hobbs, A. (2019). The application of risk–needs programming in a juvenile diversion program. *Criminal Justice and Behavior, 46*(8), 1128–1147. https://doi.org/10.1177/0093854819859045

Wilson, H. A., & Hoge, R. D. (2013). The effect of youth diversion programs on recidivism: A meta-analytic review. *Criminal Justice and Behavior, 40*(5), 497–518. https://doi.org/10.1177/0093854812451089

Winstanley, M., Webb, R. T., & Conti-Ramsden, G. (2019). Psycholinguistic and socioemotional characteristics of young offenders: Do language abilities and gender matter? *Legal and Criminological Psychology, 24*, 195–214. https://doi.org/10.1111/lcrp.12150

Wong, J. S., Bouchard, J., Gravel, J., Bouchard, M., & Morselli, C. (2016). Can at-risk youth be diverted from crime? A meta-analysis of restorative diversion programs. *Criminal Justice and Behavior, 43*(10), 1310–1329. https://doi.org/10.1177/0093854816640835

World Health Organization. (2018). *Adverse childhood experiences international questionnaire. In Adverse Childhood Experiences International Questionnaire (ACE-IQ)*. WHO. Retrieved April 5, 2023 from https://www.who.int/publications/m/item/adverse-childhood-experiences-international-questionnaire-(ace-iq)

Zelle, H., Romaine, C. L. R., & Goldstein, N. E. (2015). Juveniles' Miranda comprehension: Understanding, appreciation and totality of circumstances factors. *Law and Human Behavior, 39*(3), 281–293.

Zimring, F. E., Langer, M., & Tanenhaus, D. S. (Eds.). (2017). *Juvenile justice in global perspective* (Vol. 1). NYU Press.

CHAPTER 5

Reintegration

Abstract Article 40(1) of the CRC requires states parties to treat children in a way that takes into account the desirability of promoting their reintegration in society. As such, reintegration is a fundamental principle of the rights-based approach to children in conflict with the law. Building on Chapter 3 on 'Prevention' and Chapter 4 on 'Diversion and Justice', this chapter aims to present the evidence around reintegration, highlighting measures that support a child's desistance from offending. In this regard, it features studies that show how a child in conflict with the law can be exit the justice system and return safely to their families and communities, including following a period of detention. It begins with developing a rights-respecting approach to reintegration. After that, it explores interventions that support positive outcomes for reintegration—such as support for families, peer relationships and the right to rest and leisure, educational rights, healthcare, addressing the needs of discriminated groups and fostering positive relationships—and deprivation of liberty. The research finds that there is significant support for a focus on reintegration at all stages of the justice process in line with the rights-based approach.

Keywords Children's rights · Children in conflict with the law · Reintegration · Deprivation of liberty · Support

U. Kilkelly et al., *Children in Conflict with the Law*, Palgrave Critical Studies in Human Rights and Criminology, https://doi.org/10.1007/978-3-031-36652-9_5

Introduction

As Chapter 2 explains, the rights-based approach requires a focus on children's rights, grouped according to three themes or phases—Protection rights, considered in Chapter 3, emphasises the importance of protecting the child's fundamental rights in order to prevent them coming into conflict with the law; Diversion and Justice rights, discussed in Chapter 4, seek to protect the child from the harms of the justice system through diversion and the guarantees of legal safeguards and adapted processes, and 'Reintegration', discussed in this chapter, which requires a consistent focus on the child's long-term future, prioritising measures that protect the right of the child to return safely to their communities, following exit from the justice system. Viewing reintegration as a fundamental principle of the rights-based approach, as derived from Article 40(1) of the CRC, requires states parties to treat children in a way that 'reinforces the child's respect for the human rights and fundamental freedoms of others, and which takes into account the child's age and the desirability of promoting the child's reintegration and assuming a constructive role in society'. This is further emphasised by guidance of the Committee on the Rights of the Child which makes clear that the goal of reintegration should be prioritised for children in contact with the youth justice system (Committee on the Rights of the Child, 2019).

As discussed in previous chapters, scholarly research on children's pathways into and out of the justice system provides rich insights into the lives and experiences of children in conflict with the law. In this regard, Chapter 3 presented the research on how breaches of children's rights in relation to health, education, family care and so on can lead to increased contact with the justice system, while fostering greater respect for rights can help to prevent this contact. Chapter 4 then presented the evidence base in favour of approaches that seek to divert the child away from the justice system, when they come into conflict with the law, setting out the research emphasising the importance of ensuring that the child's rights are protected during the justice process. Building on this research, the aim of this chapter is thus to present the evidence around reintegration, highlighting measures that support a child's desistance from offending. In this regard, it features studies that show how a child in conflict with the law can leave the justice system and return safely to their families and communities, including following a period of detention. It begins with a reminder of the importance of the general principles of children's rights to all actions aiming to support the child's reintegration into society.

Developing a Rights-Respecting Approach to Reintegration

The Best Interests of the Child

Article 3 of the CRC provides that in all actions concerning the child the best interests of the child must be a primary consideration. Within the youth justice system, one of the consequences of the best interests principle is that the focus should remain on rehabilitation and reintegration for all children (Committee on the Rights of the Child, 2019; UN General Assembly, 1985) ensuring, throughout any contact with the justice system, that children are treated as children. Even where children have committed serious offences, weight should be given to the child's best interests as well as to the need to promote reintegration (Committee on the Rights of the Child, 2019, para. 76).

Adequate realisation of a child's rights under Article 3 requires states parties to adopt a rights-respecting approach to all of the rights protected within the CRC and to 'secure the holistic physical, psychological, moral and spiritual integrity of the child and promote his or her human dignity' (Committee on the Rights of the Child, 2013, section I.A.). This implies that in any intervention or measure applied within the youth justice system, the goal of reintegration must be pursued in a manner which reinforces respect for all of the rights of the child under the CRC. Throughout a child's contact with the justice system, then, the best interests of the child should be taken into account. This is especially important with regard to the sanctions or measures imposed on a child who comes into conflict with the law and is directly related to the requirement that a child should be deprived of liberty only as a measure of last resort and for the shortest appropriate period of time (Article 37, CRC). This reflects the harm that detention can cause children and the widespread international concern about the failure to protect the rights of children deprived of liberty (Nowak, 2019). The Committee on the Rights of the Child has commented that the concept of best interests aims to ensure 'the full and effective enjoyment of all the rights recognized in the Convention and the holistic development of the child' (Committee on the Rights of the Child, 2013); as such, an application of the concept within the justice context must take into account the needs and development of the child in an individualised and holistic way, and ensure that all of the rights children are entitled to under the CRC, set out in Chapter 2, are fully respected and realised.

Desistance and the Child's Right to Development

As previously discussed in Chapter 3, there is a need both to recognise that children's offending must be situated in the context of our knowledge of child development more broadly, and that continued involvement in offending behaviour represents a threat to children's rights to life, survival and development, as outlined under Article 6 of the Convention. Similar considerations apply in relation to reintegration and the need to support a child's desistance and their path out of the justice system. Research in this area reinforces the view that child offending takes place in a complex system of biology, environment, cultural factors and individual factors; it is necessary to recognise these bioecological components when considering diversion or desistence (Belciug et al., 2016; Burt, 2022; Snyder & Duchschere, 2022). Research on young people's desistance from offending reinforces the core message of the international standards that children should continue to be treated as children in their contact with the justice system, prioritising an individualised, child-centred approach. Supporting the process of desistance is crucial to ensuring that children's right to life, survival and development is adequately respected when they come into conflict with the law. A significant body of international literature helps us understand how people at different life stages break the cycle of offending. While it rarely engages with children's rights, the literature nonetheless supports the view that desistance is often linked to the process of maturation with direct relevance to children's right to development under Article 6, as well as their evolving capacity, under Article 5 of the CRC (Evans-Chase et al., 2013; Rocque, 2015; Shapland & Bottoms, 2011; Weerman, 2010).

While most children will desist from offending as they mature, a minority continue to commit offences for a longer period of time (Farrington, 1986) for a variety of reasons. Differentiating between the young people who desist from offending and those who continue to offend into adulthood has been the subject of discussion in the literature, and different typologies of offending patterns have been put forward to explain this. Scholars such as Moffitt have posited that there were two distinct types of offending patterns—'adolescent-limited' offenders and 'life-course persistent' offenders; while those in the former group tend to stop engaging in offending behaviour as they mature, the latter category continue to engage in criminal behaviour in a persistent manner into adulthood (see discussion Skardhamar, 2009). Despite concerns as to whether this approach is supported by sufficiently compelling evidence (Skardhamar, 2009), it nonetheless highlights that many young people do in fact desist from offending behaviour as they grow into adulthood. The categorisation also risks losing sight of the other pathways that young people in conflict with the law experience. For instance, a German study—Crime in the Modern City—looking at rates of self-reports of urban crime among a cohort of over 3,000 adolescents highlighted multiple different patterns that exist in adolescent offending behaviour, including categories like adolescent intensive offenders, low-level offenders, early-desistance offenders, persistent offenders and early intensive/desistance offenders (Bors & Reinecke, 2010; Mazerolle et al., 2010; Seddig & Reinecke, 2017). As mentioned in chapter 3, studies highlight the difficulties inherent in categorisation and attempts to predict trajectories of offending behaviour. More recent studies also highlight the difficulties inherent in making generalisations about young people's involvement in offending, and their desistance from it (McAra & McVie, 2022).

According to the research, both individual motivation and external supports are important for desistance. Studies have highlighted that young people who were engaged in desistance processes had often reached a point where they no longer wanted to engage in offending behaviour (Martí et al., 2021; Pyrooz & Decker, 2011; Shapland & Bottoms, 2011; Terry & Abrams, 2015). Individual motivation to change can be an important prerequisite for and play a crucial role in activating other resources in the desistance process, such as relationships with important figures in the young person's life (Cann et al., 2005). Individual motivation to enact change can also influence both successful completion of intervention programmes and successful outcomes subsequent to participation in these programmes (Araújo et al., 2021).

Internal processes and emotions may also have an impact on desistance (Hosser et al., 2008), with research suggesting that interventions that encourage young people to take responsibility for their behaviour and acknowledge the negative consequences of their actions may prevent further recidivism (Hosser et al., 2008). Some studies highlight that for some people, downplaying and distancing oneself from earlier involvement in offending and reconstructing self-identity is an important part of the desistance process (McAra & McVie, 2022). The development of resilience through introspection may also help to support desistance from crime (Fitzpatrick (née Taylor), 2011; Zemel et al., 2016). This is further evidenced by the reported effectiveness of recidivism interventions based on improving psychological resilience in young people (Hodgkinson et al., 2021). Moreover, it has been suggested that physiological and neurological development during adolescence and puberty may present a unique opportunity to 'recalibrate' previously embedded physiological mechanisms around stress and divert young people on positive developmental trajectories (Gunnar et al., 2019; Perry et al., 2020). Taken together, this suggests that there is a uniquely sensitive period of development wherein positive social environments can have a significant impact on future development and behaviour.

Where individual motivation to change exists, external sources are important to support and sustain processes of change (Shapland & Bottoms, 2011). The literature has highlighted that social opportunities facilitate or restrict individual decisions, as well as an internal motivation or need for change (Deuchar, 2009; Gormally, 2014). Studies with young people who had left detention have highlighted that supports were vital to enable young people to access services, build a routine and stay motivated (Nugent, 2015). The Edinburgh of Youth Transitions and Crime has also highlighted the importance of both individual agency and appropriate supports in the desistance journey into adulthood, emphasising that this process is heavily influenced by opportunity, structures and relationships, in addition to individual motivation (McAra & McVie, 2022).

Desistance processes can take a number of different forms, which can depend on a combination of individual factors relating to the young person themselves, and the social and economic environment in which they live (Murray, 2009). It is important to note that the desistance process is often difficult for young people; they can sometimes experience bullying and loss of status when they choose to disengage from offending behaviour and peers involved in offending (Murray, 2012). For some young people, desistance can be a long, complicated and unpredictable process (McAra & McVie, 2022; Webster et al., 2006). These messages support the fundamental concept that in responding to children in conflict with the law, an individualised and child-centred approach which takes the best interests of children into account is crucial to support children to stay out of trouble and engage more constructively in society. Engaging with children, including through participation decision-making, is critical as is the need to reinforce supports in areas such as education, health and family supports, if a child's development beyond the youth justice system is to be secured.

Intervening to Support Positive Outcomes

Article 40 (1) of the CRC sets out the right of every child in conflict with the law to 'be treated in a manner consistent with the promotion of the child's sense of dignity and worth' and in a manner 'which reinforces the child's respect for the human rights and fundamental freedoms of others'. Although public safety is a legitimate aim of youth justice, the Committee on the Rights of the Child has emphasised that this must be pursued in a manner which respects and protects the rights of the child not least because offending by young people tends to decrease in systems that adhere to these principles (Committee on the Rights of the Child, 2019, para. 3). Research has, for example, identified a number of protective factors in predicting the likelihood of reoffending, including contact with prosocial peers, access to employment or other vocational roles, education, current social skills and prosocial beliefs/attitudes (Hay et al., 2020). The issues that bring young people into contact with the justice system are intersectional and often complex (Skowyra & Cocozza, 2006); therefore significant investment of time and other resources is required to meaningfully impact change (Becroft, 2009). As discussed in Chapter 3, these factors cross multiple domains in children's lives and are strongly related to many of the rights set out in Chapter 2, including children's rights in relation to health, to family care and to rest and leisure. The scholarship on children's experiences of contact with the youth justice system and evaluations of interventions carried out with children highlight the continued importance of these rights and interests when children come into conflict with the law. The following section highlights some of the literature which discusses how interventions with children in the justice system can help to support positive outcomes and ultimately, exit from contact with the justice system, highlighting the ongoing importance of respect for the full range of rights for all children.

Support for Families

Chapter 2 highlighted the significant emphasis in the children's rights standards on family contact and parental involvement in a child's life when they come into contact with the justice system, a point reinforced in Chapter 3 under Prevention rights. It noted that parents or the extended family or community should provide direction and guidance to the child in the exercise of their rights in a manner consistent with their evolving capacities. Article 5 of the CRC has particular relevance here, highlighting the influential role of parents in the child's enjoyment of their rights in the justice system (Kilkelly, 2020). Further, Chapter 3 discussed how better support for children's rights in relation to the family may help to prevent children from becoming involved in offending and harmful contact with the justice system. The Committee on the Rights of the Child has repeatedly emphasised the importance of the family in prevention efforts, in securing the rights of the child when they are in contact with the youth justice system and in efforts to support desistance and reintegration (Committee on the Rights of the Child, 2019).

Given the importance of the family in children's development and social lives, it is perhaps unsurprising that the family has been a target for interventions by state authorities when children come into conflict with the law, and literature in the area highlights some of the associated opportunities and potential challenges. While styles of parenting can impact negatively on young people's offending behaviour, a child's family can also exert a significant positive influence to support desistance efforts (Stout et al., 2017). For this reason, and given the importance of these relationships, some research suggests that interventions to promote children's pathways out of conflict with the law need to pay attention to family members—particularly parents—as well as to the young people themselves (Baglivio et al., 2017). Studies have found that factors such as a sense of family belonging can have a significant impact on adverse behaviour (Stone et al., 2023). For example, some reviews of functional family therapy and multi-systemic therapies have shown reductions in reoffending rates following engagement, though these interventions can be resource-intensive (Whyte, 2004). In some cases, significant changes resulted from engagement, both for young people and for parents; in a study of an Australian multi-systemic therapy-based approach, for example, parents highlighted that benefits included that they were 'calmer, more focused, and used the skills they had learned' through participation in the programme, and further, it was found that the functioning of families overall was improved by participation in the programme (Stout et al., 2017). Research has demonstrated that family-based interventions are effective for children and adolescents with disruptive behaviour; however, while there is some promising research in this area, there is a dearth of high-quality research at present (Sheidow et al., 2022).

While a focus on the family is broadly in line with the importance placed on parental involvement in the children's rights standards, it is important to pay attention to how this is done. For example, some approaches which seek to stimulate family engagement have taken a more punitive approach, focusing on the imposition of responsibility on parents for children's offending behaviour, through requirements such as attendance at parenting programmes (Evans, 2012). Studies of these types of interventions have found that, overall, these orders 'had little or no positive effect' on preventing further offending by young people (Evans, 2012). In addition, they have highlighted that a high percentage of the parents studied had previous involvement with a social care or other helping agency of some form (Evans, 2012), highlighting the level of need among these families. Findings such as these further reinforce the need to prefer strong social supports for families, as well as for children in contact with the youth justice system rather than punitive measures, in line with requirements under the CRC to provide appropriate support and assistance to parents in relation to child-rearing.

In addition to supporting the development of stronger family bonds, some studies have also highlighted the need to address family and parental disadvantage and trauma. It has been noted that there are significantly high rates of trauma and post-traumatic stress disorder in the parents of young people engaged with criminal justice, highlighting the need for comprehensive supports (Pieterse et al., 2022). A number of challenges in implementing and designing effective family-based interventions—such as retention, collaboration and trust—also need to be considered when designing interventions (NeMoyer et al., 2020). It has been suggested that strengths-based and family-focused interventions can, however, hold significant potential to promote more positive outcomes for young people (Case & Browning, 2021).

Some studies have found that there can be negative outcomes where families are excluded from or not kept informed about interventions with young people in conflict with the law. For example, in one study, family members and caregivers reported feeling that they were not included in decision-making processes or the development of care plans for young people when they were in an out-of-home placement (Mullis et al., 2005). In these situations, it has been suggested that children returning home after a period of time spent in detention may benefit from individual or family counselling to prepare the family for their return home, given the importance of family bonds in supporting desistance (Bath et al., 2019; Mullis et al., 2005).

Whether interventions are focused on building family bonds or fostering parental resilience in order to provide better support for children in conflict with the law, the literature is clear about the importance of the family as a site for the development of more positive outcomes for children in conflict with the law. In addition to the crucial role that the family plays in keeping children out of the justice system, then, it is clear that promoting children's rights with regard to the family is also central to promoting their safe exit from the justice system, moving on from offending behaviour and enabling them to assume a more positive role in society.

Peer Relationships and the Right to Rest and Leisure

As discussed in Chapter 3, a young person's involvement with peers and the manner in which they spend their leisure time have been the subject of research in relation to their involvement in offending behaviour. While it appears that involvement with peers who are themselves involved in offending, and lack of resources for leisure in the community environment, may contribute to young people's involvement in offending, conversely, providing positive opportunities for young people in relation to their leisure time is equally important in supporting young people to end their contact with the justice system, and to assume more positive roles in society (see further Case & Browning, 2021; Hazel et al., 2017). This is recognised within the international children's rights standards, with the Committee on the Rights of the Child noting the importance of peer association as well as participation in cultural and leisure activities to preventing children from coming into conflict with the law (Committee on the Rights of the Child, 2019, para. 10). When children come into the justice system, including when deprived of their liberty, these rights—to association with peers, as well as to enjoy sport, arts and leisure time activities—continue to be important (Committee on the Rights of the Child, 2019, para. 95).

The significance of peers—both forming attachments to more positive peers and dissociating from negative peers—features prominently in the desistance literature. Young people engaged in such processes have reported using particular strategies to navigate risks in their environment that may lead them back into offending (Terry & Abrams, 2015). In some cases, changing outward appearance and clothing choices were important in the desistance process, particularly for young people who were previously affiliated with gangs (Terry & Abrams, 2015). It is also acknowledged in these studies that leisure time and the positive aspects of these associations need to be considered; it has been suggested, in light of this, that intervention programmes that support desistance might usefully consider providing alternatives to the 'lost pleasures' associated with offending for young people (Murray, 2012). Ensuring that young people are able to access education and the job market can also be important steps in supporting a young person's desistance (Abeling-Judge, 2019; Schubert et al., 2018), along with opportunities to build social capital (Deuchar, 2009).

A young person's relationships can be particularly important in understanding how and if a young person desists successfully from offending behaviour (Martí et al., 2021). It has been highlighted that desistance programmes and processes must be understood within the context of human relationships (Sandøy, 2018). While relationships can play a number of different roles in a young person's life, depending on the networks they are a part of, pre-existing relationships such as relationships with parents or old friends can play an important role in the desistance process, particularly where young people reinterpret these relationships as 'hooks for change' (Martí et al., 2021). Some studies have highlighted the different roles that relationships can play; others suggest the possible benefits of 'experiential peers', i.e., peers with comparable life stories to support young people's desistance, as they can positively and authentically communicate the benefits of a life away from offending (Brierley, 2023). Within the Sheffield Desistance Study, it was highlighted that while friends could play a role in pulling young adults into further offending behaviour, family and intimate relationships could help young people to desist (Shapland & Bottoms, 2011). Young people involved in some studies of desistance highlighted the importance of ongoing relationships with particular peers (Sandøy, 2018; Terry & Abrams, 2015) and its relationship to external motivation to desist.

Overall, these studies highlight the importance to young people in the process of desistance of both peer relationships and leisure time. The synergies with the children's rights standards are very clear, especially important is the recognition that children's rights to rest, play and leisure support their exit from the justice system, even if rights relating to peer relationships are notably absent. Ensuring that children have positive social connections and attachment to more constructive social activities during leisure time is an important way to support more positive outcomes for children.

Promoting Educational Rights and Inclusion

Children's rights to education, set out in Articles 28 and 29 of the CRC, are of particular importance to children in conflict with the law including as a means to ensure they can return safely and constructively to their communities. Within the international children's rights standards, Liefaard has pointed to the strong 'pedagogical character' of the guidance given to states parties about how responses to children in conflict with the law should be directed (Liefaard, 2016). The Committee on the Rights of the Child emphasises the need to ensure judges and other decision-makers in the justice system should have ample opportunities at their disposal to direct children towards social and educational measures (Committee on the Rights of the Child, 2019, para. 18). Special attention is paid to the importance of the right to education for children deprived of their liberty (Committee on the Rights of the Child, 2019, para. 95).

The research literature clearly recognises the role of education in reducing levels of offending among young people (Sabates, 2008), and in this regard, endorses interventions which contain an educational component. Accessing educational opportunities can provide both short-term and long-term benefits for children in supporting their desistance from offending (Abeling-Judge, 2019). In a US study of the impact of reenrolment in education on patterns of offending, for instance, findings suggested that education could play an important part in facilitating desistance among early school-leavers, as well as being an important prevention strategy (Abeling-Judge, 2019). Further, school-based interventions—including those that focus on educational engagement, emotional regulation and prosocial behaviour—when well-implemented, have been shown to reduce rates of suspension and contact with police, although more research is needed to understand the precise mechanisms of this relationship (Bohnenkamp et al., 2021; Mielke & Farrington, 2021).

Some studies have highlighted the need to improve opportunities for young people and build on their strengths, rather than simply seeking to address any deficits or unmet needs in education (Case & Browning, 2021; Taylor, 2016). Scholars have suggested that there is a need to focus on getting young people onto the right path, rather than merely focusing on getting them off the wrong one (Schubert et al., 2018). Desistance research with men who were involved with the criminal justice system when they were younger shows how deeply interwoven social exclusion and economic inequality are with the adoption of 'hard-man' masculinities, which can in turn validate the depreciation of education (Cambridge et al., 2022). Therefore, educational attainment in and of itself may not be enough; decreasing social inequality, ensuring greater opportunities for those at risk of social exclusion and increasing the role of families in supporting learning and preventing anti-social behaviour in early years are equally important (Sabates, 2008). This reflects the approach in the international standards of a rights-based approach that recognises the importance of the whole child, viewed in their family and societal context.

The importance of ensuring that young people have access to educational opportunities—both as a means of preventing involvement in offending in the first place and in supporting young people to desist from offending—cannot thus be overstated. The Edinburgh of Youth Transitions and Crime found that successful desistance both during adolescence and into adulthood for individuals involved in the youth justice system often depended on educational inclusion; the study also emphasised the importance of further education and lifelong learning opportunities to support individuals in accessing more secure employment (McAra & McVie, 2022). Research on educational retention rates argues that three main categories are particularly important: situational (life circumstances), dispositional (individual characteristics) and institutional (the educational setting) (Carroll et al., 2009). A systematic review of barriers and facilitating factors found 'belongingness' to be a significant factor for increasing retention rates, a sense of attachment to the school, identification with its culture and positive relationships with peers and staff (Bowles & Brindel, 2017).

The research in this area emphasises the importance of providing educational opportunities and fostering educational inclusion among young people (McAra & McVie, 2022), further reinforcing the importance of realising children's educational rights in promoting positive outcomes for children when they come into conflict with the law. In more recent years, there has been a growing interest in trauma-sensitive schools, where 'challenging' behaviour is reframed instead as adaptive stress responses; consequently, there is a shift from punitive measures to increasing supports for young people and staff (Fondren et al., 2020).

The Role of Healthcare

The child's right to health (Art 24, CRC) is also important to support a safe and healthy exit from the justice system. In highlighting the need for reactions to offences within the youth justice system to be proportionate to the circumstances of the child, the Committee on the Rights of the Child has drawn attention to the relevance of factors relating to children's health, such as any mental health needs that the child may have (Committee on the Rights of the Child, 2019, para. 76). In support of this approach, international research on interventions with children in conflict with the law has highlighted the importance of attending to children's health needs, including their mental health, when they are in the justice system, in order to advance their right to health and to the wider principle of reintegration. Mirroring the approach in Chapter 3, the literature examined here addresses two principal issues in this context—mental health and substance use.

Mental Health

As previously discussed in Chapter 3, the scholarship in this area confirms that a significant proportion of young people in the youth justice system experience some form of mental health difficulty (Case & Browning, 2021; Kim et al., 2020; Tolou-Shams et al., 2019). Contact with the justice system can entail further health risks for young people who may already be marginalised, impacting their ability to successfully desist from offending. In addition, the experience of entering detention can be highly traumatising for young people, with such children already far more likely to experience mental health difficulties than their same-age peers (Hayes & O'Reilly, 2007). Many consider youth custody a particularly inappropriate setting for children facing these difficulties for this reason (Haysom et al., 2023; Nowak, 2019). In addition, research has demonstrated that young people in detention experience a wide range of complex mental health presentations that are often improperly treated with disciplinary or punitive measures (Whitley et al., 2022).

Conversely, the literature in this area demonstrates that interventions exist to help young people to address these challenges (Jeong et al., 2014), with interventions to address mental health difficulties taking a variety of forms. Some US studies have suggested that probation services aimed at young people were most effective when combined with rehabilitative therapies such as family-functioning therapy, multidimensional treatment foster care and cognitive behavioural therapy (CBT) (Robst, 2015). While there is often support for programmes such as CBT for young people, not all analyses of existing studies indicate that these approaches are effective in reducing recidivism (Kim et al., 2013). While CBT can be very effective for many cohorts, there are groups for whom this approach does not work, particularly those who are experiencing multiple challenges (Garber et al., 2016).

The interaction of mental health difficulties with other issues, particularly substance use, can impact on young people in conflict with the law and studies have suggested that interventions for young people should address all of these issues together (Kowalski, 2019). Dual diagnosis of a mental health issue and a substance dependence issue, for instance, can be particularly problematic where relevant services are not joined up. For instance, research has indicated a need for such services to work in a holistic way in order to be effective (MacGabhann et al., 2004). If not, young people can be 'bounced' between mental health and addiction services with gaps in care that can lead to disengagement (Murphy et al., 2018). In studies which have considered interventions for young people engaged with violence, it has been noted that approaches that interfere with the provision of mental health services in favour of deterrent sanctions or other behaviour management interventions may not be advisable (Caldwell & Van Rybroek, 2005; Jeong et al., 2014). Other studies similarly found that young people who received mental health care had a lower likelihood of re-arrest than those on standard probation supervision, though this was not always consistent across types of arrest (Robst, 2015). However, there is a need for further study to identify what specific elements of mental health treatment might be helpful in reducing repeat offending (Jeong et al., 2014).

Ensuring that young people receive appropriate mental health care promptly after arrest can be of greatest benefit (Christian, 2023; Robst, 2015) whereas increasing the capacity of professionals and recognising the role of parents has been found to be important in formulating plans for young people and identifying referral pathways to appropriate mental health services (Doulas & Lurigio, 2014). As a whole, this literature reinforces the necessity to pay attention to the mental health needs of young people in conflict with the law in the reaction taken to an offence and in efforts to support their reintegration, as part of a holistic, rights-based approach (Committee on the Rights of the Child, 2019, para. 76).

Substance Use

In addition to mental health needs, it is also necessary to consider interventions which address substance use by young people; a number of studies have emphasised the importance of ensuring that young people who need services in this area are matched to appropriate treatments without undue delay, taking account of behavioural and mental health needs and substance use issues (Hoeve et al., 2013). Where substance use is the target of a particular intervention or programme, there remains a need to consider this in tandem with the impact of other factors in an individual's life. Studies of mental health treatments have highlighted the need to integrate treatments for mental illness and substance use where both issues are present (Hammersley, 2011; Hoeve et al., 2013; Jeong et al., 2014).

Some scholars have suggested that there may be an important distinction to be made between young people who use illicit substances for the purposes of social interaction which may lead to criminal activity, and those with substance use or mental health disorders, designing interventions accordingly (Sullivan et al., 2007). Exposure to substance use within the family or community can significantly impact on a young person's ability to successfully reintegrate and avoid further contact with the justice system. For instance, in one qualitative study, participants described the lack of support received after a drug-related death within the family, describing instead that their children felt over-policed (Lambert et al., 2021).

A number of other factors can have significance for someone recovering from drug use and could be influenced by particular life events;

while it is not always easy to identify the factors that will promote or support desistance, the establishment of stable partnerships, becoming a parent and employment could be important factors in the desistance processes of young people who were involved in using drugs and in offending behaviours (Webster et al., 2006). Another key factor in determining how likely a young person is to engage with supports for substance use is how welcoming and youth-friendly the service is (Hawke et al., 2019). This is important as programmes designed specifically for young people can play a significant role in reducing and preventing substance use (Tremblay et al., 2020). An additional factor in service design and delivery is treatment engagement rates; in a study of childhood trauma and residential addiction engagement, results showed that the higher the levels of trauma the more treatment attempts were required (Lambert & Murphy, 2019). Failure to complete should be viewed as an aspect of the recovery journey, given that punitive responses to treatment disengagement are likely to increase shame and stigma and decrease motivation to continue to engage. Those who have experienced the most adversity tend to struggle most with service utilisation. Rather than a client blameworthy perspective, services should instead adapt to support those with the greatest needs (Lambert & Murphy, 2019).

There is an opportunity within schools and educational settings to deliver such care these approaches; however, research in this area highlights there are several effective means of delivering approaches such as family-based, digital and community-interventions (Das et al., 2016). Overall, there are many opportunities to create interventions that are led by the needs of individual young people with research reinforcing the complex, individualised and inter-connected nature of the issues faced by young people in conflict with the law (Lambert & Murphy, 2019). Therefore, recognising the inter-dependent nature of children's rights, the research here bears out that the child's right to health can best be met in tandem with addressing rights relating to the family, leisure time, education and social needs, and with consideration for the best interests of the child in each case.

Trauma Aware Services

Trauma aware services imply an understanding of the psychological and biological mechanisms through which traumatic experiences and/or adversity (on an individual, community and societal level) impact upon a young person's behaviour, motivation, outlook and understanding of the world around them (Lambert et al., 2017). In turn, a trauma-informed service endeavours to incorporate this understanding and awareness of trauma into their ethos, practice and service delivery. While a trauma aware service does not necessitate the provision of interventions to address experiences of trauma, it does maintain a focus on trauma responsiveness and understanding through every aspect of service delivery.

Trauma aware services, important at every stage of the justice process, recognise that trauma, and the prevailing impact of a traumatic experience, is complex and enduring requiring an approach that seeks to 'do no harm and reduce the potential for re-traumatisation' (Dermody et al., 2018). An awareness and understanding of trauma applies not only to clinical staff working with young people, but to every staff member with whom the young person may engage in a service or as part of the adjudicating process (Brown et al., 2021). This increases awareness of involuntary trauma response activations, thereby, reducing the potential for behavioural and emotional responses, disengagement and re-traumatisation (Lynch & Lambert, 2016). By this, services should move towards a multi-faceted approach to trauma and should be aware of their own power to enact or worsen trauma in young people (Spacey & Thompson, 2022).

Beyond the scope of service delivery, a trauma-sensitive perspective is especially useful within research and the design of services. For instance, for populations such as crossover youth (Modrowski et al., 2022), bereaved youth (Ford, 2022) and families (Lambert et al., 2021), or survivors of sexual abuse (Wareham et al., 2022), the trauma-sensitive perspective allows for a more comprehensive understanding of current and future behaviour. This approach also acknowledges and caters for the impact on staff of working with traumatised client groups emphasising staff well-being as part of the rights-based approach (Kilkelly & Bergin, 2022).

Addressing the Needs of Discriminated Groups

In Chapter 3, it was noted that certain groups of children are significantly over-represented in the justice system. The Committee on the Rights of the Child has highlighted that safeguards against discrimination within youth justice procedures are needed from the earliest stages of contact with the youth justice system (Committee on the Rights of the Child, 2019, para. 40), highlighting the particular need for gender-sensitive provision. Some of the literature in this area has also highlighted the need for gender-specific interventions to take girls' specific needs into account and to respond to different patterns of offending on the part of girls and boys (Anderson et al., 2016; Burman & Batchelor, 2009; Veysey & Hamilton, 2007).

While evidence is mixed, there is some evidence that gender-responsive programmes can produce positive results both in relation to recidivism and in relation to other outcomes, such as the development of positive support systems, access to employment and increases in self-esteem and empowerment (Anderson et al., 2016). Gender-sensitive and trauma-informed substance use interventions have shown some promising results (Brown et al., 2021; Tolou-Shams et al., 2021). However, there is often a lack of interventions designed specifically for young women (Burman & Batchelor, 2009) and this can lead to a lack of consideration for the specific needs and pathways of girls, as opposed to boys, and in some cases disengagement due to a lack of interest on the part of young women (Kelly, 2012).

In light of this, the importance of gender-responsive interventions for girls in conflict with the law has been highlighted in a number of studies (Anderson et al., 2016; Ho & Rocheleau, 2021; Parrish et al., 2021; Veysey & Hamilton, 2007; Williams-Butler et al., 2022). Research has suggested that gender-responsive interventions should contain a number of specific elements; they should provide an integrated treatment model for young women; they should address trauma; promote resilience; and have a focus on young people's strengths and on building relationships (Anderson et al., 2016). While some studies have found young women to be especially receptive to education while they are in custody (Burman & Batchelor, 2009), there is a need to ensure that adequate supports are available in all parts of the system, including when young people leave custody and return to their communities. The specific gendered consequences of 'welfare inaction' and failure to provide appropriate assistance to young women can lead to continued interaction with and exposure to the adult criminal justice system, which in turn can have more serious consequences in terms of further exclusion and marginalisation (Myers, 2013). Equally, it has been highlighted that there is a need to consider the inter-connected factors and issues that can impact on girls' offending; some interventions are aimed at addressing one specific problem, rather than considering the inter-connected nature of the factors involved (Anderson et al., 2016). While research in this area is still nascent, findings from longitudinal assessments of gender-responsive programmes have yielded promising results in the reduction or risk of offending (Belisle et al., 2022; Davis, 2020).

It has been highlighted that there is also a need to ensure that interventions address specific issues that are faced by young men. The value of specific programmes which address boys' issues, particularly around masculinities, has been highlighted (Harland & McCready, 2014). This is particularly important given the significant over-representation of boys within the youth justice system and the extent to which males are more likely to receive harsh treatment, including transfer to adult court and a custodial sentence, especially when involved with serious offending (Cauffman et al., 2007).

Other biases also operate to prevent children in conflict with the law enjoying equal access to their right to reintegration, and research highlights the need to ensure a non-discriminatory approach to children in conflict with the law. Implicit bias in educators, for instance, can significantly impact on children's pathways into and out of contact with the youth justice system (Hughes et al., 2020) and studies have found that young people who experienced race and ethnicity-based victimisation at school were at increased risk for early school leaving and criminal justice contact (Peguero et al., 2015). In an Irish context, children from the Traveller community, an ethnic minority, face bias with respect to peer rejection and lower teacher expectation (McGinley & Keane, 2021). More widely, research has shown that underinvestment in schools can lead to the overuse of school exclusions, which disproportionately affect children most in need of positive school experiences, highlighting the need for substantial investment in schooling and education (Irwin-Rogers et al., 2020). The need to pay particular attention to the needs and respond to the particular vulnerabilities of Black, Asian and Minority Ethnic groups has also been recognised in the UK context (Case & Browning, 2021). It has further been argued that prosecution and sentencing processes often serve to further entrench black, indigenous and ethnic minority children more deeply within youth justice systems, and a case has been made for the need for greater community engagement and a process of justice reinvestment within communities to begin to counter some of these negative impacts (Cunneen, 2020; White, 2015).

Research highlights the need to proactively adapt services to the particular needs of young people. For example, traditional probation services have been said to be largely ineffective at meeting the complex needs of young people with disabilities and often result in high levels of recidivism (Kim et al., 2021). This highlights the needs for specific and person-centred interventions that are driven by individual needs in line with a rights-based approach. Similarly, other further marginalised or vulnerable groups of young people possess complex needs in terms of their aftercare and support, which should be embedded within any probation service (Lee & Taxman, 2020).

Fostering Positive Relationships with Young People

The development of positive relationships, particularly those which foster and support active participation among young people in interventions, is an important aspect of supporting young people's reintegration. In addition to being an important aspect of working towards the goals related to reintegration set out in Article 40 (1) of the CRC, this is also important when viewed through the lens of children's rights under Article 12 of the Convention and the child's right to be heard in all matters affecting them.

Research shows that the development of positive relationships may help to foster more positive outcomes for young people and assist them in their journeys towards desistance and the assumption of more positive roles in society. The Edinburgh of Youth Transitions and Crime recently highlighted that young people's experiences of the care and justice systems were 'very much dependent on the quality of the individual staff whom people encounter', reinforcing the importance of relationships with young people, and the training and specialisation of professionals (McAra & McVie, 2022). Similar findings have been documented in the evaluations of particular approaches and practices. In some diversionary interventions, the development of personal relationships between young people and mentors or facilitators was deemed to be an important factor in supporting positive outcomes (Belciug et al., 2016; Seroczynski, 2016). In studies of probation practice, the approach of practitioners has been found to be particularly important, especially where there is a focus on building relationships between youth workers, other practitioners and young people (Gunay & Bacon, 2020). In a study of a multi-systemic therapy-based programme in New South Wales, it was highlighted that the 'creative and flexible approach' adopted by facilitators was crucial to achieving successful outcomes (Stout et al., 2017). Similarly, building a helping relationship between young people and practitioners is significantly impacted by the development of trust, mutual respect and advocacy (Drake et al., 2014). Better experiences with youth services and better case management serve as a protective factor for young people exiting probation (Li et al., 2019). In other words, the value of taking time to build meaningful relationships based on respect, trust, empathy and acceptance—among other issues—is important for young people and youth workers (Harland & McCready, 2014; O'Dwyer, 2019) and fostering greater engagement on the part of young people is key to supporting positive outcomes (Case & Browning, 2021). This relationship-based approach has been found to be equally important for children deprived of liberty (Bamber et al., 2016).

Research has found that where positive relationships were established between young people and youth workers, it could have an important impact on young people by broadening their horizons and supporting positive change (Drake et al., 2014). In programmes where young people were paired with a mentor, particularly where young people engaged with mentors in an activity they found interesting, there were a number of positive outcomes, including improvements in mental health and the ability to set goals and plan ahead; in developing these gains, the 'excellent relationship' between mentors and young people was found to underpin all other advantages (Gunay & Bacon, 2020). Conversely, the absence of trust and poor communications with agencies can have a harmful impact on the outcomes of the young people engaging with them (Price, 2020).

Deprivation of Liberty

Article 37 (b) of the CRC imposes a duty on states parties to ensure that detention is only used as a last resort, for the shortest appropriate period of time. Despite this requirement, and although the rate of child detention has been in decline, the Global Study on Children Deprived of Liberty identified that there wor residentialere approximately 1.5 million children detained annually, 410,000 of which were detained in the justice system (Nowak, 2019). This caused the study to recommend that states 'rigorously apply' the CRC requirement, ensuring that children are only detained in 'truly exceptional cases' (Nowak, 2019, p. 668). While bail support schemes can be effective in reducing the use of detention on remand (Freeman, 2008), much greater longitudinal research is required to understand how to reduce the use of detention in a sustainable manner.

Healthcare and Education

Building on Article 37(c), which emphasises the need for strong protections for children's rights where they are deprived of their liberty, Chapter 2 highlights that several other international instruments stress the importance of rights-respecting approaches to detention in order to ensure that children experience the benefits of rights protections—healthcare and education, for instance—while in detention (Kilkelly & Bergin, 2022). The importance of ensuring the child's placement prepares them for their return to society when they leave is also enshrined in the rights-based approach, set out in Chapter 2. This is critical to both pursuing the overarching rights-based goal of reintegration and ensuring respect for children's rights and their best interests. While research explains the importance of these provisions, it also illustrates the challenges that surround their implementation, causing some to argue in favour of abolishing detention altogether (Goldson, 2005).

The international standard requiring the detention of children as a measure of last resort is thus predicated on the view that detention can cause children harm (Goldson & Kilkelly, 2013). It is particularly problematic when children are either detained alongside adults—a practice prohibited by Article 37 (c) of the CRC—or are detained in adult, prison-like conditions (Mendel, 2011). The European Committee for the Prevention of Torture has highlighted that the practice of detaining children with adults places children at risk of violence and ill-treatment, increases the use of solitary confinement and fails to ensure adequate contact with children's families (Kilkelly & Casale, 2012). The harms of detaining children in adult prison have also led to recommendations in favour of specialist child-centred facilities (Freeman & Seymour, 2010; Kilkelly & Bergin, 2022).

Regardless, concerns about the inadequate conditions in which children are detained are widespread, with overcrowding, poor medical care and nutrition, a lack of education and training, limited family communication and a lack of leisure and outdoor activities particularly acute (Nowak, 2019). Children interviewed for the Global Study lamented the lack of appropriate education and vocational training (p. 89) while also conveying their understanding of its importance to their future (p. 110).

On health, the Study found that children deprived of liberty will almost universally be 'distinguished with a high burden of ill-health' (Nowak, 2019, p. 117). At the same time, it noted that, in some circumstances, deprivation of liberty could be associated with positive health outcomes, even for children detained in the justice system (Nowak, 2019, p. 120). Such potential benefits are contingent on the quality of care in the place of detention and must be sustained after the child's release (Nowak, 2019, p. 121).

In addition to factors such as anxiety and depression, the capacity to regulate emotions is highly associated with offending behaviour in children. For instance, one study aimed to assess the relationship between anger, depression and other psychological problems in newly-detained young males (Kelly et al., 2019), and identified a positive relationship between anger, and both violent and non-violent offending behaviour (Kelly et al., 2019). This carries forward into future behaviour, where improvement in emotional regulation capacity has been found to significantly lower rates of recidivism (Docherty et al., 2022). Conversely, recent findings from the Edinburgh of Youth Transition and Crime highlighted that impulsive personality traits could inhibit desistance later in life as young people transition to adulthood (McAra & McVie, 2022).

The literature is replete with examples of the harms that detention causes children (Nowak, 2019) together with the illustrations of state failure to ensure detention is a safe, positive and rights-respecting experience (Cox, 2017). At the same time, there is support for detention that more closely aligns with international children's rights standards (Freeman & Seymour, 2010; Kilkelly, 2003) and a case has been made for a model of detention that centres around child-centred care and education, in line with the children's rights standards. This approach requires a range of legal and non-legal measures including specialisation, enhanced capacity of professional staff and a systematic child-centred approach throughout (Kilkelly & Bergin, 2022).

Returning to the Community

The CRC emphasises the importance of ensuring children are reintegrated into their community on release from detention and the literature in this area similarly highlights the fundamental importance of ensuring that suitable supports are available to children during this transition. When young people return to their communities, they can face a number of barriers to achieving reintegration in practice, including challenges in relation to education, employment and the possibility of re-arrest (Chung et al., 2007). Family, living circumstances and peer influence can also present difficulties for young people (Chung et al., 2007).

Research has highlighted the importance of supporting and facilitating reintegration as a protective factor in preventing future offending (Kubek et al., 2020). While programmes delivered with young people in detention can have an impact on the ability of young people to end their involvement in offending, the literature suggests that these gains can be difficult to sustain when young people return to their communities (Rajah et al., 2014), especially when the structure and support they received in the institutional setting is no longer available (Chung et al., 2007). Positive gains achieved during a period of detention or residential care can be difficult to maintain or sustain where there is a lack of meaningful supports available to young people on their return home (Myers, 2013). Young people can, for example, face challenges when attempting to re-enter education after time spent in detention (Belkin, 2020). A US-based study with young people in detention on their hopes and expectations for their educational pathways showed that ongoing support after release, post-detention, is crucial to continuing their education successfully (Noorman & Brancale, 2022).

The international standards highlight the importance of ensuring that aftercare supports are in place for children leaving detention (UN General Assembly, 1990; Committee on the Rights of the Child, 2007, 2019, para. 29). The literature emphasises the importance of adequate supports for children leaving detention, with a particular focus on supports to address social inequalities and deficiencies in the labour market (Rajah et al., 2014). Equally, the need to find stable long-term accommodation and to ensure that young people have something meaningful to do with their time following release is crucial (Myers, 2013). As research in Ireland has indicated, however, children often experience difficulties accessing appropriate supports, including aftercare placement, on leaving detention (Carr & Mayock, 2018). Scholars have highlighted the importance of ensuring that the underlying problems and needs of a young person continue to be addressed through a joint approach from mainstream children's services and those working in the youth justice system to provide appropriate services to address those needs (Gray, 2011). Research similarly highlights the continued importance of ensuring that children who leave detention continue to be treated as children (Hollingsworth, 2008). This is further reinforced in international standards which recommend that all young people should benefit from 'arrangements designed to assist them in returning to society, family life, education or employment after release' (UN General Assembly, 1990, para. 79).

It has been suggested that it may be useful to frame re-entry around a strengths-based approach, focusing on positive outcomes for children, rather than the reduction of harmful behaviour (Dempsey et al., 2021). Studies have highlighted that close supervision and effective service contacts can be important for children returning to the community, both in terms of preventing a return to offending behaviour and for supporting engagement in employment or education (Chung et al., 2007). While many stakeholders have a good awareness of the importance of interagency collaboration, there may be limitations in the awareness of stakeholders in how to effectively implement aftercare and reintegration plans (O'Neill et al., 2020). However, it is clear, from both the literature in the area and the international guidelines, that continuing to treat children in an age and developmentally appropriate manner, with consideration for their best interests and a focus on mainstream service provision, is critical to supporting children in their desistance efforts and in achieving the goals of Article 40 (1) of the CRC to promote children's reintegration and assumption of a constructive role in society.

Conclusion

This chapter presented the scholarly research that underpins measures that promote a child's reintegration into their community following contact with the justice system. Across a large body of literature, the key themes that emerged reflect strong alignment with rights-based approaches including measures that strengthen the child's health, education and family relationships. In addition, the research highlights the importance of approaches that are child-centred, focused on the child's best interests and development and seek to engage the child in positive and constructive ways. Like Chapters 3 and 4, this chapter also highlighted the need to tailor approaches and measures to the needs of especially vulnerable children or those from discriminated or minority groups, cohering with the rights-based and individualised approach. In general, it is evident that across disciplines and jurisdictions, large studies and small, lies a huge evidence base as to how to support children away from offending and the justice system. Combined with the rights-based focus, there is clearly significant support for a focus on reintegration at all stages of the justice process. Key to this, however, is the commitment to introduce this approach into practice. Implementation will be addressed in the concluding chapter which now follows.

Bibliography

Abeling-Judge, D. (2019). Stopping out and going back: The impact of educational attainment on criminal desistance among stopped-out offenders. *Crime & Delinquency, 65*(4), 527–554. https://doi.org/10.1177/0011128719828352

Anderson, V. R., Walerych, B. M., Campbell, N. A., Barnes, A. R., Davidson, W. S., Campbell, C. A., Onifade, E., & Petersen, J. L. (2016). Gender-responsive intervention for female juvenile offenders: A quasi-experimental outcome evaluation. *Feminist Criminology, 14*(1), 24–44. https://doi.org/10.1177/1557085116677749

Araújo, G. E., Cruz, O. S., & Moreira, D. (2021). Maladaptive Beliefs of young adults in interpersonal relationships: A systematic literature review. *Trauma, Violence, & Abuse, 24*(2), 646–661. https://doi.org/10.1177/15248380211038684

Baglivio, M. T., Wolff, K. T., Piquero, A. R., DeLisi, M., & Vaughn, M. G. (2017). Multiple pathways to juvenile recidivism: Examining parental drug and mental health problems, and markers of neuropsychological deficits among serious juvenile offenders. *Criminal Justice and Behavior, 44*(8), 1009–1029. https://doi.org/10.1177/0093854817714810

Bamber, J., Brolly, C., Mills, E., & Farrar, C. (2016). *Building relationships with young people in oberstown to improve pro-social outcomes*. Centre for Effective Services.

Bath, E., Kim, B. K. E., Amani, B., López, S. A., & Milburn, N. G. (2019). Lessons learned: Challenges and strategies for conducting family-based intervention research in juvenile justice settings. *Journal of the American Academy of Child & Adolescent Psychiatry, 58*(11), 1038–1041. https://doi.org/10.1016/j.jaac.2019.05.011

Becroft, A. (2009). Are there lessons to be learned from the youth justice system? *Policy Quarterly, 5*(2), 9–18.

Belciug, C., Franklin, C., Bolton, K. W., Jordan, C., & Lehmann, P. (2016). Effects of goal commitment and solution building on the completion rates for a juvenile diversion program. *Criminal Justice and Behavior, 43*(7), 923–936. https://doi.org/10.1177/0093854815626753

Belisle, L. A., Salisbury, E. J., & Keen, J. (2022). Did they move on? An outcome evaluation of the gender-responsive program, girls...moving on. *Feminist Criminology, 17*(2), 223–251. https://doi.org/10.1177/15570851211065900

Belkin, L. D. (2020). Challenges with school re-entry for incarcerated youth and inadequacies of collaborative service provision by schools and agencies. In R. Papa (Ed.), *Handbook on promoting social justice in education* (pp. 2487–2523). Springer. https://doi.org/10.1007/978-3-030-14625-2_115

Bohnenkamp, J. H., Schaeffer, C. M., Siegal, R., Beason, T., Smith-Millman, M., & Hoover, S. (2021). Impact of a school-based, multi-tiered emotional and behavioral health crisis intervention on school safety and discipline. *Prevention Science, 22*, 492–503. https://doi.org/10.1007/s11121-020-01195-3

Bors, K., & Reinecke, J. (2010). Explaining the development of adolescent violent delinquency. *European Journal of Criminology, 7*(6), 499–520. https://doi.org/10.1177/1477370810376572

Bowles, T. V., & Brindle, K. A. (2017). Identifying facilitating factors and barriers to improving student retention rates in tertiary teaching courses: A systematic review. *Higher Education Research & Development, 36*(5), 903–919. https://doi.org/10.1080/07294360.2016.1264927

Brierley, A. (2023). Experiential peers cultivate a participation culture in youth justice. *Safer Communities, 22*(2), 78–90. https://doi.org/10.1108/SC-07-2022-0024

Brown, S. L., Wanamaker, K. A., Greiner, L., Scott, T., & Skilling, T. A. (2021). Complex trauma and criminogenic needs in a youth justice sample: A gender-informed latent profile analysis. *Criminal Justice and Behavior, 48*(2), 175–194.

Burman, M., & Batchelor, S. A. (2009). Between two stools? Responding to young women who offend. *Youth Justice, 9*(3), 270–285. https://doi.org/10.1177/1473225409345104

Burt, S. A. (2022). The genetic, environmental, and cultural forces influencing youth antisocial behavior are tightly intertwined. *Annual Review of Clinical Psychology, 18*, 155–178. https://doi.org/10.1146/annurev-clinpsy-072220-015507

Caldwell, M. F., & Van Rybroek, G. J. (2005). Reducing violence in serious juvenile offenders using intensive treatment. *International Journal of Law and Psychiatry, 28*(6), 622–636. https://doi.org/10.1016/j.ijlp.2004.07.001

Cambridge, G., Lynch, O., & Windle, J. (2022). *The Desistance journey—Into recovery and out of chaos*. Palgrave Macmillan/Springer Nature Switzerland AG.

Cann, J., Falshaw, L., & Friendship, C. (2005). Understanding 'what works': Accredited cognitive skills programmes for young offenders. *Youth Justice, 5*(3), 165–179. https://doi.org/10.1177/147322540500500303

Carr, N., & Mayock, P. (2018). *Children and young people in care and contact with the criminal justice system*. Irish Penal Reform Trust.

Carroll, D., Ng, E., & Birch, D. (2009). Retention and progression of postgraduate business students: An Australian perspective. *Open Learning: The Journal of Open and Distance Learning, 24*, 197–209.https://doi.org/10.1080/02680510903201599

Case, S., & Browning, A. (2021). *Child first justice: The research evidence-base* [full Report]. Loughborough University. https://hdl.handle.net/2134/14152040.v1

Cauffman, E., Piquero, A. R., Kimonis, E., Steinberg, L., Chassin, L., & Fagan, J. (2007). Legal, individual, and environmental predictors of court disposition in a sample of serious adolescent offenders. *Law and Human Behavior, 31*(6), 519–535.

Christian, D. D. (2023). Mandatory mental health screening for justice-involved youth: A national priority. *Youth Justice, 23*(1), 49–57. https://doi.org/10.1177/14732254211052334

Chung, H. L., Schubert, C. A., & Mulvey, E. P. (2007). An empirical portrait of community reentry among serious juvenile offenders in two metropolitan cities. *Criminal Justice and Behavior, 34*(11), 1402–1426. https://doi.org/10.1177/0093854807307170

Committee on the Rights of the Child. (2007, April 25). *General Comment No. 10 (2007) Children's rights in juvenile justice*. CRC/C/GC/10.

Committee on the Rights of the Child. (2013, May 29). *General comment No. 14 (2013) on the right of the child to have his or her best interests taken as a primary consideration (art. 3, para. 1)*. CRC/C/GC/14.

Committee on the Rights of the Child. (2019, September 19). *General comment No. 24 (2019) on children's rights in the child justice system*. CRC/C/GC/24.

Cox, A. (2017). *Trapped in a vice: The consequences of confinement for young people*. Rutgers University Press.

Cunneen, C. (2020). Youth justice and racialization: Comparative reflections. *Theoretical Criminology, 24*(3), 521–539.

Das, J. K., Salam, R. A., Arshad, A., Finkelstein, Y., & Bhutta, Z. A. (2016). Interventions for adolescent substance abuse: An overview of systematic reviews. *Journal of Adolescent Health, 59*(4), S61–S75. https://doi.org/10.1016/j.jadohealth.2016.06.021

Davis, A. (2020). *Women in crisis: An analysis of the benefits of gender-responsive and trauma-responsive treatment models for women in the criminal justice system*. Princeton University Senior Theses.

Dempsey, M. P., Davis, W. M., Forbes, P., Penkoff, C. B., Gonsoulin, S., & Harris, P. W. (2021). Juvenile justice administrator perspectives: Reframing reentry around positive youth outcomes. *Behavioral Disorders, 46*(3), 187–196. https://doi.org/10.1177/0198742920965134

Dermody, A., Gardner, C., Davis, S., Lambert, S., Dermody, J., & Fein, M. (2018). Resilience in the face of trauma: Implications for service delivery. *Irish Probation Journal, 15*, 161–178.

Deuchar, R. (2009). *Gangs, marginalised youth and social capital*. Trentham Books.

Docherty, M., Lieman, A., & Gordon, B. L. (2022). Improvement in emotion regulation while detained predicts lower juvenile recidivism. *Youth Violence and Juvenile Justice, 20*(2), 164–183. https://doi.org/10.1177/15412040211053786

Doulas, A. V., & Lurigio, A. J. (2014). Juvenile Crisis Intervention Teams (CITs): A qualitative description of current programmes. *The Police Journal, 87*(2), 114–125. https://doi.org/10.1350/pojo.2014.87.2.534

Drake, D. H., Fergusson, R., & Briggs, D. B. (2014). Hearing new voices: Reviewing Youth Justice Policy through practitioners' relationships with young people. *Youth Justice, 14*(1), 22–39. https://doi.org/10.1177/1473225413520360

Evans, R. (2012). Parenting orders: The parents attend yet the kids still offend. *Youth Justice, 12*(2), 118–133. https://doi.org/10.1177/1473225412447163

Evans-Chase, M., Kim, M., & Zhou, H. (2013). Risk-taking and self-regulation: A systematic review of the analysis of delinquency outcomes in the juvenile justice intervention literature 1996–2009. *Criminal Justice and Behavior, 40*(6), 608–628. https://doi.org/10.1177/0093854812469608

Farrington, D. P. (1986). Age and crime. *Crime and Justice, 7*, 189–250. http://www.jstor.org/stable/1147518

Fitzpatrick (née Taylor), C. (2011). What is the difference between 'desistance' and 'resilience'? Exploring the relationship between two key concepts. *Youth Justice, 11*(3), 221–234. https://doi.org/10.1177/1473225411420528

Fondren, K., Lawson, M., Speidel, R., McDonnell, C. G., & Valentino, K. (2020). Buffering the effects of childhood trauma within the school setting: A systematic review of trauma-informed and trauma-responsive interventions among trauma-affected youth. *Children and Youth Services Review, 109*, 104691. https://doi.org/10.1016/j.childyouth.2019.104691

Ford, S. (2022). Losing Someone Then Losing Yourself: Helping Juveniles in the Justice System Experiencing Grief With a Trauma-Informed Pretrial Diversion Program. *The Journal of Criminal Law & Criminology. Online, 112*, 197–213.

Freeman, S. (2008). The experience of young people remanded in custody: A case for bail support and supervision schemes. *Irish Probation Journal, 5*, 91–102.

Freeman, S., & Seymour, M. (2010). 'Just waiting': The nature and effect of uncertainty on young people in remand custody in Ireland. *Youth Justice, 10*(2), 126–142.

Garber, J., Frankel, S. A., & Herrington, C. G. (2016). Developmental demands of cognitive behavioral therapy for depression in children and adolescents: Cognitive, social, and emotional processes. *Annual Review of Clinical Psychology, 12*(1), 181–216. https://doi.org/10.1146/annurev-clinpsy-032814-112836

Goldson, B. (2005). Child imprisonment: A case for abolition. *Youth Justice, 5*(2), 77–90. https://doi.org/10.1177/147322540500500202

Goldson, B., & Kilkelly, U. (2013). International human rights standards and child imprisonment: Potentialities and limitations. *The International Journal of Children's Rights, 21*(2), 345–371.

Gormally, S. (2014). 'I've been there, done that...': A study of youth gang desistance. *Youth Justice, 15*(2), 148–165. https://doi.org/10.1177/1473225414549679

Gray, P. (2011). Youth custody, resettlement and the right to social justice. *Youth Justice, 11*(3), 235–249. https://doi.org/10.1177/1473225411420529

Gunay, A., & Bacon, A. M. (2020). Experiences of youth mentoring through street dance. *Youth Justice, 20*(3), 235–251. https://doi.org/10.1177/1473225419879248

Gunnar, M. R., DePasquale, C. E., Reid, B. M., Donzella, B., & Miller, B. S. (2019). Pubertal stress recalibration reverses the effects of early life stress in postinstitutionalized children. *Proceedings of the National Academy of Sciences, 116*(48), 23984–23988. https://doi.org/10.1073/pnas.1909699116

Hammersley, R. (2011). Pathways through drugs and crime: Desistance, trauma and resilience. *Journal of Criminal Justice, 39*(3), 268–272. https://doi.org/10.1016/j.jcrimjus.2011.02.006

Harland, K., & McCready, S. (2014). Rough justice: Considerations on the role of violence, masculinity, and the alienation of young men in communities and peacebuilding processes in Northern Ireland. *Youth Justice, 14*(3), 269–283. https://doi.org/10.1177/1473225414549696

Hawke, L. D., Mehra, K., Settipani, C., Relihan, J., Darnay, K., Chaim, G., & Henderson, J. (2019). What makes mental health and substance use services youth friendly? A scoping review of literature. *BMC Health Services Research, 19*(1), 1–16. https://doi.org/10.1186/s12913-019-4066-5

Hay, C., Stults, B., Copp, J., Young, B., & Hargrove, E. (2020). *Predicting reoffending and informing treatment for Florida residential youth*. The Florida State University College of Criminology & Criminal Justice.

Hayes, J., & O'Reilly, G. (2007) *Emotional intelligence, mental health and juvenile delinquency*. Cork. Juvenile Mental Health Matters.

Haysom, L., Kasinathan, J., & Singh, Y. (2023). Youth custody is no place for mentally ill children and young people. *Australasian Psychiatry*. https://doi.org/10.1177/10398562231155753

Hazel, N., Goodfellow, P., Liddle, M., Bateman, T., & Pitts, J. (2017). *"Now all I care about is my future": Supporting the shift: Framework for the effective resettlement of young people leaving custody*. Beyond Youth Custody.

Ho, T., & Rocheleau, G. C. (2021). Gender differences in risk assessment among youth adjudicated to juvenile correctional facilities. *Women & Criminal Justice, 31*(6), 463–475. https://doi.org/10.1080/08974454.2020.1727819

Hodgkinson, R., Beattie, S., Roberts, R., & Hardy, L. (2021). Psychological resilience interventions to reduce recidivism in young people: A systematic review. *Adolescent Research Review, 6*, 333–357. https://doi.org/10.1007/s40894-020-00138-x

Hoeve, M., McReynolds, L. S., Wasserman, G. A., & McMillan, C. (2013). The influence of mental health disorders on severity of reoffending in juveniles. *Criminal Justice and Behavior, 40*(3), 289–301. https://doi.org/10.1177/0093854812459639

Hollingsworth, K. (2008). Protecting rights at the margins of youth justice in England and Wales: Intensive fostering, custody and leaving custody. *Youth Justice, 8*(3), 229–244. https://doi.org/10.1177/1473225408096462

Hosser, D., Windzio, M., & Greve, W. (2008). Guilt and shame as predictors of recidivism: A longitudinal study with young prisoners. *Criminal Justice and Behavior, 35*(1), 138–152. https://doi.org/10.1177/0093854807309224

Hughes, T., Raines, T., & Malone, C. (2020). School pathways to the juvenile justice system. *Policy Insights from the Behavioral and Brain Sciences, 7*(1), 72–79. https://doi.org/10.1177/2372732219897093

Irwin-Rogers, K., Muthoo, A., & Billingham, L. (2020). *Youth violence commission final report*. Youth Violence Commission.

Jeong, S., Lee, B. H., & Martin, J. H. (2014). Evaluating the effectiveness of a special needs diversionary program in reducing reoffending among mentally Ill youthful offenders. *International Journal of Offender Therapy and Comparative Criminology, 58*(9), 1058–1080. https://doi.org/10.1177/0306624X13492403

Kelly, E. L., Novaco, R. W., & Cauffman, E. (2019). Anger and depression among incarcerated male youth: Predictors of violent and nonviolent offending during adjustment to incarceration. *Journal of Consulting and Clinical Psychology, 87*(8), 693–705. https://doi.org/10.1037/ccp0000420

Kelly, L. (2012). Representing and preventing youth crime and disorder: Intended and unintended consequences of targeted youth programmes in

England. *Youth Justice, 12*(2), 101–117. https://doi.org/10.1177/1473225412447160
Kilkelly, U. (2003). Children detention schools: Learning from international best practice. *Irish Criminal Law Journal, 13*(3), 15–19.
Kilkelly, U. (2020). "Evolving capacities" and "parental guidance" in the context of youth justice. *The International Journal of Children's Rights, 28*(3), 500–520. https://doi.org/10.1163/15718182-02803004
Kilkelly, U., & Bergin, P. (2022). *Advancing children's rights in detention*. Bristol University Press.
Kilkelly, U., & Casale, S. (2012). *Children's rights and the European Committee for the Prevention of Torture*. Council of Europe.
Kim, B. K. E., Gilman, A. B., Thompson, N., & De Leon, J. (2020). Statewide trends of trauma history, suicidality, and mental health among youth entering the juvenile justice system. *Journal of Adolescent Health, 68*(2), 300–307. https://doi.org/10.1016/j.jadohealth.2020.05.044
Kim, B. K. E., Johnson, J., Rhinehart, L., Logan-Greene, P., Lomeli, J., & Nurius, P. S. (2021). The school-to-prison pipeline for probation youth with special education needs. *American Journal of Orthopsychiatry, 91*(3), 375–385. https://doi.org/10.1037/ort0000538
Kim, B., Merlo, A. V., & Benekos, P. J. (2013). Effective correctional intervention programmes for juveniles: Review and synthesis of meta-analytic evidence. *International Journal of Police Science & Management, 15*(3), 169–189. https://doi.org/10.1350/ijps.2013.15.3.310
Kowalski, M. A. (2019). Adverse childhood experiences and justice-involved youth: The effect of trauma and programming on different recidivistic outcomes. *Youth Violence and Juvenile Justice, 17*(4), 354–384. https://doi.org/10.1177/1541204018809836
Kubek, J. B., Tindall-Biggins, C., Reed, K., Carr, L. E., & Fenning, P. A. (2020). A systematic literature review of school reentry practices among youth impacted by juvenile justice. *Children and Youth Services Review, 110*, 104773. https://doi.org/10.1016/j.childyouth.2020.104773
Lambert, S., & Murphy, R. (2019). The role of trauma in dual diagnosis. *Forum: Journal of the Irish College of General Practitioners*, 1–10.
Lambert, S., Gill-Emerson, G., Horan, A., & Naughton, A. (2017). *Moving towards trauma-informed care. A model of research and practice*. Cork Simon Community.
Lambert, S., O'Callaghan, D., & Frost, N. (2021). 'Special death': Living with bereavement by drug-related death in Ireland. *Death Studies, 46*(10), 2335–2345. https://doi.org/10.1080/07481187.2021.1939461
Lee, J. S., & Taxman, F. S. (2020). Using latent class analysis to identify the complex needs of youth on probation. *Children and Youth Services Review, 115*, 105087. https://doi.org/10.1016/j.childyouth.2020.105087

Li, D., Chu, C. M., Xu, X., Zeng, G., & Ruby, K. (2019). Risk and protective factors for probation success among youth offenders in Singapore. *Youth Violence and Juvenile Justice, 17*(2), 194–213. https://doi.org/10.1177/15412040187788

Liefaard, T. (2016). Child-Friendly Justice: Protection and participation of children in the justice system. *Temple Law Review, 88*(4), 905–927.

Lynch, O., & Lambert, S. (2016). *EU issue paper on child returnees to Europe from ISIL held territories in Syria/Iraq*. Radicalisation Awareness Network (RAN) Centre of Excellence.

MacGabhann, L., Scheele, A., Dunne, T., Gallagher, P., MacNeela, P., Moore, G., & Philbin, M. (2004). *Mental health and addiction services and the management of dual diagnosis in Ireland*. The Stationery Office.

Martí, J., Albani, E., Ibàñez, A., & Cid, J. (2021). Personal networks and desistance from crime in young offenders. *European Journal of Criminology, 18*(2), 235–253. https://doi.org/10.1177/1477370819842207

Mazerolle, P., Piquero, A. R., & Brame, R. (2010). Violent onset offenders: Do initial experiences shape criminal career dimensions? *International Criminal Justice Review, 20*(2), 132–146. https://doi.org/10.1177/1057567710368361

McAra, L., & McVie, S. (2022). *Cause and impacts of offending and criminal justice pathways: Follow-up of the Edinburgh Cohort at Age 35*. The University of Edinburgh.

McGinley, H., & Keane, E. (2021). "The school for the travellers and the blacks": Student and teacher perspectives on "choosing" a post-primary school with a high concentration of disadvantage. *Education Sciences, 11*(12), 777. https://doi.org/10.3390/educsci11120777

Mendel, R. A. (2011). *No place for Kids: The case for reducing juvenile incarceration*. The Annie E. Casey Foundation.

Mielke, M., & Farrington, D. P. (2021). School-based interventions to reduce suspension and arrest: A meta-analysis. *Aggression and Violent Behavior, 56*, 101518. https://doi.org/10.1016/j.avb.2020.101518

Modrowski, C. A., Chaplo, S. D., & Kerig, P. K. (2022). Advancing our understanding of the risk factors associated with crossover youth in the child welfare and juvenile justice systems: A trauma-informed research agenda. *Clinical Child and Family Psychology Review, 25*, 283–299. https://doi.org/10.1007/s10567-021-00370-4

Mullis, R. L., Mullis, A. K., Cornille, T. A., Kershaw, M. A., Beckerman, A., & Perkins, D. (2005). Young chronic offenders: A case study of contextual and intervention characteristics. *Youth Violence and Juvenile Justice, 3*(2), 133–150. https://doi.org/10.1177/1541204004273315

Murphy, K. D., Lambert, S., McCarthy, S., Sahm, L. J., & Byrne, S. (2018). "You don't feel": The experience of youth benzodiazepine misuse in Ireland.

Journal of Psychoactive Drugs, 50(2), 121–128. https://doi.org/10.1080/02791072.2017.1371365

Murray, C. (2009). Typologies of young resisters and desisters. *Youth Justice, 9*(2), 115–129. https://doi.org/10.1177/1473225409105491

Murray, C. (2012). Young people's perspectives: The trials and tribulations of going straight. *Criminology & Criminal Justice, 12*(1), 25–40. https://doi.org/10.1177/1748895811423089

Myers, R. R. (2013). The biographical and psychic consequences of 'welfare inaction' for young women in trouble with the law. *Youth Justice, 13*(3), 218–233. https://doi.org/10.1177/1473225413505385

NeMoyer, A., Gale-Bentz, E., Goldstein, N. E. S., & Pema Harvey, L. (2020). Factors associated with successful completion of a community-based, postarrest juvenile diversion program and subsequent rearrest. *Crime & Delinquency, 66*(5), 603–626. https://doi.org/10.1177/0011128719842377

Noorman, K., & Brancale, J. (2022). Barriers to school reentry: Perceptions of school reentry among detained and committed youth. *Youth Violence and Juvenile Justice*. https://doi.org/10.1177/15412040221147017

Nowak, M. (2019). *Global study on children deprived of liberty*. A/74/136.

Nugent, B. (2015). Reaching the 'hardest to reach.' *Youth Justice, 15*(3), 271–285. https://doi.org/10.1177/1473225414560276

O'Dwyer, K. (2019). Reducing youth crime: The role of mentoring. *Irish Probation Journal, 16*, 153–167.

O'Neill, S. C., Mathur, S. R., Cumming, T. M., Griller-Clark, H., & Strnadová, I. (2020). Stakeholder awareness of reintegration practices for incarcerated youth: A cross-national comparison. *Preventing School Failure: Alternative Education for Children and Youth, 65*(1), 1–11. https://doi.org/10.1080/1045988X.2020.1799184

Parrish, D. E., Thompson, R., Negi, N., & Alquicira, L. (2021). A national survey of probation staff of the needs, services and barriers of female youth in juvenile justice settings. *Women & Criminal Justice, 31*(6), 445–462. https://doi.org/10.1080/08974454.2020.1813236

Peguero, A. A., Popp, A. M., & Koo, D. J. (2015). Race, ethnicity, and school-based adolescent victimization. *Crime & Delinquency, 61*(3), 323–349. https://doi.org/10.1177/0011128711398021

Perry, N. B., DePasquale, C. E., Donzella, B., & Gunnar, M. R. (2020). Associations between stress reactivity and behavior problems for previously institutionalized youth across puberty. *Development and Psychopathology, 32*(5), 1854–1863. https://doi.org/10.1017/S0954579420001297

Pieterse, D., Kim, B. E., Klomhaus, A., Comulada, W. S., López, S. A., Bath, E., Amani, B., Myers, B., Semaan, A., & Milburn, N. G. (2022). PTSD among families of juvenile justice-involved youth: Relation to mental, emotional, and behavioral health problems. *Journal of Child and Family Studies, 31*(7), 1947–1956. https://doi.org/10.1007/s10826-022-02302-4

Price, J. (2020). The experience of young people transitioning between youth offending services to probation services. *Probation Journal, 67*(3), 246–263. https://doi.org/10.1177/0264550520939166

Pyrooz, D., & Decker, S. (2011). Motives and methods for leaving the gang: Understanding the process of gang desistance. *Journal of Criminal Justice, 39*(5), 417–425. https://doi.org/10.1016/j.jcrimjus.2011.07.001

Rajah, V., Kramer, R., & Sung, H.-E. (2014). Changing narrative accounts: How young men tell different stories when arrested, enduring jail time and navigating community reentry. *Punishment & Society, 16*(3), 285–304. https://doi.org/10.1177/1462474514527148

Robst, J. (2015). Disposition of charges, out-of-home mental health treatment, and juvenile justice recidivism. *International Journal of Offender Therapy and Comparative Criminology, 61*(11), 1195–1209. https://doi.org/10.1177/0306624X15615383

Rocque, M. (2015). The lost concept: The (re)emerging link between maturation and desistance from crime. *Criminology & Criminal Justice, 15*(3), 340–360. https://doi.org/10.1177/1748895814547710

Sabates, R. (2008). Educational attainment and juvenile crime: Area-level evidence using three cohorts of young people. *The British Journal of Criminology, 48*(3), 395–409. https://doi.org/10.1093/bjc/azn003

Sandøy, T. A. (2018). Beyond personal reform: Adolescent drug-law offenders and the desistance process. *Punishment & Society, 21*(5), 578–595. https://doi.org/10.1177/1462474518809021

Schubert, C. A., Mulvey, E. P., Hawes, S. W., & Davis, M. (2018). Educational and employment patterns in serious adolescent offenders with mental health disorders: The importance of educational attainment. *Criminal Justice and Behavior, 45*(11), 1660–1687. https://doi.org/10.1177/0093854818784330

Seddig, D., & Reinecke, J. (2017). Exploration and explanation of adolescent self-reported delinquency trajectories in the Crimoc study. In A. Blokland & V. van de Geest (Eds.), *The Routledge international handbook of life-course criminology* (pp. 159–178). Routledge.

Seroczynski, A. D. (2016). Reading for life and adolescent re-arrest: Evaluating a unique juvenile diversion program. *Journal of Policy Analysis and Management, 35*(3), 662–682.

Shapland, J., & Bottoms, A. (2011). Reflections on social values, offending and desistance among young adult recidivists. *Punishment & Society, 13*(3), 256–282. https://doi.org/10.1177/1462474511404334

Sheidow, A. J., McCart, M. R., & Drazdowski, T. K. (2022). Family-based treatments for disruptive behavior problems in children and adolescents: An updated review of rigorous studies (2014–April 2020). *Journal of Marital and Family Therapy, 48*(1), 56–82. https://doi.org/10.1111/jmft.12567

Skardhamar, T. (2009). Reconsidering the theory of adolescent-limited and life-course persistent anti-social behavior. *British Journal of Criminology, 49*(6), 863–878. https://doi.org/10.1093/bjc/azp048

Skowyra, K., & Cocozza, J. J. (2006). *A blueprint for change: Improving the system response to youth with mental health needs involved with the juvenile justice system*. National Center for Mental Health and Juvenile Justice.

Snyder, S. E., & Duchschere, J. E. (2022). Revisiting ecological systems theory: Practice implications for juvenile justice youth. *Translational Issues in Psychological Science, 8*(2), 234–245. https://doi.org/10.1037/tps0000324

Spacey, M., & Thompson, N. (2022). Beyond individual trauma: Towards a multi-faceted trauma-informed restorative approach to youth justice that connects individual trauma with family reparation and recognition of bias and discrimination. *British Journal of Community Justice, 18*(1), 18–35.

Stone, K. J., Poquiz, J. L., Fite, P. J., & Pederson, C. A. (2023). Family belonging and internalizing symptoms among youth involved with the juvenile justice system. *Youth Justice, 23*(1), 117–132. https://doi.org/10.1177/14732254221096554

Stout, B., Dalby, H., & Schraner, I. (2017). Measuring the impact of juvenile justice interventions: What works, what helps and what matters? *Youth Justice, 17*(3), 196–212. https://doi.org/10.1177/1473225417741226

Sullivan, C. J., Veysey, B. M., Hamilton, Z. K., & Grillo, M. (2007). Reducing out-of-community placement and recidivism: Diversion of delinquent youth with mental health and substance use problems from the justice system. *International Journal of Offender Therapy and Comparative Criminology, 51*(5), 555–577. https://doi.org/10.1177/0306624X06296237

Taylor, C. (2016). *Review of the youth justice system in England and Wales*. Ministry of Justice.

Terry, D., & Abrams, L. S. (2015). Dangers, diversions, and decisions: The process of criminal desistance among formerly incarcerated young men. *International Journal of Offender Therapy and Comparative Criminology, 61*(7), 727–750. https://doi.org/10.1177/0306624X15602704

Tolou-Shams, M., Brown, L. K., Marshall, B. D., Dauria, E., Koinis-Mitchell, D., Kemp, K., & Poindexter, B. (2019). The behavioral health needs of first-time offending justice-involved youth: Substance use, sexual risk, and mental health. *Journal of Child & Adolescent Substance Abuse, 28*(5), 291–303. https://doi.org/10.1080/1067828X.2020.1774023

Tolou-Shams, M., Dauria, E. F., Folk, J., Shumway, M., Marshall, B. D., Rizzo, C. J., Messina, N., Covington, S., Haack, L. M., Chaffee, T., & Brown, L. K. (2021). VOICES: An efficacious trauma-informed, gender-responsive cannabis use intervention for justice and school-referred girls with lifetime substance use history. *Drug and Alcohol Dependence, 228*, 108934. https://doi.org/10.1016/j.drugalcdep.2021.108934

Tremblay, M., Baydala, L., Khan, M., Currie, C., Morley, K., Burkholder, C., Davidson, R., & Stillar, A. (2020). Primary substance use prevention programs for children and youth: A systematic review. *Pediatrics, 146*(3), e20192747. https://doi.org/10.1542/peds.2019-2747

UN General Assembly. (1985, November 29). *United Nations Standard Minimum Rules for the Administration of Juvenile Justice ("The Beijing Rules")*. 40/33.

UN General Assembly. (1990, December 14). *United Nations Rules for the Protection of Juveniles Deprived of their Liberty (The Havana Rules)*. 45/113.

Veysey, B. M., & Hamilton, Z. (2007). Girls will be girls: Gender differences in predictors of success for diverted youth with mental health and substance abuse disorders. *Journal of Contemporary Criminal Justice, 23*(4), 341–362. https://doi.org/10.1177/1043986207309435

Wareham, J., Dembo, R., Schmeidler, J., Wolff, J., & Simon, N. (2022). Sexual trauma informed understanding of longitudinal depression among repeat juvenile offenders. *The Journal of Behavioral Health Services & Research, 49*(4), 456–469. https://doi.org/10.1007/s11414-022-09804-5

Webster, C., MacDonald, R., & Simpson, M. (2006). Predicting criminality? Risk factors, neighbourhood influence and desistance. *Youth Justice, 6*(1), 7–22. https://doi.org/10.1177/1473225406063449

Weerman, F. M. (2010). Delinquency after Secondary School: Exploring the consequences of schooling, working and dropout. *European Journal of Criminology, 7*(5), 339–355. https://doi.org/10.1177/1477370810373729

White, R. (2015). Indigenous young people and hyperincarceration in Australia. *Youth Justice, 15*(3), 256–270. https://doi-org.ezproxy.brunel.ac.uk/10.1177/1473225414562293

Whitley, K., Tastenhoye, C., Downey, A., & Rozel, J. S. (2022). Mental health care of detained youth within juvenile detention facilities. *Child and Adolescent Psychiatric Clinics, 31*(1), 31–44. https://doi.org/10.1016/j.chc.2021.09.002

Whyte, B. (2004). Effectiveness, research and youth justice. *Youth Justice, 4*(1), 3–21. https://doi.org/10.1177/147322540400400102

Williams-Butler, A., Liu, F. Y., Howell, T., Menon, S. E., & Quinn, C. R. (2022). Racialized gender differences in mental health service use, adverse childhood experiences, and recidivism among justice-involved African American youth. *Race and Social Problems*, 1–14. https://doi.org/10.1007/s12552-022-09360-9

Zemel, O., Ronel, N., & Einat, T. (2016). The impact of introspection and resilience on abstention and desistance from delinquent behavior among adolescents at risk. *European Journal of Criminology, 13*(1), 111–128. https://doi.org/10.1177/1477370815587770

CHAPTER 6

Conclusions

Abstract This book sought to explore the relationship between the research literature on youth offending and youth justice and the international children's rights standards, identifying synergies to strengthen the rights-based approach to children in conflict with the law. This concluding chapter summarises the findings from this process, sets out gaps that have been identified and presents some next steps so that the exercise can be taken forward.

Keywords Children's rights · Children in conflict with the law

Introduction

This book seeks to explore the relationship between the research literature on youth offending and youth justice and the international children's rights standards, identifying synergies between these two bodies of knowledge in favour of progressive youth justice. The Convention on the Rights of the Child is the world's most widely ratified human rights treaty and thus holds particular importance for states who have committed to implementing its provisions in their national law and practice, including within states' responses to young people who come into conflict with the law.

U. Kilkelly et al., *Children in Conflict with the Law*,
Palgrave Critical Studies in Human Rights and Criminology,
https://doi.org/10.1007/978-3-031-36652-9_6

Despite some shortcomings in the international law that sets out the rights of children in conflict with the law, it has been argued that they nonetheless represent a gold standard for states seeking to improve their approach to child justice (Kilkelly, 2008). The evidence presented in this book from the research literature examining the way in which children come into conflict with the law, their engagement with youth justice processes, and interventions and supports required to facilitate reintegration gives further credence to this position, highlighting the ways in which protection of children's rights serves to advance positive outcomes for children at all stages of their contact with youth justice systems. Ultimately, this book aims to establish that there are strong links between the literature documenting children's experiences of coming into conflict with the law, and between protection of children's rights across a range of domains, as set out in the CRC and related international standards. This final concluding chapter aims to summarise the findings from this process, set out some of the gaps that it revealed and present some next steps so that the exercise can be taken forward.

A Rights-Based Approach to Children in Conflict with the Law

As Chapter 2 explained, international children's rights standards present a comprehensive and detailed set of principles and provisions that aim to guide states in their treatment of children in conflict with the law. This body of law includes children's rights standards that are universal to all children in all circumstances—like health, education, family support and protection from harm—and those that are particular to children in conflict with the law—including principles of diversion, rights to a child-friendly justice system adapted to the needs and capacities of children, and the right to reintegration as a principled approach to promote the child's return to their community and away from offending. While breaches of the rights of children in conflict with the law continue to occur across the world, despite the proliferation of standards in this area (Lynch & Liefaard, 2020; Nowak, 2019), there is also evidence that at national level, rights-based discourse and advocacy has been influential in bringing about meaningful changes in law and practice in youth justice systems (Goldson & Kilkelly, 2013; Kilkelly & Bergin, 2022). As such, the international standards have particular significance and meaning for states seeking to develop their approach to youth justice practice at national level. In addition to the Convention on the Rights of the Child, the guidance available for states has been enhanced both at UN and Council of Europe levels through the development of additional standards in relation to child-friendly justice, the treatment of children deprived of their liberty, strategies relation to prevention and early intervention, and the development of General Comments. This copious body of standards was discussed in Chapter 2 and distilled into three themes: Prevention—from contact with the justice system; Diversion and Justice—while in the justice system; and Reintegration—as a means of supporting the child to move out of the justice system towards fulfilling their potential in society. The Committee on the Rights of the Child, in developing a second General Comment on the rights of children in the justice system, have highlighted the significance of new knowledge about child development and effective practice, underscoring the importance of research and evidence in developing our understanding of the children's rights standards themselves.

The Research Base

Drawing on an extensive body of scholarly literature, across disciplines and jurisdictions, Chapters 3–5 sought to explain the extent to which children's rights-based approaches are informed and strengthened by research and evidence relating to children's involvement in offending. Although not a meta-analysis or a systematic review, this study relied on leading international studies and published authorities in the area to summarise the most authoritative and persuasive body of knowledge on these key themes. In the main, the analysis shows a large degree of alignment between the children's rights approach and the research evidence in support of a progressive system of youth justice. Although not always conclusive—nor should it be, given that rights are not earned but inherent in all children by virtue of their common dignity and childhood status—the research presents a strongly coherent set of messages about what approaches to children in conflict with the law are most likely to protect and promote their rights. Reflecting the importance of the child's fundamental rights—which are codified in international law—the research endorses the need to ensure that every child enjoys the right to education, to healthcare, to family support, to rest and leisure and to protection from harm. Whether preventing the child from coming into conflict with the law, diverting the child from the justice or prioritising the child's reintegration into society, the research unanimously endorses the critical nature of these fundamental rights and the need to ensure they are enjoyed without discrimination. The research evidence highlighting the myriad ways in which breaches of children's fundamental rights often precede contact with the justice system—and conversely, evidence which demonstrates how support for children to access their rights more fully can serve as protective factors—highlights the significance of greater realisation of children's rights for preventing young people from becoming involved in offending and into contact with the potentially harmful impacts of criminal justice contact in the first place. Another important theme from the study is the relevance of the child's development to their treatment in the justice system. Regardless of the stage of the justice process, the evidence highlights that a focus on the child's developmental stage, their capacity and their associated vulnerability is critically important to a rights-based approach. Without sufficient attention to children's rights, their meaningful and effective participation with the justice system is difficult, increasing the chances of negative outcomes for children. Equally, the research demonstrates that support for children to access their rights in relation to education, healthcare and family support is critical to helping children to begin and sustain processes of desistance further offending and to achieve the aims of the children's rights standards in relation to reintegration and assumption of a more positive role in society. Here, the synergy between the child's best interests and the importance in the literature of an individualised approach that takes account of a child's circumstances in a child-centred way is particularly strong.

Rights Standards and Research—Some Gaps

Notwithstanding the importance of the rights standards, they are not without their flaws, and it is equally important to recognise that gaps remain in the international framework setting out children's rights, as well as in the research base in this area. Viewed from the perspective of the research, the children's rights standards could be said to be weak in a number of areas—chiefly with regard to children's unequal experience in their enjoyment of rights and their marginalisation as a result of poverty and disadvantage. In particular, it is evident from the literature that disproportionate contact with the justice system is experienced by multiple groups of children who suffer complex layers of disadvantage, vulnerability and prejudice that means they are not only likely to suffer discrimination in the enjoyment of their rights, but they are also more likely to be subjected to a more punitive approach, with frequently devastating consequences. In this regard, although Article 2 of the CRC prohibits discrimination in the enjoyment of CRC rights on all grounds including race and other status, the questions of racial bias, the over-representation of children with disabilities and children who have experience of state care, and the disproportionate impact on children from poor or marginalised communities have received insufficient little attention from the bodies responsible for monitoring and standard setting in children's rights. While the need for both safeguards against discrimination occurring in the first instance and processes to provide redress for any discriminatory practices has been highlighted by the Committee on the Rights of the Child (Committee on the Rights of the Child, 2019, para. 40), much more direct and substantive guidance should be set out regarding the urgent need to address children's realities of these rights in practice. If the gap in the children's rights standards needs to be addressed so that they can retain their legitimacy and currency, equally, a case can be made for greater research on approaches that have successfully countered these issues. In this regard, the Committee on the Rights of the Child has acknowledged the need for more knowledge in this area, recommending that evaluations of the justice system should enquire into issues relating to discrimination (Committee on the Rights of the Child, 2019, para. 114).

The second area where alignment between the research evidence and the international children's rights standards is not especially strong is with regard to the child's right to a say in decision-making. Here, although Article 12 presents a strongly worded right, which international bodies have applied creatively to the justice context, the research has yet to catch up. Many of the studies reported have of course involved children, but as research subjects, whose lives are studied, rather than as research participants whose views and experiences are valued as part of the research process. While the engagement of children in research, on a rights-basis, is improving, it is still relatively rare to involve children directly in studies and to give them a say in a process that clearly, as Article 12 indicates, affects their lives. Some studies have begun to engage directly with children so as to demonstrate the importance of children's contribution to research on the justice system (Forde & Kilkelly, 2023), and indeed, ground was broken with the inclusion in the Global Study on Children Deprived of Liberty of research that involved a substantial international consultation with children deprived of their liberty on their experiences of their rights (Nowak, 2019). This proves that research can routinely engage with children in the justice system on these issues, in line with the CRC. Moreover, involving children in such research is imperative if the literature itself is to reflect the rights-basis that so much of it appears to advocate. In this and in other ways, both those responsible for children's rights standard setting and the research community have much to do if the full potential of both fields is to be realised in fulfilment of the child's right to be heard.

Implementation—The Next Frontier

One of the frequent criticisms of children's rights standards is that they are strong on 'what'—in terms of the treatment to which children are entitled—and weak on the 'how'—as in how these rights are to be realised. While this arguably stems from the fact that, under international law, states parties have discretion as to how international obligations are to be fulfilled, it can lead to frustration as to how *best* to implement these standards. In the last decade or so, researchers in children's rights have begun to focus more directly on the implementation question, with important contributions to the literature focusing on measures of national and local implementation (Chaney, 2017; Kilkelly, 2019; Kilkelly & Liefaard, 2019; Kilkelly et al., 2021). With respect to children in conflict with the law, this is beginning to yield fruit also, with studies increasingly seeking to examine how children's rights standards are implemented—in courts, in policing and in detention for instance. Although valuable, this work has relatively limited potential to reach across disciplines and jurisdictions given how important the context of the setting under analysis can be. This is where this study can make a useful contribution, by providing some useful insights and suggestions as to how to advance research in this area into the future.

First, the discussion set out in Chapter 2 highlights the relevance of the international standards to every aspect of a child's contact with the youth justice system. Instead of simply focusing on the specific rights related to the child's contact with the justice system which are engaged when a young person commits a crime, it seeks to emphasise the importance of a holistic approach to ensuring that *all* of the rights children are entitled to under the Convention are critical to both preventing children from coming into contact with the justice system and its harmful effects in the first place, and to supporting positive outcomes for children who do come into conflict with the law. It demonstrates that across domains related to Prevention, Diversion and Justice, and Reintegration, a focus on the children's rights standards can add much to states' efforts to develop principled responses to children who become involved in committing offences. Second, by exploring the research evidence in light of the international standards, this study seeks to explore not whether the rights standards have been implemented but *how*. Chapters 3–5, for instance, are replete with illustrations of the ways in which practical effect can be given to the child's rights across all aspects of the justice system in the three themes of the book—Prevention, Diversion and Justice, and Reintegration. These examples highlight that while there are myriad ways of responding to children in conflict with the law, approaches which seek to strengthen children's rights across a range of domains—in relation to their health, securing access to education and strengthening supports for families—can be key to securing more positive outcomes for children. In this way, the principal idea behind this book was to begin to explore this process, by bringing together disciplines, approaches and methodologies so that the mutual strengths of rights and research can combine to aid greater advances in an evidence- and rights-based approach to children in conflict with the law.

Bibliography

Chaney, P. (2017). Limited gains, enduring violations: Civil society perspectives on the implementation of the United Nations' convention on the rights of the child in Bangladesh. *Journal of South Asian Development, 12*(3), 286–307. https://doi-org.ucc.idm.oclc.org/10.1177/0973174117735213

Committee on the Rights of the Child. (2019, September 19). *General comment No. 24 (2019) on children's rights in the child justice system*. CRC/C/GC/24.

Forde, L., & Kilkelly, U. (2023). Children and police questioning: A rights-based approach. *Criminology and Criminal Justice*, 1–22. https://doi.org/10.1177/17488958231161423

Goldson, B., & Kilkelly, U. (2013). International human rights standards and child imprisonment. *International Journal of Children's Rights, 21*(2), 345.

Kilkelly, U. (2008). Youth courts: The Irish experience. *Youth Justice, 8*, 39.

Kilkelly, U. (2019). The UN convention on the rights of the child: Incremental and transformative approaches to legal implementation. *The International Journal of Human Rights, 23*(3), 323–337. https://doi.org/10.1080/13642987.2018.1558974

Kilkelly, U., & Bergin, P. (2022). *Advancing Children's Rights in detention*. Bristol University Press.
Kilkelly, U., & Liefaard, T. (2019). Legal implementation of the UNCRC: Lessons to be learned from the constitutional experience of South Africa. *De Jure Law Journal, 52*, 521–539.
Kilkelly, U., Lundy, L., & Byrne, B. (Eds.). (2021). *Incorporating the UN convention on the rights of the child into National Law*. Intersentia.
Lynch, N., & Liefaard, T. (2020). What is left in the "Too Hard Basket"? Developments and challenges for the rights of children in conflict with the law. *The International Journal of Children's Rights, 28*(1), 89–110.
Nowak, M. (2019). *Global study on children deprived of liberty*. A/74/136.

Index

U. Kilkelly et al., *Children in Conflict with the Law*, Palgrave Critical Studies in Human Rights and Criminology, https://doi.org/10.1007/978-3-031-36652-9

GPSR Compliance
The European Union's (EU) General Product Safety Regulation (GPSR) is a set of rules that requires consumer products to be safe and our obligations to ensure this.

If you have any concerns about our products, you can contact us on

ProductSafety@springernature.com

In case Publisher is established outside the EU, the EU authorized representative is:

Springer Nature Customer Service Center GmbH
Europaplatz 3
69115 Heidelberg, Germany

www.ingramcontent.com/pod-product-compliance
Ingram Content Group UK Ltd.
Pitfield, Milton Keynes, MK11 3LW, UK
UKHW020836290926
15470UKWH00004B/1376
* 9 7 8 3 0 3 1 3 6 6 5 1 2 *